Collins

PUB QUIZ 2

HarperCollins Publishers
Westerhill Road
Bishopbriggs
Glasgow
G64 2QT

First Edition 2013

Reprint 10 9 8 7 6 5

ISBNs:
978-0-00-752562-1
978-0-00-793828-5
978-0-00-796719-3

Collins® is a registered trademark of
HarperCollins Publishers Limited

www.collinsdictionary.com

A catalogue record for this book is
available from the British Library

Typeset by Davidson Publishing
Solutions, Glasgow

Printed in Great Britain by Clays Ltd,
St Ives plc

Acknowledgements

AUTHOR
Chris Bradshaw

EDITOR
Ian Brookes

FOR THE PUBLISHER
Gerry Breslin
Lucy Cooper
Kerry Ferguson
Evelyn Sword

Introduction

Samuel Johnson, the famous dictionary compiler and wit, once noted: "There is nothing contrived by man by which so much happiness is produced as by a good tavern or inn." It is interesting to ponder what Dr Johnson would make of modern pubs. Would he wonder why people prefer to stare at Sky Sports News on mute rather than talk to one another? Would he be shocked by how much is charged for a gourmet burger? Would he be bemused by people putting ice in their cider? Maybe. But one thing is for certain, a man of his breadth of learning would make a great addition to any pub quiz team.

The pub quiz is a relative newcomer to the list of attractions that draw people into hostelries. People may be mystified by bar billiards, underwhelmed by shove ha'penny, and reaching for their ear plugs during karaoke but a pub quiz unites patrons like no other entertainment. No evening of the week draws in more punters (apart from curry night, perhaps) and it is remarkable to behold the sudden sobering up of drinkers as they try to sharpen their wits for an hour of intense cerebral competition. The prize may be disappointing (usually twelve bottles of the pub's cheapest beer) but that is of no consequence. It is the thrill of competition and the glory of winning that counts.

The beating heart of every good quiz is a first-class quizmaster, and the key to achieving this status is having the right questions. That's where *Collins Pub Quiz 2* comes in. *Collins Pub Quiz 2* is designed to give you, the quizmaster, the questions that will guarantee that everyone in the pub gives you their full attention during the quiz. Turn over to find out how it works...

The quizzes

There are two hundred quizzes in this book. Half of them are themed with classic pub quiz themes. There are animal quizzes, movie quizzes, politics, sport, television and history quizzes. The natural world, space, and the human body are covered. So too are food and drink, books, and geography. Every subject you could want really. The other half of the quizzes are pot luck rounds, because you can never have enough of these.

The quizzes are grouped together according to how tricky they are. First come the easy ones, then medium and finally the difficult quizzes.

Easy

The easy questions should not have you scratching your head too much. If they do, you'll need to have your head examined to see if there's anything inside. A few of them are trickier than others and might even be described as 'challenging'. These have been included to keep things interesting. If questions are too simple people might switch off.

Medium

The medium-level quizzes should get a good hum of conferring going in each team. Someone will be positive of the answer, someone else will be positive that person is wrong but won't quite be able to provide the right answer themselves. Someone else will think it begins with the letter 'c'.

Difficult

These questions are tricky. Very tricky. As tricky as translating the complete works of Shakespeare into Klingon. Anyone who gets all of these questions right is probably cheating. If they've got a former winner of *Mastermind* on speed-dial be ready to give them a red card. You might not want to throw in too many of this level into your quiz, but they are excellent for spicing things up or as tie-breaker questions.

The answers

The answers to each quiz are printed at the end of the following quiz. For example, the answers to Quiz 1-Pot Luck appear at the bottom of Quiz 2-Art, Architecture, and Design. The exception to this rule is the last quiz in every level. The answers to these quizzes appear at the end of the very first quiz in the level.

Running a quiz

Collins Pub Quiz 2 is only half-finished. (Wait! Don't demand a refund yet, read on!) People don't go to the theatre to sit and read a script. Likewise, the quizzes in this book need someone to read them out. That's you.

If you're just quizzing your family during a car journey, or your mates of an afternoon, then there's probably no need to put in lots of preparation. If you're planning on using this book to run a more organized and formal quiz however, there are a few things you need to get right before you start:

❖ Rehearse: don't just pick this book up and read out the questions cold. Go through all the quizzes you're going to use by yourself beforehand. Note down all the questions (notes look better in a quiz environment than reading from a book) and answers. Although every effort has been made to ensure that all the answers in *Collins Pub Quiz 2* are correct, despite our best endeavours, mistakes may still appear. If you see an answer you are not sure is right, or if you think there is more than one possible answer, then check.

❖ Paper and writing implements: do yourself a favour and prepare enough sheets of paper for everyone to write on. The aim of the game here is to stop the mad impulse certain people feel to 'help'. They will spend ten minutes running around looking for 'scrap' paper, probably ripping up your latest novel in the process. The same problem applies to pens. Ideally, have enough for everyone. Remember, though, that over half of them will be lost forever once you've given them out.

❖ Prizes: everyone likes a prize. No matter how small, it's best to have one on offer.

Good luck! We hope you enjoy *Collins Pub Quiz 2*.

Contents

Easy Quizzes

1. Pot Luck
2. Art, Architecture, and Design
3. Pot Luck
4. Numbers part 1
5. Pot Luck
6. Films
7. Pot Luck
8. Pop Music
9. Pot Luck
10. Connections part 1
11. Pot Luck
12. History
13. Pot Luck
14. Connections part 2
15. Pot Luck
16. Advertising Slogans
17. Pot Luck
18. Politics
19. Pot Luck
20. Television part 1
21. Pot Luck
22. Alliterative Answers
23. Pot Luck
24. Olympics Games
25. Pot Luck
26. Animals part 1
27. Pot Luck
28. Famous Martins
29. Pot Luck
30. Love and Marriage
31. Pot Luck
32. Numbers part 2
33. Pot Luck
34. Days and Months
35. Pot Luck
36. Animals part 2
37. Pot Luck
38. Anagrams part 1
39. Pot Luck
40. Countries Ending in Vowels
41. Pot Luck
42. Sporting Nicknames
43. Pot Luck
44. Big and Small
45. Pot Luck
46. Duets
47. Pot Luck
48. Fill in the Blank
49. Pot Luck
50. Name the Year
51. Pot Luck
52. Television part 2
53. Pot Luck
54. Sun, Moon, and Stars
55. Pot Luck
56. Colours
57. Pot Luck
58. Sport part 1
59. Pot Luck
60. Football Teams
61. Pot Luck
62. Ireland
63. Pot Luck
64. Sport part 2
65. Pot Luck
66. Anagrams part 2

Medium Quizzes

67. Pot Luck
68. Art, Architecture, and Design
69. Pot Luck
70. Barack Obama
71. Pot Luck
72. Films part 1
73. Pot Luck
74. Films part 2
75. Pot Luck
76. History part 1
77. Pot Luck
78. England
79. Pot Luck
80. Famous Elizabeths
81. Pot Luck
82. Colours
83. Pot Luck
84. Sport part 1
85. Pot Luck
86. Transport
87. Pot Luck
88. Anagrams
89. Pot Luck
90. Famous Pauls
91. Pot Luck
92. Sport part 2
93. Pot Luck
94. Places
95. Pot Luck
96. Doctors
97. Pot Luck
98. Natural World
99. Pot Luck
100. Television part 1

101. Pot Luck
102. Alliterative Answers
103. Pot Luck
104. Numbers
105. Pot Luck
106. Pop Music
107. Pot Luck
108. Olympic Games
109. Pot Luck
110. Television part 2
111. Pot Luck
112. Big and Small
113. Pot Luck
114. Firsts and Lasts
115. Pot Luck
116. Connections part 1
117. Pot Luck
118. Dance
119. Pot Luck
120. Days and Months
121. Pot Luck
122. Myth and Legend
123. Pot Luck
124. Connections part 2
125. Pot Luck
126. Sport part 3
127. Connections part 3
128. History part 2
129. Pot Luck
130. The Name Is James
131. Pot Luck
132. Famous Toms
133. Pot Luck

Difficult Quizzes

134. Pot Luck
135. Places part 1
136. Pot Luck
137. Art, Architecture, and Design
138. Pot Luck
139. Sports Governing Bodies
140. Pot Luck
141. Films part 1
142. Pot Luck
143. Natural World
144. Pot Luck
145. Ologies
146. Pot Luck
147. Sport part 1
148. Pot Luck
149. Alliterative Answers
150. Pot Luck
151. Politics
152. Pot Luck
153. Connections
154. Pot Luck
155. Television part 1
156. Pot Luck
157. Pop Music part 1
158. Pot Luck
159. Transport part 1
160. Pot Luck
161. History
162. Pot Luck
163. Pop Music part 2
164. Pot Luck
165. Anagrams
166. Pot Luck
167. Food and Drink

168. Pot Luck
169. Films part 2
170. Pot Luck
171. Television part 2
172. Pot Luck
173. Olympic Games
174. Pot Luck
175. Anatomy and Medicine
176. Pot Luck
177. Sport part 2
178. Pot Luck
179. Places part 2
180. Pot Luck
181. Television part 3
182. Pot Luck
183. First and Last
184. Pot Luck
185. Sport part 3
186. Pot Luck
187. Movie Taglines
188. Pot Luck
189. Transport part 2
190. Pot Luck
191. Sport part 4
192. Pot Luck
193. Books
194. Pot Luck
195. Fill in the Blank
196. Pot Luck
197. Pop Music part 3
198. Pot Luck
199. Colours
200. Pot Luck

EASY QUIZZES

Quiz 1: Pot Luck

1. Which football team won its 20th English domestic league title in 2012/13?

2. Weatherfield is the setting for which long-running TV drama?

3. The Bull Ring is a large shopping centre in which English city?

4. Which Australian actor played The Joker in the 2008 film 'The Dark Knight'?

5. In Roman numerals, which number is represented by the letter X?

6. Cirrus, cumulus, and stratus are examples of what type of meteorological feature?

7. In computing, what do the initials www stand for?

8. According to the proverb, ask a silly question and you'll get what?

9. Which word describes a person who breaks into a website and an inept golfer?

10. Peking is the former name of which Asian capital city?

11. How many players are on each side in a game of cricket?

12. In relation to television, what do the initials HD stand for?

13. Which piece of furniture is also the name given to a group of high-ranking government officials?

14. The national flag of Scotland is named after which saint?

15. The hit TV show 'Downton Abbey' is set in a fictional country house in which English county?

16. The Terrence Higgins Trust is a charity that raises funds to combat which disease?

17. What name describes the meeting of the College of Cardinals that decides a new pope?

18. 'Water Lilies' is a series of paintings by which French Impressionist?

19. How many degrees is a right angle?
    a) 45
    b) 90
    c) 180

20. Which of the following animals is not the name of a year in the Chinese calendar?
    a) cat
    b) dog
    c) rabbit

Answers to Quiz 66: Anagrams part 2

1.	Germany	11.	New Zealand
2.	Denmark	12.	Romania
3.	South Africa	13.	Bulgaria
4.	Luxembourg	14.	Saudi Arabia
5.	Argentina	15.	Slovenia
6.	Czech Republic	16.	Sri Lanka
7.	Ethiopia	17.	Ireland
8.	Indonesia	18.	Cameroon
9.	Lebanon	19.	Belgium
10.	Australia	20.	Bangladesh

Quiz 2: Art, Architecture, and Design

1. '200 Campbell's Soup Cans' is a work by which American pop artist?

2. What is the base of a statue called?

3. What type of artwork takes its name from the French for 'paste-up'?

4. What is the name of the upright support on which an artist places his or her canvas?

5. Which British artist is famous for his 'spot paintings'?

6. CM Coolidge produced a famous painting of which animals playing poker?

7. By what name was the Italian artist Giovanni Antonio Canal better known?

8. Which well-spoken art critic wrote the 2011 autobiography, 'Outsider: Always Almost: Never Quite'?

9. What nationality was the painter Goya?

10. 'Starry Night over the Rhone' is by which Dutch painter?

11. What type of pottery derives its name from the Italian for 'baked earth'?

12. What nationality were the painters Rembrandt and Vermeer?

13. Which Spanish painter, who died in 1973, had blue and rose periods?

14. In 1914, Vincenzo Peruggia was sent to prison for a year for stealing which famous painting?

15. By what name is the painter Doménikos Theotokópoulos better known?

16. Salvador Dali was most commonly associated with which artistic movement?

17. The artistic movement Impressionism took its name from a painting by which French artist?

18. What was the first name of the French artist Matisse?

19. Which of the following is the title of a painting by Botticelli?
a) The Birth of Venus b) The Birth of Earth
c) The Birth of Jupiter

20. A painting called 'Flag' by Jasper Johns sold for over $28m in 2010. Which flag did it depict?
a) Royal Standard b) Stars and Stripes c) Union Flag

Answers to Quiz 1: Pot Luck

1.	Manchester United	11.	11
2.	Coronation Street	12.	High Definition
3.	Birmingham	13.	Cabinet
4.	Heath Ledger	14.	Saint Andrew
5.	10	15.	Yorkshire
6.	Clouds	16.	HIV/AIDS
7.	World Wide Web	17.	Conclave
8.	A silly answer	18.	Claude Monet
9.	Hacker	19.	90
10.	Beijing	20.	Cat

Quiz 3: Pot Luck

1. The city of Nottingham stands on which river?

2. What type of confectionery is also the name given to a piece of information placed on a computer user's hard drive by a web server?

3. The Bolshoi Ballet is based in which European capital?

4. Antwerp is the second largest city in which country?

5. What is the name of the alternative therapy that uses scented plant oils to aid relaxation?

6. Mary Berry and Paul Hollywood are the judges on which culinary talent show?

7. Which branch of medicine specializes in mental illness and its treatment?

8. In a game of cricket, how many balls make up an over?

9. In the Christian calendar, which feast is celebrated each year on 1 November?

10. Which silent film won the Best Film Oscar in 2011?

11. William Shakespeare is buried in which English town?

12. The song 'I'm Forever Blowing Bubbles' is associated with which London football club?

13. The Glitterball Trophy is awarded to the winner of which TV show?

14. Prior to joining the Euro, what was the currency of Portugal?

15. Which part of the UK is known as Cymru?

16. What is US president Barack Obama's middle name?

17. Which religious leader said 'It seemed like the Lord was sleeping at times' shortly before his 2013 resignation?

18. What is the name of the pub in the TV sitcom 'Only Fools and Horses'?

19. La Scala is an opera house in which European city?
    a) Madrid
    b) Milan
    c) Paris

20. What is the Security Service also known as?
    a) MI5
    b) MI6
    c) MI7

Answers to Quiz 2: Art, Architecture, and Design

1.	Andy Warhol	11.	Terra cotta
2.	Plinth	12.	Dutch
3.	Collage	13.	Picasso
4.	Easel	14.	Mona Lisa
5.	Damien Hirst	15.	El Greco
6.	Dogs	16.	Surrealism
7.	Canaletto	17.	Claude Monet
8.	Brian Sewell	18.	Henri
9.	Spanish	19.	The Birth of Venus
10.	Vincent van Gogh	20.	Stars and Stripes

Quiz 4: Numbers part 1

EASY

1. Cruella de Vil is the central character in which 1961 Disney animation?

2. A decagon is a shape with how many sides?

3. What was the title of Adele's first album?

4. After how many years of marriage would a couple celebrate a diamond wedding anniversary?

5. How many strings does a standard guitar have?

6. In a game of cricket, how many wickets must the bowling team take to dismiss the batting team?

7. How many stars appear on the Australian flag?

8. How many players are on a rugby league team?

9. Which novel by Alexandre Dumas featured the adventures of a trio of friends called Athos, Porthos, and Aramis?

10. How many points are there on a 'Star of David'?

11. What is the name of the orbital motorway that circles Manchester?

12. How many colonies originally declared independence from Britain and formed the United States of America?

13. What is the square root of 625?

14. On a football pitch, how far in yards is the penalty spot from the goal line?

15. In the Charles Dickens classic 'A Christmas Carol', Scrooge was visited by how many ghosts?

16. 'Slam Dunk (Da Funk)', 'Keep on Movin'' and 'Let's Dance' were big hits for which British boyband?

17. At the start of a frame of snooker, how many balls are on the table?

18. What is the lowest number that cannot be scored with a single dart on a standard dartboard?

19. In a rugby union team, which number shirt does the full back wear?
    a) 1
    b) 7
    c) 15

20. How many teams make up football's Premier League?
    a) 18
    b) 20
    c) 22

Answers to Quiz 3: Pot Luck

1. River Trent
2. Cookie
3. Moscow
4. Belgium
5. Aromatherapy
6. The Great British Bake Off
7. Psychiatry
8. Six
9. All Saints' Day
10. The Artist
11. Stratford-upon-Avon
12. West Ham United
13. Strictly Come Dancing
14. Escudo
15. Wales
16. Hussein
17. Pope Benedict XVI
18. The Nag's Head
19. Milan
20. MI5

Quiz 5: Pot Luck

1. Who succeeded David Tennant as Dr Who?

2. According to the proverb, familiarity breeds what?

3. Mont Blanc is the highest peak in which mountain range?

4. Mansion House is the official residence of the holder of which office?

5. Which sporting organization has the initials IOC?

6. Murcia, Cantabria, and Aragon are regions of which European country?

7. What metal has the atomic symbol Pb?

8. In 2013, David Beckham joined which French football club?

9. What form of alternative therapy uses thin metal needles to stimulate parts of the body?

10. Which spirit is the main ingredient in the liqueur Tia Maria?

11. The annual Promenade Concerts are held at which London venue?

12. Whom did Margaret Thatcher succeed as British prime minister?

13. McPartlin and Donnelly are the surnames of which British TV double act?

14. Nicky Wire and James Dean Bradfield are members of which Welsh rock group?

15. The novel 'Ulysses' by James Joyce is set in which European capital city?

16. Who is the first female in line to the British throne?

17. Which two football teams meet in a derby match called 'El Clasico'?

18. On a London Tube map, what colour is the Bakerloo line?

19. In which year did the Titanic sink?
    a) 1902
    b) 1912
    c) 1922

20. What is the occupation of the classic film character Indiana Jones?
    a) archaeologist
    b) physician
    c) stuntman

Answers to Quiz 4: Numbers part 1

1. One Hundred and One Dalmatians
2. Ten
3. 19
4. 60
5. Six
6. Ten
7. Six
8. 13
9. The Three Musketeers
10. Six
11. M60
12. 13
13. 25
14. 12
15. Four
16. Five
17. 22
18. 23
19. 15
20. 20

Quiz 6: Films

1. Woody, Buzz, and Mr Potato Head are characters in which animated film trilogy?

2. 'A long time ago in a galaxy far, far away' was the tagline to which film?

3. The 1940 film 'A Wild Hare' was the first to feature which cartoon character?

4. Which silent movie actor starred in 'The General', 'The Navigator', and 'Sherlock Jr'?

5. Meryl Streep won the Best Actress Oscar in 2011 for her portrayal of which British politician?

6. The 1987 film 'The Last Emperor' was set in which Asian country?

7. Which film director, the subject of a 2013 biopic, was known as 'The Master of Suspense'?

8. Which series of vampire fantasies is based on a series of novels by Stephanie Meyer?

9. Who played the Queen in the 2006 film of the same name?

10. 'The Searchers', 'Unforgiven', and 'True Grit' are films in which genre?

11. What are the Golden Raspberry Awards more commonly known as?

12. Which member of the Monty Python comedy team played 'R' in the 1999 Bond film 'The World Is Not Enough'?

13. Which British director's films include 'Trainspotting', '127 Hours', and 'Slumdog Millionaire'?

14. Which English actor played Edward Cullen in the 'Twilight' films?

15. Sean Connery made his last appearance as James Bond in which 1983 film?

16. Which New York borough gave its name to a 1979 classic directed by Woody Allen?

17. 'Who ya gonna call?' was the tagline to which supernatural 1984 comedy?

18. Who directed the film 'Django Unchained'?

19. Which film was not nominated in the Best Picture category at the 2012 Oscars?
a) Life of Pi b) Skyfall c) Zero Dark Thirty

20. What was the title of the 1940 romantic comedy starring Cary Grant and Katharine Hepburn?
a) The Cleveland Story b) The Philadelphia Story
c) The Pittsburgh Story

Answers to Quiz 5: Pot Luck

1.	Matt Smith	11.	Royal Albert Hall
2.	Contempt	12.	James Callaghan
3.	The Alps	13.	Ant and Dec
4.	Lord Mayor of London	14.	Manic Street Preachers
5.	International Olympic Committee	15.	Dublin
		16.	Princess Beatrice
6.	Spain	17.	Real Madrid and Barcelona
7.	Lead		
8.	Paris St Germain	18.	Brown
9.	Acupuncture	19.	1912
10.	Rum	20.	Archaeologist

Quiz 7: Pot Luck

EASY

1. Pope Francis I is from which South American country?

2. Brie and Camembert are cheeses from which country?

3. Which sport would you expect to see at Roland Garros and Flushing Meadows?

4. Kilimanjaro is a mountain in which African country?

5. In relation to the internet, what are Opera, Safari, and Firefox?

6. The Élysée Palace is the official residence of the president of which country?

7. By what name was Ivan IV of Russia better known?

8. Which Welshman was the only man to play and score in all of the first 20 seasons of football's Premier League?

9. Who were the two politicians to hold the post of Chancellor of the Exchequer during the 1997–2010 Labour government?

10. O'Hare International Airport serves which American city?

11. Which England cricketer made his heavyweight boxing debut against Richard Dawson in November 2012?

12. On a London Tube map, what colour is the Jubilee line?

13. Which desert takes its name from the Mongolian for 'waterless place'?

14. Who resigned as manager of the England football team in February 2012?

15. Which former EastEnder won the 2012 series of 'I'm a Celebrity, Get Me out of Here'?

16. Which word means a horse that is yet to win a race or an over in cricket when no runs are scored?

17. From 2005 until 2013, Mahmoud Ahmadinejad was the president of which Middle Eastern country?

18. The Great Victoria is a desert in which Commonwealth country?

19. Complete the title of a 1981 horror film: 'An American Werewolf in ...'
    a) Liverpool
    b) London
    c) Luton

20. Which part of the United Kingdom is not represented on the Union Flag?
    a) England
    b) Northern Ireland
    c) Wales

Answers to Quiz 6: Films

1. Toy Story
2. Star Wars
3. Bugs Bunny
4. Buster Keaton
5. Margaret Thatcher
6. China
7. Alfred Hitchcock
8. Twilight
9. Helen Mirren
10. Westerns
11. The Razzies
12. John Cleese
13. Danny Boyle
14. Robert Pattinson
15. Never Say Never Again
16. Manhattan
17. Ghostbusters
18. Quentin Tarantino
19. Skyfall
20. The Philadelphia Story

Quiz 8: Pop Music

1. Belieber is a nickname given to a fan of which teen idol?

2. 'Live Forever' was the first top ten single by which band?

3. Which female singer's number one hit singles include 'Like a Prayer' and 'Who's That Girl'?

4. 'Carry On up the Charts' was a best-selling album by which group?

5. 'Rehab' was the only top ten UK single from which singer, who died in 2011?

6. Which female singer was born Stefani Joanne Angelina Germanotta?

7. By what name are the musical duo Charles Hodges and David Peacock better known?

8. Tony Hadley was the lead singer with which New Romantic outfit?

9. Which famous 19th-century battle was also the title of a 1974 number one hit single?

10. Which Rat Pack singer recorded the classic album 'Songs for Swingin' Lovers!'?

11. Which Irish band had a big hit in 2012 with 'Hall of Fame'?

12. 'Baby One More Time' was the first UK number one single by which singer?

13. The Wailers were the backing band of which reggae legend?

14. NKOTB are the initials of which boy band who topped the charts in the late 1980s and early 1990s?

15. 'What Makes You Beautiful' was the debut single from which popular boy band?

16. 'We Are Never Ever Getting Back Together' was a top five hit in 2012 for which American singer-songwriter?

17. Which veteran rock band's 2013 tour was called '50 & Counting'?

18. Nicky Byrne, Kian Egan, Mark Feehily, Shane Filan, and Brian McFadden were members of which boy band?

19. Tracy Marrow is the real name of which rapper, who later found acting fame in 'Law and Order: Special Victims Unit'?
    a) Ice Cube b) Ice T c) Vanilla Ice

20. What is the name of Bruce Springsteen's backing band?
    a) The C Street Band b) The D Street Band
    c) The E Street Band

Answers to Quiz 7: Pot Luck

1. Argentina
2. France
3. Tennis
4. Tanzania
5. Web browsers
6. France
7. Ivan the Terrible
8. Ryan Giggs
9. Gordon Brown and Alistair Darling
10. Chicago
11. Andrew Flintoff
12. Silver (grey)
13. Gobi
14. Fabio Capello
15. Charlie Brooks
16. Maiden
17. Iran
18. Australia
19. London
20. Wales

Quiz 9: Pot Luck

1. Lily Savage is the alter ego of which Liverpool comedian?

2. Who was the British prime minister from 1990 until 1997?

3. Which actor made his debut as the 'Caped Crusader' in the 2005 film 'Batman Begins'?

4. The retina, iris, and pupil are parts of which organ of the human body?

5. Ag is the chemical symbol for which precious metal?

6. Kelly Jones is the lead singer with which Welsh rock group?

7. Which spice is used to describe a move in football where the ball is played through an opponent's legs?

8. According to the proverb, fortune favours the ...?

9. Who is Britain's richest living artist?

10. The Battle of Jutland was a naval engagement in which war?

11. Brazil was formerly a colony of which European country?

12. The Beatles named their last album after which London thoroughfare?

13. Titan is the largest moon of which planet of the Solar System?

14. Which planet of the Solar System orbits closest to the sun?

15. The Amazon River flows into which ocean?

16. Rhinoplasty is a cosmetic surgery procedure on which part of the body?

17. Who was the British prime minister at the start of World War II?

18. Which British rock star is nicknamed 'The Prince of Darkness'?

19. Baffin Island is part of which Commonwealth country?
    a) Australia
    b) Canada
    c) New Zealand

20. What is the title of the classic film and West End play?
    a) The 39 Steps
    b) The 49 Steps
    c) The 59 Steps

Answers to Quiz 8: Pop Music

1. Justin Bieber
2. Oasis
3. Madonna
4. The Beautiful South
5. Amy Winehouse
6. Lady Gaga
7. Chas and Dave
8. Spandau Ballet
9. Waterloo
10. Frank Sinatra
11. The Script
12. Britney Spears
13. Bob Marley
14. New Kids on the Block
15. One Direction
16. Taylor Swift
17. The Rolling Stones
18. Westlife
19. Ice T
20. The E Street Band

Quiz 10: Connections part 1

EASY

1. What is the central family in the sitcom 'Only Fools and Horses'?

2. In the 'Chronicles of Narnia' books, what type of creature was Aslan?

3. 'U Can't Touch This' was the biggest UK hit for which big-trousered rapper?

4. Which TV presenter hosted 'Supermarket Sweep' and the National Lottery tie-in 'In It to Win It'?

5. 'Hotel California' was the only UK top ten single for which band?

6. Muddy Waters, Robert Johnson, and John Lee Hooker are associated with which genre of music?

7. In astrology, which animal symbolizes the star sign Aries?

8. 'Never Ever', 'Pure Shores', and 'Black Coffee' were number one hit singles for which girl group?

9. Johnny Depp plays Captain Jack Sparrow in which film series?

10. In addition to woods and a putter, what type of clubs are used by golfers?

11. The clear, colourless fruit brandy Kirsch is traditionally made from what fruit?

12. 'Wishing (If I Had a Photograph of You)' was the only top ten hit from which 80s band, noted for the amazing haircut of its lead singer?

13. Barn, Tawny, and Long-eared are examples of what type of nocturnal bird?

14. Which weapon featured in the title of the only top five hit by Scottish rockers The Fratellis?

15. What is the name of the wheelchair-bound character played by Peter Kay in the TV comedy 'Phoenix Nights'?

16. Tenerife and Lanzarote are part of which island group?

17. Robert Lindsay played Wolfie Smith in which Tooting-set TV comedy?

18. Britt Reid is the alter ego of which comic-book superhero?
    a) Green Hornet
    b) Green Lantern
    c) Green Goblin

19. What was the name of the 1981 film starring Warren Beatty about the Russian Revolution?
    a) Blues
    b) Greens
    c) Reds

20. What is the connection between all the answers?

Answers to Quiz 9: Pot Luck

1. Paul O'Grady
2. John Major
3. Christian Bale
4. The eye
5. Silver
6. Stereophonics
7. Nutmeg
8. Bold
9. Damien Hirst
10. World War I
11. Portugal
12. Abbey Road
13. Saturn
14. Mercury
15. Atlantic
16. The nose
17. Neville Chamberlain
18. Ozzy Osbourne
19. Canada
20. The 39 Steps

Quiz 11: Pot Luck

1. In the human body, what are molars, premolars, and incisors?

2. Sumatra is the second largest island of which country?

3. Easter Island is situated in which ocean?

4. The Artful Dodger and Bill Sikes are characters from which novel by Charles Dickens?

5. In economics, which countries are collectively known as BRIC?

6. What is the largest sports stadium in Britain?

7. Which award-winning actress plays the fierce, elderly matriarch Violet Crawley, dowager countess of Grantham, in 'Downton Abbey'?

8. The stage musical 'Spamalot' is based on which comedy team?

9. What name is given to the side opposite the right angle in a right-angled triangle?

10. What is the UK equivalent of an American freeway?

11. Which measure of weight represents the letter K in the NATO Phonetic Alphabet?

12. Who became President of the United States following the assassination of John F Kennedy?

13. In 2009, Angela Merkel was elected for a second term as the leader of which country?

14. Which element of the periodic table has the atomic number 2?

15. What was the first name of the composer Beethoven?

16. Which Cornish town appears in the title of an opera by Gilbert and Sullivan?

17. In 2011, Dr Conrad Murray was convicted of the involuntary manslaughter of which pop star?

18. Which actor played Gollum in the 2012 film 'The Hobbit'?

19. If a football team plays in a highly defensive style they are said to have
    a) parked the bus
    b) parked the car
    c) parked the taxi

20. Prince Edward is the Earl of where?
    a) Essex
    b) Sussex
    c) Wessex

EASY

Answers to Quiz 10: Connections part 1

1. The Trotters
2. Lion
3. MC Hammer
4. Dale Winton
5. The Eagles
6. Blues
7. Ram
8. All Saints
9. Pirates of the Caribbean
10. Irons
11. Cherries
12. A Flock of Seagulls
13. Owl
14. (Chelsea) Dagger
15. Brian Potter
16. The Canaries
17. Citizen Smith
18. Green Hornet
19. Reds
20. Nicknames of English football teams

Quiz 12: History

1. Which volcano erupted in 79AD, burying the Roman towns of Pompeii and Herculaneum?

2. The Boxer Rebellion was an uprising in which country?

3. Which British prime minister established the Metropolitan Police, giving rise to the nickname 'bobbies'?

4. Who was the first US president to resign from office?

5. From 1919 until 1933, the Weimar Republic was a name given to the government of which country?

6. Killed in 1918, Nicholas II was the last emperor of which country?

7. Who was the father of Queen Elizabeth I?

8. The scene of a famous Japanese aerial attack, Pearl Harbor is in which American state?

9. In 1941, Josef Jakobs became the last person to be executed at which famous London landmark?

10. The French collaborationist government in World War II was based in which town?

11. In 2003, actor Arnold Schwarzenegger was elected governor of which American state?

12. Which English king sealed the Magna Carta?

13. The first Opium War was fought between Britain and which country?

14. Which suffragette died after throwing herself in front of the king's horse at the 1913 Epsom Derby?

15. Which politician's 1946 speech spoke of an 'iron curtain' that had descended across Europe?

16. The Charge of the Light Brigade took place during which war?

17. What were stolen from the Tower of London by Irish adventurer Colonel Thomas Blood in 1671?

18. The Battle of Monte Cassino was fought in which war?

19. What was the name of the 1944 Allied landings in Normandy?
    a) B-Day
    b) D-Day
    c) E-Day

20. In which year did the Battle of Culloden take place?
    a) 1546
    b) 1746
    c) 1946

Answers to Quiz 11: Pot Luck

1. Teeth
2. Indonesia
3. Pacific
4. Oliver Twist
5. Brazil, Russia, India, and China
6. Wembley
7. Dame Maggie Smith
8. Monty Python
9. Hypotenuse
10. Motorway
11. Kilo
12. Lyndon Johnson
13. Germany
14. Helium
15. Ludwig
16. Penzance
17. Michael Jackson
18. Andy Serkis
19. Parked the bus
20. Wessex

Quiz 13: Pot Luck

1. Which chamber of the the UK parliament is known as the Upper House?

2. Which English actor played Commissioner Gordon in 'The Dark Knight Rises'?

3. What is the name of the long bone that runs from the shoulder to the elbow?

4. 'At a Glance: An Absolutely Fabulous Life' is the title of the autobiography of which veteran British actress?

5. What was the first name of the British composer Holst?

6. Who was the first former presidential First Lady to be elected to the US Senate?

7. George Orwell's book 'Homage to Catalonia' is set in which conflict?

8. Who was elected Russian president for a third time in 2012?

9. Detective drama 'Scott and Bailey' is set in which English city?

10. Who made his debut as James Bond in the 1987 film 'The Living Daylights'?

11. Which Democratic Party candidate did George W Bush defeat in the 2000 US presidential election?

12. Assam, Bihar, and Kerala are states in which country?

13. What national radio station broadcasts on 1053 and 1089 AM?

14. Nell Gwyn was the mistress of which English monarch?

15. In computing, what do the initials CPU stand for?

16. Who played the title character in the 1964 family favourite 'Mary Poppins'?

17. What was the first country to win football's World Cup three times?

18. On a standard computer keyboard, which letter lies between C and B?

19. What nationality is the dapper fictional detective Hercule Poirot?
    a) Belgian
    b) French
    c) Swiss

20. Which month represents a letter in the NATO Phonetic Alphabet?
    a) October
    b) November
    c) December

Answers to Quiz 12: History

1. Mt. Vesuvius	11. California
2. China	12. King John
3. Sir Robert Peel	13. China
4. Richard Nixon	14. Emily Davison
5. Germany	15. Winston Churchill
6. Russia	16. The Crimean War
7. Henry VIII	17. The Crown Jewels
8. Hawaii	18. World War II
9. The Tower of London	19. D-Day
10. Vichy	20. 1746

Quiz 14: Connections part 2

EASY

1. What name is given to a young kangaroo?

2. Which internet search engine was launched by Microsoft in May 2009?

3. What is the traditional name for a person who makes and sells candles?

4. In the Old Testament, who was the first wife of Jacob and the mother of Joseph and Benjamin?

5. Which four-letter word can be a verb meaning 'to become more cheerful or lively' or a noun meaning 'a benefit received by an employee in addition to a salary'?

6. Which TV regular found fame for his spoon-bending abilities?

7. What is the branch of science that is concerned with fossils of animals and plants?

8. The former flag of Libya was made up entirely of which colour?

9. Which radio presenter is the sister of broadcaster Keith Chegwin?

10. Which boy's name provided Michael Jackson with a number 7 hit in 1972?

11. Steve Guttenberg and Ted Danson were two of the three men in the film 'Three Men and a Baby'. Who was the third?

12. Which actor married Madonna in 1985?

13. What was the name of the female baddie in the 1989 Disney animation 'The Little Mermaid'?

14. Who succeeded Barry Norman as the host of BBC TV's 'Film' programme?

15. Which French artist created the work 'Fountain' which featured a urinal signed 'R.Mutt'?

16. 'The Night Watch' is a famous painting by which 17th-century Dutch master?

17. Albany is the capital of which American state?

18. Which of the following is a moon of the planet Saturn?
    a) Patty
    b) Penny
    c) Phoebe

19. In 'Masterchef: The Professionals' what is the name of Michel Roux's sous-chef?
    a) Martha
    b) Mary
    c) Monica

20. What is the connection between all the answers?

Answers to Quiz 13: Pot Luck

1. The House of Lords
2. Gary Oldman
3. Humerus
4. June Whitfield
5. Gustav
6. Hillary Clinton
7. Spanish Civil War
8. Vladimir Putin
9. Manchester
10. Timothy Dalton
11. Al Gore
12. India
13. talkSPORT
14. Charles II
15. Central Processing Unit
16. Julie Andrews
17. Brazil
18. V
19. Belgian
20. November

Quiz 15: Pot Luck

1. Which hugely popular contemporary costume drama is filmed at Highclere Castle in Hampshire?

2. In a game of cricket, what do the initials LBW stand for?

3. Which Irish actor played Hannibal in the 2010 film version of 'The A Team'?

4. According to the proverb, what speak louder than words?

5. Stretching some 137 miles, what is the longest canal in Britain?

6. What is the most commonly used word in the English language?

7. The phrase 'a pound of flesh' derives from which Shakespeare play?

8. Complete the proverb: If a job's worth doing it's worth doing ...

9. Controversial striker Luis Suarez plays international football for which country?

10. Which British motorway runs from Rugby to Carlisle?

11. On a standard computer keyboard, what is the only vowel that isn't on the top row of letters?

12. What is Britain's best-selling daily newspaper?

13. In relation to technology, what do the initials GPS stand for?

14. What is the only number in English that is equal to the number of letters in its name?

15. Florence Welch is the lead singer with which British band?

16. What was the name of the protest movement that camped outside St Paul's Cathedral in late 2011?

17. How is 2013 written in Roman numerals?

18. Which animal-inspired play, which was later turned into a 2011 film directed by Steven Spielberg, was based on a book by Michael Morpurgo?

19. In October 2011 the world's population topped how many billion?
    a) 3 billion
    b) 5 billion
    c) 7 billion

20. What was name given to the series of political protests that started in 2010?
    a) Arab Spring
    b) Arab Summer
    c) Arab Winter

Answers to Quiz 14: Connections part 2

1. Joey
2. Bing
3. Chandler
4. Rachel
5. Perk
6. Uri Geller
7. Palaeontology
8. Green
9. Janice Long
10. Ben
11. Tom Selleck
12. Sean Penn
13. Ursula
14. Jonathan Ross
15. Marcel Duchamp
16. Rembrandt
17. New York
18. Phoebe
19. Monica
20. They all relate to the sitcom 'Friends'.

Quiz 16: Advertising Slogans

EASY

Identify the companies associated with the following slogans:

1. 'Every little helps.'

2. 'What's the worst that could happen?'

3. 'The world's local bank'

4. 'I'm lovin' it.'

5. 'Think different.'

6. 'Eat fresh.'

7. 'Just do it.'

8. 'It does exactly what it says on the tin.'

9. 'Because I'm worth it'

10. 'It's the real thing.'

11. 'Live well for less.'

12. 'Simples!'

13. 'Zoom zoom'

14. 'Good with food'

15. 'It gives you wings.'

EASY

16. 'Taste the rainbow.'

17. 'Connecting people'

18. 'Buy it. Sell it. Love it.'

19. 'It could be you!'

20. 'It's got our name on it.'

Answers to Quiz 15: Pot Luck

1. Downton Abbey
2. Leg before wicket
3. Liam Neeson
4. Actions
5. The Grand Union
6. The
7. The Merchant of Venice
8. Well
9. Uruguay
10. M6
11. A
12. The Sun
13. Global Positioning System
14. Four
15. Florence and the Machine
16. Occupy
17. MMXIII
18. War Horse
19. 7 billion
20. Arab Spring

Quiz 17: Pot Luck

1. According to Oscar Wilde, what is 'the curse of drinking classes'?

2. A parliament that is bicameral has how many chambers?

3. Which motorway runs from London to South Wales?

4. What does a barometer measure?

5. 'Vert' is the French word for which colour?

6. Who is older – Prince William or his cousin, Zara Phillips?

7. In internet slang, what does the acronym 'YOLO' stand for?

8. Which imperial measurement is equivalent to 2.54cm?

9. Bungle, George, and Zippy were characters in which long-running children's TV show?

10. What title is given to the wife of a duke?

11. Brass is an alloy of copper and what metal?

12. Which composer wrote the piece of music known as the 'Moonlight Sonata'?

13. Which letter sits between I and P on a standard computer keyboard?

14. In America they're known as morticians, but what are they called in the UK?

15. Which British overseas territory is situated near the southern tip of Spain?

16. In relation to the changing of clocks, what does the S in BST stand for?

17. Which detective appeared in the novels 'Murder on the Orient Express' and 'Death on the Nile'?

18. Which branch of science deals with the motion of projectiles, especially bombs and bullets?

19. 'How you doin'?' was a catchphrase of which character from the TV comedy 'Friends'?

20. 'The Owls' is the nickname of which English football team?
    a) Huddersfield Town
    b) Leeds United
    c) Sheffield Wednesday

21. The Ashmolean Museum is located in which English city?
    a) Cambridge
    b) Oxford
    c) London

EASY

Answers to Quiz 16: Advertising Slogans

1. Tesco
2. Dr Pepper
3. HSBC
4. McDonald's
5. Apple
6. Subway
7. Nike
8. Ronseal
9. L'Oréal
10. Coca-Cola
11. Sainsbury's
12. CompareTheMarket.com
13. Mazda
14. The Co-operative
15. Red Bull
16. Skittles
17. Nokia
18. eBay
19. The National Lottery
20. Wickes

Quiz 18: Politics

1. In the UK, elections usually take place on which day of the week?

2. IDS are the initials of which former leader of the Conservative Party?

3. How often do US presidential elections take place?

4. Which chamber of parliament has more members – the House of Commons or the House of Lords?

5. Which politician famously said, 'You turn if you want to. The lady's not for turning'?

6. What are the names of the two houses of the US Congress?

7. On which day of the week does Prime Minister's Questions take place?

8. What is the only state of America that is named after a US president?

9. Who originally played Jim Hacker in the classic political comedy 'Yes, Minister'?

10. In UK politics, which government department has the initials DEFRA?

11. What name describes an MP who is not a member of the government or a shadow minister?

12. The SDLP and the DUP are political parties found in which part of the UK?

13. In 1998 US president Bill Clinton admitted to having an inappropriate relationship with which intern?

14. Which Labour politician did Vince Cable describe as having undergone a transformation from 'Stalin to Mr Bean'?

15. Nineteen British prime ministers have been educated at which public school?

16. Which MP, who found fame on a reality TV show, called David Cameron and George Osborne 'two posh boys who don't know the price of milk'?

17. What is the minimum age that a person in Britain can stand in local council elections?

18. Which Conservative politician had a four-year affair with prime minister John Major?

19. Who officially calls a UK general election?
    a) the prime minister b) the speaker of the House of Commons
    c) the Queen

20. The 'Gang of Four' founded which UK political party?
    a) the Green Party b) the SDP c) UKIP

Answers to Quiz 17: Pot Luck

1. Work
2. Two
3. M4
4. Atmospheric pressure
5. Green
6. Zara Phillips
7. You only live once
8. Inch
9. Rainbow
10. Duchess
11. Zinc
12. Beethoven
13. O
14. Undertakers
15. Gibraltar
16. Summer (British Summer Time)
17. Hercule Poirot
18. Ballistics
19. Joey
20. Sheffield Wednesday
21. Oxford

Quiz 19: Pot Luck

1. What is the oldest university in Scotland?

2. What nationality is Formula One driver Fernando Alonso?

3. The Riddler, the Penguin, and Catwoman were enemies of which superhero?

4. Which element of the periodic table has the atomic number 7 and the chemical symbol N?

5. What is western Europe's highest mountain?

6. IMF are the initials of which global financial organization?

7. According to the proverb, what is in the eye of the beholder?

8. Which savoury dish of meat, jelly, and pastry is also the name of a type of hat?

9. What is the national motto of France?

10. John S Pemberton was the inventor of which famous drink?

11. According to the proverb, an army marches on its what?

12. Which actor made his debut as James Bond in the 1995 film 'Goldeneye'?

13. The bands Elbow, James, and The Stone Roses are from which British city?

14. The musical 'We Will Rock You' is based on the songs of which band?

15. How many strings are on a standard double bass?

16. Which popular tomato-based dip takes its name from the Spanish word for sauce?

17. 'Mardi' is the French word for which day of the week?

18. The 1996 film 'Trainspotting' was based on a novel by which Scottish author?

19. Which Olympian was granted the freedom of the city of Sheffield in 2013?
    a) Jessica Ennis
    b) Mo Farah
    c) Greg Rutherford

20. Pop star Madonna was formerly married to which British film director?
    a) Dexter Fletcher
    b) Guy Ritchie
    c) Matthew Vaughn

Answers to Quiz 18: Politics

1. Thursday
2. Iain Duncan Smith
3. Every four years
4. House of Lords
5. Margaret Thatcher
6. The Senate and the House of Representatives
7. Wednesday
8. Washington
9. Paul Eddington
10. Department for Environment, Food, and Rural Affairs
11. Backbencher
12. Northern Ireland
13. Monica Lewinsky
14. Gordon Brown
15. Eton
16. Nadine Dorries
17. 18
18. Edwina Currie
19. The Queen
20. The SDP

Quiz 20: Television part 1

EASY

1. 'EastEnders' is set in which fictional London suburb?

2. How many 'Dragons' are there on the TV show 'Dragons' Den'?

3. Which long-standing 'Coronation Street' character is played by Simon Gregson?

4. Which TV programme features a mysterious driver known as 'The Stig'?

5. 'Torchwood' is a spin-off from which science-fiction programme?

6. Which member of the Monty Python team went 'Pole to Pole' and 'Around the World in 80 Days'?

7. Tom, Barbara, Jerry, and Margo were the central characters in which 1970s sitcom?

8. Which comedy duo present 'The Great British Bake Off'?

9. Who is the host of the TV quiz show 'University Challenge'?

10. In which TV game show are contestants asked to 'say what you see'?

11. Tony Hutchinson, Jack Osborne, and Cindy Cunningham are long-serving characters in which TV drama?

12. Which former Dr Who played Alec Hardy in crime drama 'Broadchurch'?

13. Who plays dot.com billionaire Walden Schmidt in the TV comedy 'Two and a Half Men'?

14. Which actor has played characters called George Carter, Terry McCann, and Gerry Standing?

15. Which TV channel bought the rights to show the Derby, the Grand National, and Royal Ascot from 2013?

16. 'Just one more thing' was the catchphrase of which dishevelled TV detective?

17. Which actor has appeared in 'Coronation Street' and also hosted game shows 'The Chase' and 'Wheel of Fortune'?

18. Which character was the host of the TV chat show 'Knowing Me, Knowing You'?

19. Classic TV comedy Cheers was set in which American city?
    a) Boston
    b) Chicago
    c) Los Angeles

20. What is the name of the Channel 4 topical satire show?
    a) 9 O'Clock Live
    b) 10 O'Clock Live
    c) 11 O'Clock Live

Answers to Quiz 19: Pot Luck

1. St Andrews
2. Spanish
3. Batman
4. Nitrogen
5. Mont Blanc
6. International Monetary Fund
7. Beauty
8. Pork pie
9. Liberté, égalité, fraternité (Liberty, equality, and fraternity)
10. Coca-Cola
11. Stomach
12. Pierce Brosnan
13. Manchester
14. Queen
15. Four
16. Salsa
17. Tuesday
18. Irvine Welsh
19. Jessica Ennis
20. Guy Ritchie

Quiz 21: Pot Luck

1. Arachnology is the study of what type of creatures?

2. In the 'Mr Men' series, what colour is Mr Strong?

3. Which American author said, 'A classic is something that everybody wants to have read and nobody wants to read'?

4. What title is given to the wife of an earl?

5. 'Just like that' was the catchphrase of which comedian and magician?

6. Which American soap returned to TV screens in 2012, 21 years after the previous series was aired?

7. Antonio Stradivari was a renowned maker of which musical instrument?

8. How many sides does a 50p coin have?

9. Which medal is awarded to military personnel displaying conspicuous bravery?

10. Which creepy family calls North Cemetery Ridge, USA home?

11. What is the nickname of the darts champion Phil Taylor?

12. A Neapolitan is the name given to a resident of which European city?

13. What is the Sunday prior to Easter Sunday commonly known as?

14. What is the only Canadian province or territory that begins with the letter Y?

15. Simba, Musafa, and Scar are the central characters in which animated film that was later turned into a hit West End show?

Answers – page 45

16. What was the name of the character played by Harrison Ford in the 'Star Wars' films?

17. Which English town is home to famous jazz, science, literature, and horse racing festivals?

18. Which British prime minister gave his name to a fragrant tea that is flavoured with bergamot oil?

19. What is the currency of Vietnam?
    a) Dong
    b) Pong
    c) Song

20. Author John le Carré is associated with which genre of fiction?
    a) espionage
    b) romance
    c) science fiction

EASY

Answers to Quiz 20: Television part 1

1. Walford
2. Four
3. Steve McDonald
4. Top Gear
5. Doctor Who
6. Michael Palin
7. The Good Life
8. Mel Giedroyc and Sue Perkins
9. Jeremy Paxman
10. Catchphrase
11. Hollyoaks
12. David Tennant
13. Ashton Kutcher
14. Dennis Waterman
15. Channel 4
16. Columbo
17. Bradley Walsh
18. Alan Partridge
19. Boston
20. 10 O'Clock Live

Quiz 22: Alliterative Answers

EASY

1. Which actress played Monica in the long-running TV comedy 'Friends'?

2. Which cartoon character is married to Wilma and has a child called Pebbles?

3. What is the name of the character played by Patsy Palmer in BBC soap 'EastEnders'?

4. The films 'ET', 'Close Encounters of the Third Kind', and 'Schindler's List' were directed by which American film-maker?

5. Which celebrity married American basketball star Kris Humphries in August 2011?

6. Who wrote the classic novel 'Robinson Crusoe'?

7. Max Bygraves, Bob Monkhouse, Les Dennis, and Vernon Kay have all hosted which TV game show?

8. 'Boom! Boom!' is the catchphrase of which talking fox?

9. Which Swede won 11 tennis grand slam titles including five successive Wimbledon titles?

10. Which Birmingham-born singer was the lead singer with heavy rockers Black Sabbath?

11. 'The Little Tramp' was the alter ego of which silent movie star?

12. Who is the primary love interest of the superhero Superman?

13. What was the original name of boxing champion Muhammad Ali?

14. Which American tennis player won his only Wimbledon men's singles title in 1992?

EASY

15. Which 1987 romantic drama starred Patrick Swayze as Johnny Castle and Jennifer Grey as Frances 'Baby' Houseman'?

16. 'Eh ... What's up, doc?' is the catchphrase of which animated character?

17. Which fictional character, created by JM Barrie, was also known as 'The Boy Who Wouldn't Grow Up'?

18. 'Terrible Tudors', 'Groovy Greeks', and 'Vicious Vikings' are works in which children's book series?

19. Which fictional children's book character was played on film by Gene Wilder in 1971 and Johnny Depp in 2005?

20. Which TV show starring John Hamm is set in a 1950s New York advertising agency?

Answers to Quiz 21: Pot Luck

1.	Spiders	11.	The Power
2.	Red	12.	Naples
3.	Mark Twain	13.	Palm Sunday
4.	Countess	14.	Yukon
5.	Tommy Cooper	15.	The Lion King
6.	Dallas	16.	Han Solo
7.	Violin	17.	Cheltenham
8.	Seven	18.	Earl Grey
9.	The Victoria Cross	19.	Dong
10.	The Addams Family	20.	Espionage

Quiz 23: Pot Luck

1. What nationality is Formula One champion Sebastian Vettel?

2. Which politician has the most followers on Twitter?

3. Which religious leader would write a letter known as an encyclical?

4. In which branch of mathematics are symbols used in place of numbers?

5. Which weighty nautical object is dropped below the sea to keep a ship stationary?

6. What is measured using an anemometer?

7. Which country won football's World Cup for the third time in 1982?

8. The M40 runs from London to which British city?

9. According to the Bible, man cannot live on what alone?

10. Salop is an alternative name for which English county?

11. Business mogul Rupert Murdoch was born in which country?

12. 'The Tale of Peter Rabbit' was the first book by which children's author?

13. Basmati, arborio, and long grain are varieties of what type of food?

14. Who has been a judge on both 'Strictly Come Dancing' and 'Britain's Got Talent'?

15. 'Bangers' are a nickname for what type of food?

16. The song 'Eye of the Tiger' is associated with which fictional boxer?

17. Which sport features teams called Mumbai Indians, Royal Challengers Bangalore, and Chennai Super Kings?

18. In chess, each player starts with how many rooks?

19. What is the maximum possible finish in a game of tournament darts?
    a) 160
    b) 170
    c) 180

20. The 'smokie' is a type of haddock associated with which Scottish town?
    a) Arbroath
    b) Falkirk
    c) Montrose

Answers to Quiz 22: Alliterative Answers

1. Courteney Cox
2. Fred Flintstone
3. Bianca Butcher
4. Steven Spielberg
5. Kim Kardashian
6. Daniel Defoe
7. Family Fortunes
8. Basil Brush
9. Bjorn Borg
10. Ozzy Osbourne
11. Charlie Chaplin
12. Lois Lane
13. Cassius Clay
14. Andre Agassi
15. Dirty Dancing
16. Bugs Bunny
17. Peter Pan
18. Horrible Histories
19. Willy Wonka
20. Mad Men

Quiz 24: Olympic Games

EASY

1. Who won gold for Britain on the track at the 2012 Olympics in the 5000m and 10,000m?

2. Foil, épée, and sabre are disciplines in which Olympic sport?

3. Which Olympic track event is nicknamed the 'metric mile'?

4. Which sprinter in 2012 became the first man to defend the men's 100m and 200m titles?

5. Which British athlete won the men's 100m at the 1992 Olympic Games in Barcelona?

6. Swimming races at the Olympics feature which four strokes?

7. The Glasgow Velodrome is named after which record-breaking Olympian?

8. In 2012, Beth Tweddle became the first British woman since 1928 to win a solo Olympic medal in which sport?

9. Which city hosted the 1996 Olympic Games?

10. Which was the first city to host the Olympic Games three times?

11. True or false – the Olympic Games have never been hosted in Africa?

12. Which British athlete won gold in the heptathlon in 2000?

13. In 2012, Nicola Adams became the first woman to win a gold medal in which sport?

14. Daley Thompson won Olympic gold in 1980 and 1984 in which event?

15. In an Olympic decathlon, what is the first field event?

16. A star at the 2000 Games, by what name was Eric Moussambani Malonga better known?

17. True or false – tug of war was once an Olympic sport?

18. What is the only city that starts with the letter H to have hosted the Summer Olympics?

19. In which year did the first modern Olympics take place?
    a) 1892
    b) 1896
    c) 1900

20. Which city hosted the inaugural games?
    a) Athens
    b) London
    c) Los Angeles

Answers to Quiz 23: Pot Luck

1. German
2. Barack Obama
3. The Pope
4. Algebra
5. An anchor
6. Wind
7. Italy
8. Birmingham
9. Bread
10. Shropshire
11. Australia
12. Beatrix Potter
13. Rice
14. Alesha Dixon
15. Sausages
16. Rocky Balboa
17. Cricket
18. Two
19. 170
20. Arbroath

Quiz 25: Pot Luck

1. The RCN is a trade union that represents people in which profession?

2. The car manufacturer Volvo is based in which country?

3. Hillsborough is the home ground of which English football team?

4. 'Tomorrow' and 'Hard Knock Life' are songs from which hit stage musical?

5. In which TV game show does the host say, 'Our survey says'?

6. From what country does the flamenco originate?

7. What is the only US state that begins with the letter L?

8. The Order of the Rising Sun is an honour awarded in which country?

9. In medicine, for what do the initials GP stand?

10. Who played the eponymous schoolboy wizard in the 'Harry Potter' films?

11. Rhino, Shadow, and Wolf were characters in which physical TV game show?

12. England cricketers Kevin Pietersen, Jonathan Trott, and Matt Prior were all born in which country?

13. Oncology is the scientific study of which disease?

14. The zloty is the currency of which European country?

15. In a game of chess, each player starts with how many pieces?

16. Which imperial measure is equivalent to 0.57 litres?

17. Which name connects a British soldier and statesman and a dish that features beef coated in pastry?

18. 'Jaune' is the French word for which colour?

19. In which year did the Battle of Agincourt take place?
    a) 1415
    b) 1615
    c) 1815

20. Jarvis Cocker is the lead singer with which band?
    a) Blur
    b) Oasis
    b) Pulp

EASY

Answers to Quiz 24: Olympic Games

1. Mo Farah
2. Fencing
3. 1500 metres
4. Usain Bolt
5. Linford Christie
6. Backstroke, breaststroke, butterfly, and crawl (freestyle)
7. Sir Chris Hoy
8. Gymnastics
9. Atlanta
10. London
11. True
12. Denise Lewis
13. Boxing
14. Decathlon
15. Long jump
16. Eric the Eel
17. True
18. Helsinki
19. 1896
20. Athens

Quiz 26: Animals part 1

1. Which golfer won his first major title at the US Masters in 1997?

2. 'The Hamster' is the nickname of which presenter of TV's 'Top Gear'?

3. Which adventurer, writer, and broadcaster, who starred in the TV show 'Born Survivor' is also the Chief Scout?

4. Which actor played Archie Mitchell in 'EastEnders'?

5. 'Pitbull' is the nickname of which former England rugby international turned controversial commentator?

6. What was the title of the 1986 film starring Paul Hogan as an adventurer from the Aussie outback who travels to New York?

7. 'The Cat' is the nickname of which team captain on 'A Question of Sport'?

8. Which singer-songwriter converted to Islam and changed his name to Yusuf Islam?

9. Which actor played Marty McFly in the 'Back to the Future' film trilogy?

10. The lawyer Atticus Finch is the central character in which classic novel, which was turned into a film starring Gregory Peck?

11. What was the title of director Quentin Tarantino's first feature film?

12. Which architect designed St Paul's Cathedral?

13. 'Monkey Business', 'Horse Feathers', and 'Duck Soup' were films starring which comedic siblings?

14. Which cricket umpire and best-selling author celebrated his 80th birthday in 2013?

15. What is the nickname of Leicestershire County Cricket Club?

16. In the TV soap 'Neighbours', what is the name of the character played by Ryan Moloney?

17. Which radio DJ was a judge on the TV talent show 'Pop Idol' from 2001 until 2003?

18. In the hit TV comedy 'Frasier', what is the title character's surname?

19. In the 'Star Wars' films, what was the name of Han Solo's ship?
    a) Millennium Eagle
    b) Millennium Falcon
    c) Millennium Swift

20. What was the name of the 1995 sci-fi adventure directed by Terry Gilliam and starring Bruce Willis?
    a) Eleven Monkeys
    b) Twelve Monkeys
    c) Thirteen Monkeys

Answers to Quiz 25: Pot Luck

1. Nursing
2. Sweden
3. Sheffield Wednesday
4. Annie
5. Family Fortunes
6. Spain
7. Louisiana
8. Japan
9. General Practitioner
10. Daniel Radcliffe
11. Gladiators
12. South Africa
13. Cancer
14. Poland
15. 16
16. A pint
17. Wellington
18. Yellow
19. 1415
20. Pulp

Quiz 27: Pot Luck

1. Which American singer had a big hit in 2012 with 'Stronger (What Doesn't Kill You)'?

2. The dance known as the tango originated in which South American city?

3. Which country did Spain beat in the final of the 2010 World Cup?

4. What is the longest man-made object on earth?

5. Which method of execution was last used in France in 1977?

6. The name of which popular school-based TV show also describes a piece of music for three or more solo unaccompanied voices?

7. Ganesh is a deity in which religion?

8. The Eden Project is located in which English county?

9. According to the proverb, what can't be cured must be ...?

10. 'The Watchtower' is a periodical published by which religious organization?

11. Which former captain of the England cricket team appeared on 'Strictly Come Dancing' in 2012?

12. In America they're known as realtors, but what is the job called in the UK?

13. 'American Idiot' is a jukebox musical based on the songs of which rock band?

14. In Greek mythology, who carried the world on his shoulders?

15. Which rodent is also the name of a device used to control a computer cursor?

16. Which actress gave up film stardom after marrying Prince Rainier of Monaco in 1956?

17. In relation to television sets, for what do the initials LCD stand?

18. Which actor plays the title character in the TV detective drama 'Lewis'?

19. In the 'Mr Men' series, what colour is Mr Bounce?
    a) Blue
    c) Red
    c) Yellow

20. Rosencrantz and Guildenstern are characters in which Shakespeare play?
    a) Antony and Cleopatra
    b) Hamlet
    c) A Midsummer Night's Dream

Answers to Quiz 26: Animals part 1

1. Tiger Woods
2. Richard Hammond
3. Bear Grylls
4. Larry Lamb
5. Brian Moore
6. Crocodile Dundee
7. Phil Tufnell
8. Cat Stevens
9. Michael J Fox
10. To Kill a Mockingbird
11. Reservoir Dogs
12. Sir Christopher Wren
13. The Marx Brothers
14. Dickie Bird
15. The Foxes
16. Jarrod 'Toadfish' Rebecchi
17. 'Dr' Neil Fox
18. Crane
19. Millennium Falcon
20. Twelve Monkeys

Quiz 28: Famous Martins

Identify the famous Martins from the clues below:

1. The lead singer with stadium rockers Coldplay.

2. Captained England to victory in the 2003 Rugby World Cup.

3. Film director whose works include 'The Aviator', 'Shutter Island', and 'Hugo'.

4. Actor who played Dr Watson alongside Benedict Cumberbatch's Sherlock Holmes.

5. Broadcaster and journalist who created MoneySavingExpert.com website.

6. Pop star who enjoyed 'Livin' la Vida Loca'.

7. He became deputy First Minister of Northern Ireland in May 2007.

8. Creator of the fantasy series 'Game of Thrones'.

9. Bass player with New Romantics Spandau Ballet.

10. The eighth president of the USA.

11. Seth Pecksniff, Sarah Gamp, and Mark Tapley are characters in this Dickens novel.

12. Banjo-playing actor, comedian, and writer who starred in 'The Jerk' and 'The Man with Two Brains'.

13. Actor whose real name is Ramon Estevez.

14. German theologian whose writings helped inspire the Protestant Reformation.

Answers – page 59

15. EastEnders character played by James Alexandrou from 1996 to 2007.

16. Formula One commentator who won the 24 Hours of Le Mans race in 1990.

17. German golfer who won the 2010 US PGA Championship and topped the world rankings in 2011.

18. He scored a goal for England in the 1966 World Cup final.

19. He played the title character in the short-lived 2009 remake of 'Reggie Perrin'.

20. US actor whose films include 'Bad Boys' and 'Big Momma's House'.

Answers to Quiz 27: Pot Luck

1. Kelly Clarkson
2. Buenos Aires
3. The Netherlands
4. The Great Wall of China
5. Guillotine
6. Glee
7. Hinduism
8. Cornwall
9. Endured
10. Jehovah's Witnesses
11. Michael Vaughan
12. Estate agent
13. Green Day
14. Atlas
15. Mouse
16. Grace Kelly
17. Liquid Crystal Display
18. Kevin Whately
19. Yellow
20. Hamlet

Quiz 29: Pot Luck

1. What nationality is the footballer Lionel Messi?

2. The character John McClane appears in which long-running film franchise?

3. What is the only capital city of a European Union country that starts with the letter H?

4. In Roman numerals, which letter represents 50?

5. The koala bear is native to which country?

6. Alencon, Honiton, and Chantilly are varieties of what type of fabric?

7. In the Christian church, what is the 40-day period before Easter known as?

8. In relation to the naval rescue service, for what do the initials RNLI stand?

9. What is the speed of 1 sea mile per hour more commonly known as?

10. What are the three member countries of the United Nations that begin with the letter H?

11. In the Christian calendar, which day precedes Good Friday?

12. Dusty Bin was the booby prize on which long-running TV game show?

13. In connection with mobile phones, for what do the initials SMS stand?

14. Which element combines with oxygen to form water?

15. Which rare gas element is also the name of the native world of Superman?

16. Which fictional broadcaster hosts a show called 'Mid Morning Matters' on radio station North Norfolk Digital?

17. What name is shared by a Scottish actor who once played Hannibal Lecter and a former keyboard player turned TV scientist?

18. What is the currency of Russia?

19. Which of the following represents a letter in the NATO Phonetic Alphabet?
    a) brother
    b) mama
    c) papa

20. What name is given to an angle that is higher than 90 but lower than 180 degrees?
    a) acute
    b) obtuse
    c) right

Answers to Quiz 28: Famous Martins

1. Chris Martin
2. Martin Johnson
3. Martin Scorsese
4. Martin Freeman
5. Martin Lewis
6. Ricky Martin
7. Martin McGuinness
8. George RR Martin
9. Martin Kemp
10. Martin Van Buren
11. Martin Chuzzlewit
12. Steve Martin
13. Martin Sheen
14. Martin Luther
15. Martin Fowler
16. Martin Brundle
17. Martin Kaymer
18. Martin Peters
19. Martin Clunes
20. Martin Lawrence

Quiz 30: Love and Marriage

1. Hugh Grant played the British prime minister in which 2003 romantic comedy?

2. Who was the ancient Roman god of love?

3. Tatiana Romanova and Rosa Klebb were characters in which James Bond film?

4. Which band spent 15 weeks at the top of the charts in 1994 with 'Love Is All Around'?

5. Who 'Just Called to Say I Love You' in 1984?

6. Which singer and actress was married to rock star Kurt Cobain?

7. The Bundy family were the central characters in which American sitcom that ran from 1987 until 1997?

8. Who played the title character in the 1998 romantic comedy 'The Wedding Singer'?

9. Which composer wrote the opera 'The Marriage of Figaro'?

10. What metal is traditionally associated with a 25th wedding anniversary?

11. In which sport is Davis Love III a notable name?

12. The 1977 hit 'I Feel Love' was the only UK number one single for which disco diva?

13. Which American actress's credits include 'I Know What You Did Last Summer', 'Ghost Whisperer', 'Party of Five', and 'Hot in Cleveland'?

14. Gwyneth Paltrow won Best Actress and Judi Dench Best Supporting Actress for their performances in which 1998 romantic comedy?

15. UB40 topped the charts in 1993 with a cover of which Elvis Presley classic?

16. The Love Unlimited Orchestra was the backing band for which American soul man?

17. Which Nottinghamshire author wrote the 1920 novel 'Women in Love'?

18. What was Dusty Springfield's only UK number one hit single?

19. 'Love You More', the official BBC Children in Need song in 2010, was sung by which boy band?
    a) JLS b) One Direction c) Westlife

20. Which American singer was 'Crazy in Love' in 2003?
    a) Beyoncé b) Christina Aguilera c) Britney Spears

Answers to Quiz 29: Pot Luck

1. Argentine
2. Die Hard
3. Helsinki
4. L
5. Australia
6. Lace
7. Lent
8. Royal National Lifeboat Institution
9. A knot
10. Haiti, Honduras, and Hungary
11. Maundy Thursday
12. 3-2-1
13. Short Message Service
14. Hydrogen
15. Krypton
16. Alan Partridge
17. Brian Cox
18. Rouble
19. Papa
20. Obtuse

Quiz 31: Pot Luck

EASY

1. Maine Road was the former ground of which Premier League football club?

2. Which city in England is home to more canals than Venice?

3. Shem, Ham, and Japheth were the sons of which Biblical figure?

4. The Azores lie in which ocean?

5. The kiwi bird is native to which country?

6. Which month was named after Julius Caesar?

7. Which educational establishment has the initials LSE?

8. The Royal Botanic Gardens are located in which London suburb?

9. What do the initials IQ stand for?

10. Which metallic element derives its chemical symbol Fe from the Latin 'ferrum'?

11. Which veteran rocker's farewell series of 2013 shows was called 'The Last at Bat Tour'?

12. What is the imaginary line that runs along the 180 degree meridian to mark the difference in time between the east and west?

13. Hydrophobia is an alternative name for which potentially fatal disease?

14. The ISBN coding system is used to identify what type of objects?

15. The US base at Guantanamo Bay is on which Caribbean island?

16. Drums, cymbals, and tambourines are members of which family of musical instruments?

17. Which one time 'voice of an angel' released the 2013 album 'One & Two'?

18. Conkers are the seed of which tree?

19. What would you do with something called a hurdy-gurdy?
    a) play it
    b) ride it
    c) wear it

20. Which chef appeared in the TV series 'Kitchen Nightmares', 'The F Word', and 'Beyond Boiling Point'?
    a) Jamie Oliver
    b) Gordon Ramsay
    c) Marco Pierre White

Answers to Quiz 30: Love and Marriage

1. Love Actually
2. Cupid
3. From Russia With Love
4. Wet Wet Wet
5. Stevie Wonder
6. Courtney Love
7. Married with Children
8. Adam Sandler
9. Mozart
10. Silver
11. Golf
12. Donna Summer
13. Jennifer Love Hewitt
14. Shakespeare in Love
15. (I Can't Help) Falling in Love with You
16. Barry White
17. DH Lawrence
18. You Don't Have to Say You Love Me
19. JLS
20. Beyoncé

Quiz 32: Numbers part 2

1. In snooker, how many points is the red worth?

2. According to the rhyme, what can you expect if you see two magpies?

3. How many holes are there in a round of championship golf?

4. Frankie Valli was the lead singer with which vocal group?

5. What was the sequel to the film '101 Dalmatians'?

6. An octahedron is a shape with how many faces?

7. In a game of darts, what is the second highest score than can be made with three darts?

8. A ruby anniversary is celebrated after how many years of marriage?

9. Which Soviet assault rifle was designed by Mikhail Timofeyevich Kalashnikov?

10. Hugh Grant played Charles and Andie MacDowell played Carrie in which hit 1994 romantic comedy?

11. What is the name of the transpennine motorway that runs from Liverpool to Hull?

12. How many dots are there on a die?

13. 'Love Shack' was the only top ten hit for which group?

14. According to a song by De La Soul, what is the 'Magic Number'?

15. Also the title of a Shakespeare play, by what name is the evening of 5 January also known?

16. Which 2013 film, starring Jessica Chastain, was about the operation that killed al-Qaeda leader Osama bin Laden?

17. Which 1949 film was based on a novella by Graham Greene and starred Orson Welles as the infamous Harry Lime?

18. Which amendment of the US constitution protects witnesses from being forced to incriminate themselves?

19. In cricket, 111 is considered unlucky. What is the nickname of 111?
    a) Napoleon
    b) Nelson
    c) Wellington

20. How many balls does a player have to pot to complete a maximum 147 break in snooker?
    a) 32
    b) 34
    c) 36

Answers to Quiz 31: Pot Luck

1. Manchester City
2. Birmingham
3. Noah
4. Atlantic
5. New Zealand
6. July
7. London School of Economics
8. Kew
9. Intelligence Quotient
10. Iron
11. Meat Loaf
12. International Date Line
13. Rabies
14. Books
15. Cuba
16. Percussion
17. Charlotte Church
18. Horse chestnut
19. Play it
20. Gordon Ramsay

Quiz 33: Pot Luck

1. Ankara is the capital city of which country?

2. What is measured using a thermometer?

3. Eleanor Gow is the real name of which supermodel?

4. What is the official document issued by a government that allows its citizens to travel abroad?

5. Which metal has the atomic number 50 and the chemical symbol Sn?

6. Over half of the world's population lives in which continent?

7. The Grimaldis are the royal family of which European principality?

8. Designed by Sir Christopher Wren, the Monument of London marks the starting point of which tragic event?

9. Which annual festival celebrates the life of a 3rd-century Christian martyr?

10. What is the currency of Japan?

11. Which word describes the government taking over ownership and operation of an industry or service?

12. Which American holiday takes place annually on the fourth Thursday in November?

13. On a standard computer keyboard, which letter sits between Z and C?

14. Which annual classic horse race usually takes place on the first Saturday in June?

15. The Tomb of the Unknown Warrior is in which London church?

16. Lewis, Donegal, and Harris are types of which fabric?

17. Which spirit is the central ingredient of the cocktail known as the Bloody Mary?

18. The Tynwald is the parliament of which part of the British Isles?

19. Brisbane is the largest city in which Australian state?
    a) New South Wales
    b) Queensland
    c) Victoria

20. A person in which occupation would wear a mitre?
    a) barrister
    b) bishop
    c) soldier

Answers to Quiz 32: Numbers part 2

1. One
2. Joy
3. 18
4. The Four Seasons
5. 102 Dalmatians
6. Eight
7. 177
8. 40
9. AK-47
10. Four Weddings and a Funeral
11. M62
12. 21
13. B52s
14. Three
15. Twelfth Night
16. Zero Dark Thirty
17. The Third Man
18. Fifth
19. Nelson
20. 36

Quiz 34: Days and Months

1. The French celebrate Bastille Day on the 14th of which month?

2. Which day of the week do Italians call 'sabato'?

3. In the northern hemisphere, the shortest day of the year occurs in which month?

4. And in which month does the longest day of the year occur?

5. Americans celebrate Independence Day on the 4th of which month?

6. Which day of the week was 'Manic' for the girl group The Bangles?

7. On which day of the week did Roman Catholics traditionally refrain from eating meat?

8. Which veteran rock guitarist is married to former 'EastEnders' star Anita Dobson?

9. In 'The Addams Family' what was the name of Gomez and Morticia's daughter?

10. Which American author wrote 'Little Women'?

11. Which actress plays Edina's mother in the sitcom 'Absolutely Fabulous'?

12. What is the name of the 16-day beer festival that takes place each year in Munich, Germany?

13. 'Captain Slow' is the nickname of which broadcaster?

14. In Britain, the clocks go forward an hour on the last Sunday of which month?

15. American director Oliver Stone won his first Best Director Oscar for which Vietnam War film?

16. In which month do Scots celebrate St Andrew's Day?

17. Which American rockers had a number 4 hit in 1992 with 'November Rain'?

18. By what name is St Stephen's Day more commonly known in the UK?

19. In the Christian church, which day marks the first day of Lent?
    a) Ash Wednesday
    b) Elm Wednesday
    c) Oak Wednesday

20. In which month is the London Marathon usually run?
    a) March
    b) April
    c) May

Answers to Quiz 33: Pot Luck

1. Turkey
2. Temperature
3. Elle Macpherson
4. Passport
5. Tin
6. Asia
7. Monaco
8. The Great Fire of London
9. St Valentine's Day
10. The yen
11. Nationalization
12. Thanksgiving
13. X
14. The Derby
15. Westminster Abbey
16. Tweed
17. Vodka
18. Isle of Man
19. Queensland
20. Bishop

Quiz 35: Pot Luck

1. Tennis star Roger Federer is from which country?

2. In use from 1840 until 1841, the Penny Black is a famous example of what type of object?

3. A rabbi is an ordained official in which religion?

4. Which word connects a piece of gold and a lump of breaded chicken?

5. The Suez Canal connects the Mediterranean Sea with which body of water?

6. Which country music legend was known as the 'Man in Black'?

7. Which nautical term refers to the left-hand side of a ship?

8. What type of chocolate biscuit is also the name of the ruling royal family of Spain?

9. Which alliterative two-word phrase was used to describe mental disorientation suffered by troops in the First World War caused by the constant bombardment of artillery?

10. Which charity for British military personnel was founded by Bryn and Emma Parry in October 2007?

11. Constantinople was the former name of which major city?

12. Which mythical Scandinavian being is also a name given to someone who posts inflammatory or off-topic messages on an internet message board?

13. Which word describes the undertaking of a journey to a religious site or shrine?

14. What is the only capital city of a European Union country that starts with the letter T?

15. Which cocktail is made from tequila, triple-sec, and lemon or lime juice?

16. The Jules Rimet Trophy was a trophy awarded to the winners of which sporting competition?

17. 'Under Milk Wood' is a famous play by which Welsh writer?

18. Which Swiss folk hero reputedly had to shoot an apple from his son's head?

19. The US Defense Department is based in which building?
    a) The Pentagon
    b) The Hexagon
    c) The Heptagon

20. Which classic Hitchcock film was based on a novel by Boileau and Narcejac called 'The Living and the Dead'?
    a) Psycho
    b) Rear Window
    c) Vertigo

Answers to Quiz 34: Days and Months

1. July
2. Saturday
3. December
4. June
5. July
6. Monday
7. Friday
8. Brian May
9. Wednesday Addams
10. Louisa May Alcott
11. June Whitfield
12. Oktoberfest
13. James May
14. March
15. Born on the Fourth of July
16. November
17. Guns n Roses
18. Boxing Day
19. Ash Wednesday
20. April

Quiz 36: Animals part 2

EASY

1. Mallard, wigeon, and shoveller are species of which animal?

2. What name is given to mammals that carry their young in a pouch?

3. What is the heaviest land mammal on earth?

4. Which animal appears on the logo of the World Wide Fund for Nature (WWF)?

5. The giraffe is native to which continent?

6. What is the largest of the great apes?

7. On the children's TV show 'Blue Peter', what type of animals were Smudge, Socks, and Cookie?

8. An elver is the young of which animal?

9. In addition to flying forwards, which bird can also fly straight up and down, sideways, and backwards?

10. Which animal takes its name from the Greek for 'river horse'?

11. Balinese, Bengal, and Burmese are breeds of which domestic animal?

12. What type of creature is a guillemot?

13. How many tentacles does an octopus have?

14. The wombat is native to which country?

15. The gnu is another name for which African herbivore?

16. What type of creature is a merlin?

17. What is a female swan called?

18. Cats called Larry, Sybil, Humphrey, and Nemo have all lived at which famous address?

19. What is the nickname of Hull City Football Club?
    a) the Eagles
    b) the Foxes
    c) the Tigers

20. A praying mantis is what type of animal?
    a) insect
    b) reptile
    c) bird

Answers to Quiz 35: Pot Luck

1. Switzerland
2. A postage stamp
3. Judaism
4. Nugget
5. The Red Sea
6. Johnny Cash
7. Port
8. Bourbon
9. Shell shock
10. Help for Heroes
11. Istanbul
12. Troll
13. Pilgrimage
14. Tallinn
15. Margarita
16. The World Cup
17. Dylan Thomas
18. William Tell
19. The Pentagon
20. Vertigo

Quiz 37: Pot Luck

EASY

1. 'The Adventures of Tom Sawyer' and 'The Adventures of Huckleberry Finn' are works by which American author?

2. Which English monarch was known as 'The Conqueror'?

3. What are the two capital cities of European Union countries that start with the letter P?

4. Ceylon is the former name of which country?

5. What does the A in the acronym NATO stand for?

6. Which bird is also the name given to a score of 2 under par in a single hole of golf?

7. How many humps does a Bactrian camel have?

8. Which major British art gallery is located on the south bank of the River Thames at Bankside?

9. The Tay Bridge spans the River Tay in which Scottish city?

10. The Taoiseach is the prime minister of which country?

11. 'The God Delusion' was a book written by which biologist and atheist?

12. Who has won the Formula One Drivers' Championship the most times?

13. 'Messiah' is a famous piece of music by which German-born British composer?

14. The flag of Ukraine is made up of horizontal stripes of which two colours?

15. The Battle of Marston Moor was fought during which conflict?

16. James Thomson wrote the words and Thomas Arne the music to which patriotic song?

17. What type of music is commonly associated with Glyndebourne?

18. What is the second largest city in Russia?

19. The UK National Lottery is drawn from how many balls?
    a) 48
    b) 49
    c) 50

20. In the 'Mr Men' series, what colour is Mr Nosey?
    a) blue
    b) green
    c) red

Answers to Quiz 36: Animals part 2

1. Duck
2. Marsupials
3. African elephant
4. Panda
5. Africa
6. Gorilla
7. Cats
8. Eel
9. Hummingbird
10. Hippopotamus
11. Cat
12. Bird
13. Eight
14. Australia
15. Wildebeest
16. Bird
17. Pen
18. 10 Downing Street
19. The Tigers
20. Insect

Quiz 38: Anagrams part 1

Re-arrange the letters to make the name of a famous Hollywood actor or actress.

1. Out Crimes

2. I Nap Coal

3. Restyle Perm

4. Chino Flirt

5. Link Comedian

6. Silent Tweak

7. Rioted Reborn

8. Harry Belle

9. Jag Much Hank

10. Brute Jailors

11. Her Inner Elm

12. Monk Hats

13. Tab Dript

14. Shank Warily

15. Anaemic Chile

EASY

16. Once Ere Googly

17. Ivy Kneecaps

18. Deer Of Joist

19. Mere Java Bird

20. Held Deacon

Answers to Quiz 37: Pot Luck

1. Mark Twain
2. William I
3. Paris and Prague
4. Sri Lanka
5. Atlantic
6. Eagle
7. Two
8. Tate Modern
9. Dundee
10. Republic of Ireland
11. Richard Dawkins
12. Michael Schumacher
13. Handel
14. Blue and yellow
15. The English Civil War
16. Rule, Britannia!
17. Opera
18. St Petersburg
19. 49
20. Green

Quiz 39: Pot Luck

1. Salisbury is the former name of which African capital city?

2. What is the largest instrument of the violin family?

3. Built by John Nash for the Prince Regent, the Royal Pavilion is in which English resort?

4. If all of the states of America were listed alphabetically, which would be first on the list?

5. And what state would be last on the list?

6. The word 'Monegasque' is used to describe people from which sovereign principality?

7. In which TV show would you expect to hear members of the panel say 'I'm out'?

8. International Workers' Day is celebrated on the 1st of which month?

9. Which American city is known as the 'Mile High City'?

10. Crown-green and flat-green are variations of which sport?

11. The Hawthorns is the home ground of which English football club?

12. A jalapeno is a variety of what type of food?

13. What spirit is added to mint, sugar, soda water, and lime to make a mojito cocktail?

14. The Australian Open tennis championship is held in which city?

15. The Gold Dagger Award is a prize awarded to writers of which genre of fiction?

EASY

16. Which word connects a moustachioed private investigator and a large bottle of champagne?

17. In Roman numerals, which number is represented by the letter C?

18. What nationality is the snooker player Ding Junhui?

19. In chess, each player starts the game with how many bishops?
    a) one
    b) two
    c) three

20. What was former prime minister Margaret Thatcher's middle name?
    a) Annie
    b) Betty
    c) Hilda

Answers to Quiz 38: Anagrams part 1

1. Tom Cruise
2. Al Pacino
3. Meryl Streep
4. Colin Firth
5. Nicole Kidman
6. Kate Winslet
7. Robert De Niro
8. Halle Berry
9. Hugh Jackman
10. Julia Roberts
11. Helen Mirren
12. Tom Hanks
13. Brad Pitt
14. Hilary Swank
15. Michael Caine
16. George Clooney
17. Kevin Spacey
18. Jodie Foster
19. Javier Bardem
20. Don Cheadle

Quiz 40: Countries Ending in Vowels

EASY

1. What is the world's second largest country by area?

2. The Hellenic Republic is the official name of which country?

3. Cricketers from which country wear a cap called a 'baggy green'?

4. Which country lies directly across the Strait of Gibraltar from Spain?

5. Sprint legend Usain Bolt is from which country?

6. Which country won football's World Cup for the first time in 1978?

7. Sinology is the academic study of which country?

8. 'The Hexagon' is a nickname for which western European country?

9. Which tiny country in the Pyrenees is bordered by France to the north and Spain to the south?

10. Robert Mugabe is the long-time leader of which African country?

11. Mombasa is the chief port of which east African country?

12. The flag of which European country features white, green, and red horizontal stripes?

13. Which Asian country is home to the fourth largest population in the world?

14. Which European country's flag features a checkerboard of red and white?

15. In 2007, Cristina Kirchner was elected president of which country?

EASY

16. Which country jointly hosted football's 2002 World Cup with Japan?

17. Which West African country, the oldest republic on the continent, was established on land acquired for freed US slaves?

18. What is Europe's second largest country by area after Russia?

19. Tata Motors is a car manufacturer based in which country?
    a) China
    b) India
    c) Russia

20. The FARC is a Marxist guerrilla movement in which South American country?
    a) Argentina
    b) Colombia
    c) Chile

Answers to Quiz 39: Pot Luck

1. Harare
2. Double bass
3. Brighton
4. Alabama
5. Wyoming
6. Monaco
7. Dragons' Den
8. May
9. Denver
10. Bowls
11. West Bromwich Albion
12. Pepper
13. White rum
14. Melbourne
15. Crime
16. Magnum
17. 100
18. Chinese
19. Two
20. Hilda

Quiz 41: Pot Luck

1. How many valves does a trumpet have?

2. The ancient massage therapy shiatsu originated in which country?

3. Chemotherapy is a treatment used to combat which disease?

4. In relation to weight, what do the initials BMI stand for?

5. Which fictional superhero is the alter ego of Dick Grayson?

6. Molineux is the home ground of which English football club?

7. The House of Orange-Nassau is the ruling family of which European country?

8. In which sport do teams compete for the America's Cup?

9. Which Russian city was formerly known as Leningrad?

10. An internet domain ending .za is from which country?

11. Texas hold 'em, stud, and draw are variants of which card game?

12. What is the only American state to end with the letter K?

13. Complete the title of a popular TV detective pairing: 'Dalziel and ...'

14. What was the first country to use adhesive postage stamps?

15. Teams from which two countries compete for rugby union's Calcutta Cup?

16. Vulcanology is the study of what?

17. What does a cartographer make?

18. Who was South Africa's first black president?

19. Russian businessman Roman Abramovich is the owner of which English football club?
    a) Chelsea
    b) Fulham
    c) Queens Park Rangers

20. Motor manufacturer SEAT is based in which country?
    a) France
    b) Italy
    c) Spain

EASY

Answers to Quiz 40: Countries Ending in Vowels

1. Canada
2. Greece
3. Australia
4. Morocco
5. Jamaica
6. Argentina
7. China
8. France
9. Andorra
10. Zimbabwe
11. Kenya
12. Bulgaria
13. Indonesia
14. Croatia
15. Argentina
16. South Korea
17. Liberia
18. Ukraine
19. India
20. Colombia

Quiz 42: Sporting Nicknames

Identify the sportsmen who have the following nicknames:

1. Goldenballs (football)

2. The Greatest (boxing)

3. Barney (darts)

4. The Whirlwind (snooker)

5. The Hayemaker (boxing)

6. Lightning (athletics)

7. Beefy (cricket)

8. The Golden Bear (golf)

9. Flymo (athletics)

10. The Manx Missile (cycling)

11. Mrs Doubtfire (golf)

12. BOD (rugby union)

13. Fedex (tennis)

14. Wolfie (darts)

15. The Wizard of Wishaw (snooker)

16. The Romford Pele (football)

17. Very Very Special (cricket)

18. Whispering Death (cricket)

19. Britney (formula one)

20. Britsa (cricket)

Answers to Quiz 41: Pot Luck

1. Three
2. Japan
3. Cancer
4. Body Mass Index
5. Robin
6. Wolverhampton Wanderers
7. The Netherlands
8. Yachting
9. St Petersburg
10. South Africa
11. Poker
12. New York
13. Pascoe
14. The UK
15. England and Scotland
16. Volcanoes
17. Maps
18. Nelson Mandela
19. Chelsea
20. Spain

Quiz 43: Pot Luck

1. The opera 'Aida' was written by which Italian composer?

2. Who wrote 'The Communist Manifesto'?

3. Which actor played the Caped Crusader in the 1960s TV series 'Batman'?

4. 'Motor City' is the nickname of which American city?

5. Which French author wrote the novels 'The Count of Monte Cristo' and 'The Three Musketeers'?

6. The town of Ypres, the scene of a number of major battles in the First World War, is in which country?

7. By what name is Israel's 'Central Institute for Intelligence and Security' better known?

8. The rocky promontory Cape of Good Hope is in which country?

9. Which name connects a World War II general and the capital of the US state of Alabama?

10. The white rose is the official flower of which county?

11. The Millennium Stadium is in which British city?

12. Dartmoor and Exmoor National Parks are in which English county?

13. What is the name of the manual counting device that consists of coloured beads on parallel bars?

14. Which now defunct discriminatory form of government took its name from the Afrikaans word for 'apartness'?

15. Oranges from which Spanish city are traditionally used to make marmalade?

16. Don Warrington played Philip in which classic comedy?

17. Headingley cricket ground is in which English city?

18. 'Pompey' is the nickname of which English town?

19. What is the first name of the TV detective 'Monk'?
    a) Adrian
    b) Anthony
    c) Arthur

20. The name of which famous English football ground was changed to the Sports Direct Arena in November 2011?
    a) Anfield
    b) St James' Park
    c) White Hart Lane

EASY

Answers to Quiz 42: Sporting Nicknames

1. David Beckham
2. Muhammad Ali
3. Raymond van Barneveld
4. Jimmy White
5. David Haye
6. Usain Bolt
7. Ian Botham
8. Jack Nicklaus
9. Mo Farah
10. Mark Cavendish
11. Colin Montgomerie
12. Brian O'Driscoll
13. Roger Federer
14. Martin Adams
15. John Higgins
16. Ray Parlour
17. VVS Laxman
18. Michael Holding
19. Nico Rosberg
20. Stuart Broad

Quiz 44: Big and Small

EASY

1. Sheldon Cooper and Leonard Hofstadter are the central characters in which TV comedy?

2. What is the name of the great hour bell at the Houses of Parliament in London?

3. 'The Big Apple' is the nickname of which American city?

4. Who was the arch-nemesis of the Three Little Pigs?

5. Chris Evans and Gaby Roslin were the original hosts of which morning TV show?

6. 'The smallest room' is a euphemism for which room of a house?

7. What is the nickname of the constellation Ursa Major?

8. 'Big Girls Don't Cry' was a number two hit single for which member of the Black Eyed Peas?

9. Derek Smalls was the bass player in which fictional rock band?

10. Jack Whitehall and James Corden caused controversy following their appearance on which annual TV panel show in December 2012?

11. Christopher Timothy played James Herriot in which TV drama?

12. Variola major is another name for which disease?

13. Big Brother is a major character in which novel by George Orwell?

14. Which 'Great Train Robber' was released from prison on compassionate grounds in 2009?

15. Standing some 8 feet 2 inches tall, who resides in a nest at 123 1/2 Sesame Street?

16. Tom Welling played a young Clark Kent in which TV series?

17. Which reality TV show aired for the first time on 18 July 2000?

18. Who was the lead singer with 90s pop favourites M People?

19. What was the name of the howitzer used by German forces at the start of the First World War?
    a) Big Bertha
    b) Big Bessie
    c) Big Edna

20. Complete the title of a 1986 film starring Kurt Russell: 'Big Trouble in Little …'
    a) China
    b) Italy
    c) Vietnam

EASY

Answers to Quiz 43: Pot Luck

1. Verdi
2. Karl Marx and Friedrich Engels
3. Adam West
4. Detroit
5. Alexandre Dumas
6. Belgium
7. Mossad
8. South Africa
9. Montgomery
10. Yorkshire
11. Cardiff
12. Devon
13. Abacus
14. Apartheid
15. Seville
16. Rising Damp
17. Leeds
18. Portsmouth
19. Adrian
20. St James' Park

Quiz 45: Pot Luck

1. Which composer was the subject of the 1984 film 'Amadeus'?

2. Who is the host of the TV panel show 'A League of Their Own'?

3. Lazio, Liguria, and Lombardy are regions of which country?

4. Biryani is a dish common in the cuisine of which country?

5. 'The Big Easy' is the nickname of which American city?

6. The MMR jab is a vaccine against which three diseases?

7. Ian Hislop is the editor of which satirical magazine?

8. Which actor and comedian is the host of the TV panel show 'Would I Lie to You'?

9. A cineaste is a lover of what?

10. What name is shared by a mythical bird and the capital of the US state of Arizona?

11. What was the name of the character played by Joe Swash in the TV soap 'EastEnders'?

12. What is the maiden name of cartoon character Marge Simpson and US First Lady Jackie Kennedy?

13. Which place in England is known as 'the city of dreaming spires'?

14. Which TV show features a star in a reasonably priced car?

15. Which Scandinavian buffet meal takes its name from the Swedish for 'open sandwich' and 'table'?

16. Which sport, played on horseback, is also a type of collared, short-sleeved shirt?

17. Iago is a major character in which Shakespeare play?

18. Coolmore and Godolphin are major organizations in which sport?

19. Leopold Bloom is the central character in which classic novel?
    a) Great Expectations
    b) The Great Gatsby
    c) Ulysses

20. What was Elvis Presley's middle name?
    a) Aaron
    b) Albert
    c) Arthur

Answers to Quiz 44: Big and Small

1. The Big Bang Theory
2. Big Ben
3. New York
4. The Big Bad Wolf
5. The Big Breakfast
6. The lavatory
7. The Big Dipper (also the Plough)
8. Fergie
9. Spinal Tap
10. The Big Fat Quiz of the Year
11. All Creatures Great and Small
12. Smallpox
13. Nineteen Eighty Four
14. Ronnie Biggs
15. Big Bird
16. Smallville
17. Big Brother
18. Heather Small
19. Big Bertha
20. China

Quiz 46: Duets

EASY

Identify the pair that duetted on the following chart hits:

1. 'Especially for You' (1988)

2. 'Summer Nights' (1978)

3. 'Don't Go Breaking My Heart' (1976)

4. 'Under Pressure' (1981)

5. 'I'll Be Missing You' (1997)

6. 'Empire State of Mind' (2009)

7. 'Endless Love' (1981)

8. 'I Got You Babe' (1965)

9. '(I've Had) The Time of My Life' (1987 and 1990)

10. 'The Sound of Silence' (1965)

11. 'Stan' (2001)

12. 'Dancing in the Street' (1985)

13. 'I Believe' / 'Up on the Roof' (1995)

14. 'Barcelona' (1987 and 1992)

15. 'I Knew You Were Waiting (For Me)' (1987)

16. The Best Things in Life Are Free' (1992)

17. 'Somethin' Stupid' (2001)

18. 'Up Where We Belong' (1983)

19. 'Easy Lover' (1985)

20. 'Baby Boy' (2003)

EASY

Answers to Quiz 45: Pot Luck

1. Mozart
2. James Corden
3. Italy
4. India
5. New Orleans
6. Measles, mumps, and rubella
7. Private Eye
8. Rob Brydon
9. Cinema and films
10. Phoenix
11. Mickey Miller
12. Bouvier
13. Oxford
14. Top Gear
15. Smorgasbord
16. Polo
17. Othello
18. Horse racing
19. Ulysses
20. Aaron

Quiz 47: Pot Luck

1. Which dinosaur's name translates into English as 'three-horned face'?

2. Which nickname was shared by boxers Thomas Hearns and Ricky Hatton?

3. On a standard computer keyboard, which letter sits between T and U?

4. Bob Cryer, Frank Burnside, and June Ackland were characters in which long-running TV drama?

5. 'Pet Sounds' was an iconic album by which American band?

6. Which former Soviet republic is also the name of a state in America?

7. Trent Bridge cricket ground is in which English city?

8. Which haulage company features in the TV show 'Trucks and Trailers'?

9. Who is the host of the TV game show 'The Cube'?

10. Holden Caulfield is the central character in which classic coming-of-age novel?

11. 'Peloton' is a term used in which sport?

12. What charity has the initials RNIB?

13. Gastritis is the inflammation of which part of the body?

14. Which animal appears on the logo of clothes by the manufacturer Lacoste?

15. Which size of paper measures 297mm by 210mm?

16. 'The Barber of Seville' is an opera by which Italian composer?

17. Claustrophobia is the fear of what?

18. Mayo and Sligo are counties in which province of Ireland?

19. The famous Maracana Stadium is in which city?
    a) Buenos Aires
    b) Mexico City
    c) Rio de Janeiro

20. What was the name of the superstorm that devastated much of New Jersey, New York, and New England?
    a) Mandy
    b) Randy
    c) Sandy

Answers to Quiz 46: Duets

1. Kylie Minogue and Jason Donovan
2. John Travolta and Olivia Newton-John
3. Elton John and Kiki Dee
4. Queen and David Bowie
5. Puff Daddy and Faith Evans
6. Jay-Z and Alicia Keys
7. Lionel Richie and Diana Ross
8. Sonny and Cher
9. Bill Medley and Jennifer Warnes
10. Simon and Garfunkel
11. Eminem and Dido
12. David Bowie and Mick Jagger
13. Robson and Jerome
14. Freddie Mercury & Montserrat Caballé
15. George Michael and Aretha Franklin
16. Janet Jackson and Luther Vandross
17. Robbie Williams and Nicole Kidman
18. Joe Cocker and Jennifer Warnes
19. Phil Collins and Philip Bailey
20. Beyoncé and Sean Paul

Quiz 48: Fill in the Blank

Fill in the missing word in the following sequences:

1. Sydney, Athens, Beijing, _____

2. England, Mexico, West Germany, _____

3. Thatcher, _____, Blair, Brown

4. _____, Reagan, Bush, Clinton

5. Rook, _____, bishop, king

6. _____, John Paul II, Benedict XVI, Francis I

7. 1979, 1983, 1987, _____, 1997

8. France, Brazil, _____, Spain

9. Alpha, beta, _____, delta

10. Bob Monkhouse, _____, Les Dennis, Andy Collins, Vernon Kay

11. Australia, _____, South Africa, New Zealand

12. 'Off The Wall', 'Thriller', _____, 'Dangerous'

13. Leo, Virgo, _____, Scorpio, Sagittarius

14. Geese-a-laying, swans-a-swimming, _____, ladies dancing

15. Matthew, Mark, Luke, John, _____

16. Red, orange, yellow, green, blue, _____, violet

17. Zoe Ball, _____, Chris Moyles, Nick Grimshaw

18. Maurice Green, Justin Gatlin, Usain Bolt, _____

19. Jupiter, Saturn, _____, Neptune

20. 'A Hard Day's Night', 'Beatles For Sale', _____,
    'Rubber Soul'

Answers to Quiz 47: Pot Luck

1. Triceratops
2. The Hit Man
3. Y
4. The Bill
5. The Beach Boys
6. Georgia
7. Nottingham
8. Eddie Stobart
9. Philip Schofield
10. The Catcher in the Rye
11. Cycling
12. Royal National Institute for the Blind
13. The stomach
14. Crocodile
15. A4
16. Rossini
17. Confined spaces
18. Connacht
19. Rio de Janeiro
20. Sandy

Quiz 49: Pot Luck

1. What type of gun was also the title of an album by the Beatles?

2. What name connects a former British motor manufacturer and the state capital of Texas?

3. An internet address ending with the letters .nl is from which country?

4. 'Dienstag' is the German word for which day of the week?

5. Noddy Holder was the lead singer with which glam rock band?

6. How many suspects are there in the board game 'Cluedo'?

7. The fortified wine port originates from which country?

8. Podiatry is a branch of medicine that deals with which part of the body?

9. Suomi is the local name for which country?

10. Alsace, Aquitaine, and Auvergne are regions of which European country?

11. Polytheism is a belief in more than one what?

12. By what name is the Oxford Committee for Famine Relief better known?

13. Natalie Coleman was the 2013 winner of which culinary TV show?

14. In 1991, Helen Sharman became the first Briton to travel where?

15. Which name connects the actress and creator of the contemporary drama 'Stella' and the classic sitcom 'Rising Damp'?

16. Which 'Pop Idol' winner made his West End debut in 2012, playing the MC in 'Cabaret'?

Answers – page 101

17. Which English monarch was known as the 'Virgin Queen'?

18. Tito was the long-time ruler of which Eastern European country?

19. Where in Britain is Parkhurst Prison?
    a) Isle of Man b) Isle of Sheppey c) Isle of Wight

20. Which of the following is not a weapon in the board game 'Cluedo'?
    a) candlestick b) jemmy c) rope

EASY

Answers to Quiz 48: Fill in the Blank

1. London (Olympic host cities 2000 to 2012)
2. Argentina (World Cup hosts 1966 to 1978)
3. Major (British prime ministers)
4. Carter (US Presidents)
5. Knight (chess pieces moving inwards from the outer square at the start of a game)
6. John Paul I (Popes)
7. 1992 (years of UK general elections)
8. Italy (World Cup winners 1998 to 2010)
9. Gamma (letters of the Greek alphabet)
10. Max Bygraves (Hosts of 'Family Fortunes')
11. England (Rugby World Cup winners 1999 to 2011)
12. Bad (Michael Jackson albums)
13. Libra (star signs)
14. Maids-a-milking (in the song '12 Days of Christmas')
15. Acts of the Apostles (books of the New Testament)
16. Indigo (colours in the rainbow)
17. Sara Cox (hosts of the Radio 1 Breakfast Show)
18. Usain Bolt (gold medallists in the Olympic men's 100m from 2000 to 2012)
19. Uranus (planets in order from the sun)
20. Help! (albums by the Beatles)

Quiz 50: Name the Year

EASY

Identify the year that the follow events happened:

1. The Battle of Hastings was fought.

2. The 7 July London bombings were carried out.

3. Queen Elizabeth II celebrated her Diamond Jubilee.

4. The Indian Ocean tsunami devastated large parts of Asia killing thousands or people.

5. Margaret Thatcher was elected prime minister for a third time.

6. Riots engulfed London and other English cities following the death of Mark Duggan in Tottenham.

7. Sydney hosted the Summer Olympics.

8. The first Rugby World Cup took place.

9. Adele topped the UK album charts with '19'.

10. World War II ended.

11. Michael Jackson died.

12. Man walked on the moon for the first time.

13. The Battle of Waterloo took place.

14. US President John F Kennedy was assassinated.

15. William Shakespeare died.

16. Football's World Cup was hosted in Africa for the first time.

17. Gordon Brown replaced Tony Blair as British prime minister.

18. England's cricketers won the Ashes for the first time since 1986/87.

19. Euro coins and banknotes went into circulation.

20. The first 'Harry Potter' film was released.

Answers to Quiz 49: Pot Luck

1. Revolver	11. God
2. Austin	12. Oxfam
3. The Netherlands	13. Masterchef
4. Tuesday	14. Space
5. Slade	15. Ruth Jones
6. Six	16. Will Young
7. Portugal	17. Elizabeth I
8. Feet	18. Yugoslavia
9. Finland	19. Isle of Wight
10. France	20. Jemmy

Quiz 51: Pot Luck

1. 'Walk the Line' was a 2005 film biopic about which musician?

2. Who is the host of the TV panel show 'QI'?

3. Toxicology is the scientific study of what?

4. The Titanic was built in which UK city?

5. How many sides does a rhombus have?

6. Plonk is a slang term for what type of drink?

7. Who are the team captains on the TV panel show 'Have I Got News for You'?

8. Halitosis is another name for what?

9. Who marked his diamond jubilee in broadcasting in 2012 on the programe '60 Years in the Wild'?

10. Which animal features on the logo of fashion designer Ralph Lauren?

11. Which name connects a variety of apple and the gang of girls in the film 'Grease'?

12. 'The Ring Cycle' is a collection of operas by which German composer?

13. What type of rectangular roof tile is also an anagram of the word 'English'?

14. 'Waiting for Godot' is the title of a play by which Irish playwright?

15. Sam Malone, Carla Tortelli, Woody Boyd, and Rebecca Howe worked at which fictional bar?

16. The period drama 'Call the Midwife' is set in which city?

17. Which left-handed England batsman scored a century on his Test debut against India at Nagpur in 2006?

18. Who resigned his job as a reporter at the Daily Planet in October 2012?

19. Tinnitus is a condition that affects which part of the body?
a) eyes
b) ears
c) nose

20. What nationality is actress Pamela Anderson?
a) American
b) Australian
c) Canadian

Answers to Quiz 50: Name the Year

1.	1066	11.	2009
2.	2005	12.	1969
3.	2012	13.	1815
4.	2004	14.	1963
5.	1987	15.	1616
6.	2011	16.	2010
7.	2000	17.	2007
8.	1987	18.	2005
9.	2008	19.	2002
10.	1945	20.	2001

Quiz 52: Television part 2

1. 'Don't just watch the adverts, win them' is a catchphrase from which weekend TV favourite?

2. Who is the host of property development show 'Grand Designs'?

3. Moe's Tavern is a the name of a bar in which animated TV series?

4. Craggy Island was the setting for which sitcom?

5. Who played Jim Royle in the TV comedy 'The Royle Family'?

6. Which TV illusionist and showman has appeared in shows called 'The Heist', 'Trick of the Mind', and 'Hero at 30,000 Feet'?

7. Which actor is the central character in the TV comedy 'Life's Too Short'?

8. Which member of the 'Last of the Summer Wine' cast provides the voice for one half of animated award winners 'Wallace and Gromit'?

9. Mr Bronson, Mr Baxter, and Miss Booth were teachers at which school?

10. Which actor plays Robert Crawley, Earl of Grantham in the costume drama 'Downton Abbey'?

11. Which Sunday night drama was set in the Yorkshire village of Aidensfield?

12. How many contestants take on the chaser in the TV quiz show 'The Chase'?

13. What was the name of the dodgy businessman played by George Cole in the TV drama 'Minder'?

14. Which famous drummer was the narrator on children's favourite 'Thomas the Tank Engine'?

15. 'Bergerac' was set on which of the Channel Islands?

16. Nick Hewer and Karren Brady are judges on which TV talent show?

17. Which 'Loose Women' regular was married to DJ and broadcaster Chris Evans?

18. Lassiter's Hotel appears in which TV soap?

19. How many letters does each contestant choose in a letters round in 'Countdown'?
    a) eight
    b) nine
    c) ten

20. How many numbered boxes are used in a game of 'Deal or No Deal'?
    a) 18
    b) 20
    c) 22

Answers to Quiz 51: Pot Luck

1. Johnny Cash
2. Stephen Fry
3. Poisons
4. Belfast
5. Four
6. Wine
7. Paul Merton and Ian Hislop
8. Bad breath
9. Sir David Attenborough
10. Pony
11. Pink Lady
12. Wagner
13. Shingle
14. Samuel Beckett
15. Cheers
16. London
17. Alastair Cook
18. Clark Kent
19. Ears
20. Canadian

Quiz 53: Pot Luck

1. Which word is used to describe an animal that eats both plants and animals?

2. Which branch of mathematics deals with the collection, analysis, and interpretation of numerical data?

3. What name connects a Northern Irish comedian who died in 2012 and the capital of the US state of Nevada?

4. Ornithology is the study of what type of creatures?

5. Edgbaston cricket ground is in which English city?

6. Who was sacked as manager of Manchester City in May 2013?

7. What name is given to physical ailments such as high blood pressure and gastric ulcers that have emotional causes?

8. The 1992 Olympic Games were hosted in which city?

9. Which Hollywood superstar has played characters called Michael Clayton, Ryan Bingham, and Danny Ocean?

10. Detective drama 'Ashes to Ashes' was a spin-off from which cop show?

11. Which English county is known as 'Shakespeare's County'?

12. What colour shirts did England wear in their only World Cup final appearance?

13. Reef, hitch, sheepshank, and granny are types of what?

14. By what name is the landmark 'Uluru' also known in English?

15. Who succeeded Sir Alex Ferguson as manager of Manchester United FC?

16. Which part of the foot is also used to describe baddies in profesional wrestling contests?

17. Which animal appears on the logo of the airline Qantas?

18. 'Eine Kleine Nachtmusik' is a piece of music written by which composer?

19. The mysterious region known as the Bermuda Triangle is in which ocean?
    a) Atlantic
    b) Indian
    c) Pacific

20. 'The Bears' is the nickname of which English county cricket team?
    a) Lancashire
    b) Surrey
    c) Warwickshire

Answers to Quiz 52: Television part 2

1. Ant and Dec's Saturday Night Takeaway
2. Kevin McCloud
3. The Simpsons
4. Father Ted
5. Ricky Tomlinson
6. Derren Brown
7. Warwick Davis
8. Peter Sallis
9. Grange Hill
10. Hugh Bonneville
11. Heartbeat
12. Four
13. Arthur Daley
14. Ringo Starr
15. Jersey
16. The Apprentice
17. Carol McGiffin
18. Neighbours
19. Nine
20. 22

Quiz 54: Sun, Moon, and Stars

1. Shane Ritchie plays which character in the TV soap 'EastEnders'?

2. Leslie Crowther, Matthew Kelly, and Cat Deeley have all hosted which TV talent show?

3. What is the national anthem of the USA?

4. Bruce Willis and Cybill Shepherd played private detectives David Addison and Maddie Hayes in which 1980s comedy drama?

5. What illicitly produced spirit is also known as hooch, mountain dew, and Tennessee white whiskey?

6. Which multinational corporation takes its name from a character in the novel 'Moby Dick'?

7. What was the second UK number one single by The Police?

8. Which film was released first – 'Star Wars' or 'Star Trek: The Motion Picture'?

9. What was the first sequel to the film 'Twilight'?

10. Which Birmingham singer released the 2013 album 'Sing To The Moon'?

11. What was the only number one hit single from 1970s teddy boys Showaddywaddy?

12. Played by Katee Sackhoff, Starbuck was a character in which sci-fi drama?

13. Shirley Bassey sang the theme song for a James Bond film for the third time in which film?

14. Featuring vocals from Noel Gallagher, 'Setting Sun' was the first number one single from which indie dance duo?

15. In 2007, who became Secretary General of the United Nations?

16. Whom did readers of 'Rolling Stone' magazine vote the second greatest drummer of all time in a 2011 poll?

17. Which British rapper topped the charts in 2010 with 'Written in the Stars'?

18. What was the name of the character played by Jane Leeves in the hit sitcom 'Frasier'?

19. 'You Stole the Sun from My Heart' was a top five hit for which band?
    a) Manic Street Preachers
    b) Stereophonics
    c) Super Furry Animals

20. What was the title of the best-selling album by Air?
    a) Sun Safari
    b) Moon Safari
    c) Star Safari

Answers to Quiz 53: Pot Luck

1. Omnivore
2. Statistics
3. Carson (Frank Carson and Carson City)
4. Birds
5. Birmingham
6. Roberto Mancini
7. Psychosomatic diseases
8. Barcelona
9. George Clooney
10. Life on Mars
11. Warwickshire
12. Red
13. Knots
14. Ayers Rock
15. David Moyes
16. Heel
17. Kangaroo
18. Mozart
19. Atlantic
20. Warwickshire

Quiz 55: Pot Luck

1. In Roman numerals, which number is represented by the letter D?

2. Which footballer scored the infamous 'Hand of God' goal at the 1986 World Cup?

3. The name of which extinct group of reptiles derives from the Greek for 'terrible lizard'?

4. Which actor plays private detective Jackson Brodie in the BBC drama 'Case Histories'?

5. The two teams that reached the final of football's Champions League in 2013 both came from which country?

6. In relation to fertility, for what do the initials IVF stand?

7. A carcinogen is a substance that can cause what disease?

8. Which word describes a plant that flowers and dies within a year of germination?

9. Septicaemia is an infection which results from poisoning of what substance of the human body?

10. The Governess, The Beast, The Dark Destroyer, and The Sinner Man appear on which TV game show?

11. The Honey Monster advertised which breakfast cereal?

12. Kings Heath, Balsall Heath, and Highters Heath are districts of which English city?

13. Gareth Bale plays international football for which country?

14. What was Kylie Minogue's maiden UK number one single?

15. A character called the Mock Turtle appeared in which book?

Answers – page 113

16. 'The Addicks' is the nickname of which London football club?

17. Which team has won football's FA Cup the most times?

18. Which actor played TV detective Jim Bergerac?

19. Prior to becoming a successful author, what was John Grisham's occupation?
    a) doctor
    b) lawyer
    c) police officer

20. The St Valentine's Day Massacre took place in which city?
    a) Chicago
    b) Los Angeles
    c) New York

Answers to Quiz 54: Sun, Moon, and Stars

1. Alfie Moon
2. Stars in Their Eyes
3. The Star-Spangled Banner
4. Moonlighting
5. Moonshine
6. Starbucks
7. Walking on the Moon
8. Star Wars
9. The Twilight Saga: New Moon
10. Laura Mvula
11. Under the Moon of Love
12. Battlestar Galactica
13. Moonraker
14. Chemical Brothers
15. Ban Ki-moon
16. Keith Moon of The Who
17. Tinie Tempah
18. Daphne Moon
19. Manic Street Preachers
20. Moon Safari

Quiz 56: Colours

1. In snooker, which colour ball is worth 2 points?

2. What is the nickname of football clubs Birmingham City and Chelsea?

3. What was the name of the army created by the government of the Soviet Union after the Bolshevik Revolution of 1917?

4. 'Another Brick in the Wall Part II' was the only number one hit for which band?

5. On UK traffic lights, what colour appears after green?

6. Anthony Kiedis is the lead vocalist with which American rock band?

7. Ewood Park is the home ground of which English football team?

8. Which body of water separates the coasts of Egypt, Sudan, and Eritrea to the west from those of Saudi Arabia and Yemen to the east?

9. What is the name of the actress who plays Dot Cotton in the TV soap 'EastEnders'?

10. Who was re-elected MP for Kirkcaldy and Cowdenbeath in 2010?

11. John Anthony Gillis is the real name of which singer and guitarist, best known for his work with The White Stripes?

12. What was the first film to feature the bumbling French detective Inspector Clouseau?

13. Which diminutive pop star had a top ten hit in 1984 with 'Purple Rain'?

14. Sebastien Vettel and Mark Webber drove for which Formula One team in 2013?

15. Which Hollywood star, best known for 'School of Rock', 'Kung Fu Panda', and 'Nacho Libre', is the lead singer with rock band Tenacious D?

16. 'Tired of Being Alone' and 'Let's Stay Together' were the only UK top ten singles by which soul singer?

17. Swiss pair Henry Dunant and Gustave Moynier were the founders of which international charitable organization?

18. Located primarily in the state of Wyoming, what is the oldest National Park in America?

19. The White Nile is one of two main tributaries of the River Nile. What is the other?
    a) Blue Nile b) Green Nile c) Red Nile

20. Which of the following is a middle name of popstar Adele?
    a) Blue b) Green c) White

Answers to Quiz 55: Pot Luck

1. 500
2. Diego Maradona
3. Dinosaur
4. Jason Isaacs
5. Germany
6. In Vitro Fertilization
7. Cancer
8. Annual
9. Blood
10. The Chase
11. Sugar Puffs
12. Birmingham
13. Wales
14. I Should Be So Lucky
15. Alice's Adventures in Wonderland
16. Charlton Athletic
17. Manchester United
18. John Nettles
19. Lawyer
20. Chicago

Quiz 57: Pot Luck

EASY

1. Which black and white flag featuring a skull and crossbones was traditionally flown by pirates?

2. Cirrhosis is a disease that affects which organ of the body?

3. The Sugar Plum Fairy features in which ballet?

4. The Battle of the Atlantic was fought during which war?

5. What is the boiling point of water in degrees Celsius?

6. Rabat is the second largest city in which country?

7. Which TV rogue was married to 'Er indoors'?

8. The red rose is the symbol of which English county?

9. Which word connects a receptacle for keeping tea and a person who carries golf clubs?

10. 'Auf Wiedersehen' means goodbye in which language?

11. Which American director's films include 'Vicky Cristina Barcelona', 'To Rome with Love', and 'Midnight in Paris'?

12. KLM is the national airline of which country?

13. Jim Hawkins is the central character in which adventure story by Robert Louis Stevenson?

14. Comedian John Bishop is from which English city?

15. The American Glazer family are the majority owners of which English football club?

16. In computing, which two words are combined to make the word 'malware'?

17. Which family lives at 742 Evergreen Terrace?

18. The Arch of Constantine is in which European capital?

19. Trevor Eve played Detective Superintendent Peter Boyd in which police procedural?
    a) Silent Witness
    b) Waking the Dead
    c) Cracker

20. The disease scurvy is caused by a deficiency of which vitamin?
    a) vitamin A
    b) vitamin B
    c) vitamin C

EASY

Answers to Quiz 56: Colours

1. Yellow
2. The Blues
3. Red Army
4. Pink Floyd
5. Amber
6. Red Hot Chili Peppers
7. Blackburn Rovers
8. The Red Sea
9. June Brown
10. Gordon Brown
11. Jack White
12. The Pink Panther
13. Prince
14. Red Bull
15. Jack Black
16. Al Green
17. Red Cross
18. Yellowstone
19. Blue Nile
20. Blue

Quiz 58: Sport part 1

1. In darts, how much is scored for hitting the bullseye?

2. Who won his fifth World Snooker Championship title in 2013?

3. Who was the only Englishman to win golf's Open Championship between 1970 and 2012?

4. Which football team plays its home games at Loftus Road?

5. Which Northern Irishman won golf's US Open in 2011 and the US PGA Championship in 2012?

6. Which major sporting event takes place each year at a venue with the postcode SW19 5AE?

7. Which colour jersey is worn by the British and Irish Lions rugby team?

8. 'The Terriers' is the nickname of which northern English football club?

9. In which month does the FA Cup final take place?

10. Who is older – Serena or Venus Williams?

11. Which country hosted the last ever edition of cricket's Champions Trophy in 2013?

12. Before becoming manager of Tottenham Hotspur, Andre Villas-Boas was the manager of which club?

13. Who is the only German player to have won the men's singles at Wimbledon more than once?

14. Which tennis player won the men's singles at the French Open seven times out of eight between 2005 and 2012?

15. Which British team beat Barcelona in the group stages of the 2012/13 Champions League?

16. When the New York Giants met the Miami Dolphins in 2007 it was the first regular-season NFL game hosted at which stadium?

17. Sometimes called the fifth major, which golf tournament takes place each year at Sawgrass in America?

18. 'The Vikings' is the nickname of the one-day side of which English county cricket team?

19. Sir Alex Ferguson was the manager of Manchester United for how many years?
    a) 22
    b) 24
    c) 26

20. The Canadian Formula One Grand Prix is hosted in which city?
    a) Montreal
    b) Toronto
    c) Vancouver

EASY

Answers to Quiz 57: Pot Luck

1. Jolly Roger
2. Liver
3. The Nutcracker
4. World War II
5. 100 degrees
6. Morocco
7. Arthur Daley
8. Lancashire
9. Caddy
10. German

11. Woody Allen
12. The Netherlands
13. Treasure Island
14. Liverpool
15. Manchester United
16. Malicious software
17. The Simpsons
18. Rome
19. Waking the Dead
20. Vitamin C

Quiz 59: Pot Luck

EASY

1. The Palace of Holyroodhouse is in which British city?

2. If it is 12 noon GMT in London, what time is it in New York?

3. Based on a fairy-tale character created by Hans Christian Andersen, the statue of the Little Mermaid can be seen in which city?

4. David Keene is the president of which American lobby group which has the initials NRA?

5. What are the first names of the male members of the band Abba?

6. And what are the first names of the two female members?

7. What colour jersey is worn by the leader of the Giro d'Italia cycle race?

8. Bowler, fedora, and trilby are examples of what item of clothing?

9. The first FA Cup final held outside England took place in which city?

10. Who played the title character in the film 'Edward Scissorhands'?

11. Maris Piper, Anya, and Rooster are varieties of what type of vegetable?

12. Which member of the Monty Python team performed a series of shows called the 'Alimony Tour' after a high-profile divorce?

13. Margaret Rutherford and Joan Hickson both played which fictional sleuth?

14. The 2014 Tour de France will start in which English county?

15. Who is the only rower to win the BBC Sports Personality of the Year Award?

16. The Guardian newspaper was originally published in which English city?

17. According to Alexander Pope, a little of what 'is a dangerous thing'?

18. How many players make up a hockey team?

19. The Walker Cup is a competition in which sport?
    a) athletics
    b) golf
    c) tennis

20. What is the title of the 2011 JJ Abrams family drama about a gang of children who witness a mysterious train crash?
    a) Super 6
    b) Super 7
    c) Super 8

Answers to Quiz 58: Sport part 1

1. 50
2. Ronnie O'Sullivan
3. Nick Faldo
4. Queens Park Rangers
5. Rory McIlroy
6. Wimbledon
7. Red
8. Huddersfield Town
9. May
10. Venus
11. England
12. Chelsea
13. Boris Becker
14. Rafa Nadal
15. Celtic
16. Wembley
17. The Players Championship
18. Yorkshire
19. 26
20. Montreal

Quiz 60: Football Teams

In which city are the following European football teams based?

1. Crystal Palace

2. Rangers

3. Aston Villa

4. Juventus

5. PSG

6. St Patrick's Athletic

7. Benfica

8. Heart of Midlothian

9. Lazio

10. Galatasaray

11. Ajax

12. Grasshopper Club

13. Feyenoord

14. Anderlecht

15. Sampdoria

16. Panathinaikos FC

17. Schalke 04

18. Young Boys

19. RCD Espanyol

20. Honved

Answers to Quiz 59: Pot Luck

1. Edinburgh
2. 7 am
3. Copenhagen
4. National Rifle Association
5. Benny and Bjorn
6. Agnetha and Anni-Frid
7. Pink
8. Hats
9. Cardiff
10. Johnny Depp
11. Potato
12. John Cleese
13. Miss Marple
14. Yorkshire
15. Sir Steve Redgrave
16. Manchester
17. Learning
18. 11
19. Golf
20. Super 8

Quiz 61: Pot Luck

1. Sushi is a common dish in what type of cuisine?

2. In UK politics, which party has the initials SNP?

3. Ellie Simmonds is a Paralympic gold medallist in which sport?

4. Honolulu is the capital city of which American state?

5. Who are the hosts of musical talent show 'The Voice'?

6. Which Hollywood star had a double mastectomy operation in 2013 after being told she was at high risk of developing breast cancer?

7. Which book of the Old Testament provided Bob Marley with the title for a 1977 album?

8. 'Boat race' is rhyming slang for which part of the body?

9. In which city is the academic institution UCL based?

10. What are the two countries of South America that end in the letter Y?

11. In relation to elections, for what do the initials FPTP stand?

12. 'Ike' was the nickname of which post-war US president?

13. In Australia they're called thongs. What are they known as in the UK?

14. Which Lib Dem politician was jailed in 2013 after admitting to perverting the course of justice?

15. In 2000, Bashar al Assad succeeded his father as the leader of which Middle East country?

16. Which football team has won the European Cup / Champions League the most times?

17. Which Swiss city gives its name to a convention regarding the humane treatment of the sick and wounded in war?

18. Which high-profile businessman dressed up as an air stewardess in 2013 after losing a bet about the performance of his Formula One team?

19. What was the name of the 1967 conflict between Israel and its Arab neighbours?
    a) The Five-Day War
    b) The Six-Day War
    c) The Seven-Day War

20. How many players take part in snooker's World Championship?
    a) 16
    b) 32
    c) 64

Answers to Quiz 60: Football Teams

1. London
2. Glasgow
3. Birmingham
4. Turin
5. Paris
6. Dublin
7. Lisbon
8. Edinburgh
9. Rome
10. Istanbul
11. Amsterdam
12. Zurich
13. Rotterdam
14. Brussels
15. Genoa
16. Athens
17. Gelsenkirchen
18. Bern
19. Barcelona
20. Budapest

Quiz 62: Ireland

EASY

1. Who is the patron saint of Ireland?

2. Which three colours feature on the flag of the Republic of Ireland?

3. Prior to adopting the euro, what was the currency of the Republic of Ireland?

4. In Irish sport, what do the initials GAA stand for?

5. Which two Irish counties are also a girl's name?

6. The Republic of Ireland shares a land border with which country?

7. True or false – the Republic of Ireland has a larger population than Wales?

8. What is the name of the Irish police force?

9. Whom did Enda Kenny succeed as the Irish prime minister?

10. Which member of England's 1966 World Cup winning team led the Republic of Ireland to the World Cup finals in 1990 and 1994?

11. Which two letters can a member of the Irish parliament put after his name?

12. Which Irishman won the Eurovision Song Contest with 'What's Another Year'?

13. What is Ireland's most southerly county?

14. FF are the initials of which Irish political party?

15. 'The Kingdom' is the nickname of which Irish county?

16. Which Irish author wrote the novels 'The Commitments', 'The Van', and 'The Snapper'?

17. What is the smallest county of the Republic of Ireland by population?

18. A novel by which author is celebrated on Bloomsday?

19. The island of Ireland is divided into how many counties?
    a) 26
    b) 32
    c) 38

20. Castlebar is the biggest town in which county?
    a) Kerry
    b) Mayo
    c) Meath

EASY

Answers to Quiz 61: Pot Luck

1. Japanese
2. Scottish National Party
3. Swimming
4. Hawaii
5. Reggie Yates and Holly Willoughby
6. Angelina Jolie
7. Exodus
8. Face
9. London
10. Paraguay and Uruguay
11. First Past The Post
12. Dwight Eisenhower
13. Flip-flops
14. Chris Huhne
15. Syria
16. Real Madrid
17. Geneva
18. Richard Branson
19. The Six-Day War
20. 32

Quiz 63: Pot Luck

1. In terms of passenger numbers, what is Britain's busiest airport?

2. By what name is the motor manufacturer Fabbrica Italiana Automobili Torino better known?

3. 'Sixteen Going on Seventeen' is a song from which musical?

4. The car manufacturer Toyota is based in which country?

5. Which member of the Monty Python team was awarded a BAFTA Fellowship award in 2013?

6. The poet Wilfred Owen is associated with which conflict?

7. Highbury was the former home of which English football club?

8. In April 2013, bombers set off a series of explosions near the finish line of a marathon taking place in which American city?

9. Who are the hosts of culinary talent show 'Masterchef: The Professionals'?

10. What was Hillary Clinton's maiden name?

11. Benedict Cumberbatch, Basil Rathbone, and Jeremy Brett have all played which fictional detective?

12. The Nebula Award is a prize awarded in which genre of fiction?

13. The Cape Verde islands lie off the coast of which continent?

14. The giant statue of Christ the Redeemer overlooks which major South American city?

15. The name Peggy derives from which name?

16. Who played 007 in the Bond film 'The World Is Not Enough'?

17. The imperial palace known as The Forbidden City is in which Asian capital?

18. Which city is also known as the 'Square Mile'?

19. Which mobster killed JFK assassin Lee Harvey Oswald?
    a) Jack Diamond
    b) Jack Pearl
    c) Jack Ruby

20. Which saint gives his name to the capital of the US state of Minnesota?
    a) St Paul
    b) St Peter
    c) St Thomas

Answers to Quiz 62: Ireland

1. St Patrick
2. Green, white, and gold
3. Irish pound (punt)
4. Gaelic Athletic Association
5. Kerry and Clare
6. The United Kingdom
7. True
8. Garda Síochána
9. Brian Cowen
10. Jack Charlton
11. TD
12. Johnny Logan
13. Cork
14. Fianna Fail
15. Kerry
16. Roddy Doyle
17. Leitrim
18. James Joyce
19. 32
20. Mayo

Quiz 64: Sport part 2

1. Which is the only tennis grand slam tournament that is played on grass?

2. Which German team did Chelsea beat in the 2012 Champions League final?

3. Which county cricket team plays its home matches at Lord's?

4. The Claret Jug is awarded to the winner of which major sporting event?

5. Which Lancashire team reached the FA Cup final for the first time in its history in 2013?

6. How often does golf's Ryder Cup take place?

7. Which country won football's European Championship in 2008 and 2012?

8. 'The Baggies' is the nickname of which English football club?

9. Who won the 2012 BBC Sports Personality of the Year award?

10. Eldrick is the real first name of which record-breaking sportsman?

11. What nationality is the Formula One driver Mark Webber?

12. In which month does the Grand National usually take place?

13. In snooker, five points are awarded for potting what colour ball?

14. The Suzuka Formula One circuit is in which country?

15. Arsenal, Chelsea, Manchester City, and Manchester United are four of the five teams to have won the Premier League. Who is the fifth?

16. Which of golf's four major tournaments takes place latest in the year?

17. Ted Hankey, Simon Whitlock, and James Wade are notable names in which sport?

18. Which South American country hosted the first football World Cup?

19. Bloomfield Road is the home ground of which English football club?
    a) Blackburn Rovers
    b) Blackpool
    c) Bolton Wanderers

20. Which is the first tennis grand slam tournament of the year?
    a) Australian Open
    b) French Open
    c) Wimbledon

Answers to Quiz 63: Pot Luck

1. Heathrow
2. Fiat
3. The Sound of Music
4. Japan
5. Michael Palin
6. The First World War
7. Arsenal
8. Boston
9. Gregg Wallace and Michel Roux Jr
10. Rodham
11. Sherlock Holmes
12. Science fiction
13. Africa
14. Rio de Janeiro
15. Margaret
16. Pierce Brosnan
17. Beijing
18. The City of London
19. Jack Ruby
20. St Paul

Quiz 65: Pot Luck

1. Who made his debut as James Bond in the 1973 film 'Live and Let Die'?

2. In a game of snooker, how many red balls are on the table at the start of a frame?

3. 'The Green Green Grass' and 'Rock and Chips' are spin-offs from which TV show?

4. What is the square root of 196?

5. If it is 12 noon GMT in London, what time is it in Moscow?

6. Which word is used to describe a genetically identical copy of an animal?

7. What type of food is mascarpone?

8. The Nikkei Index is a share market in which city?

9. In relation to taxation, for what do the initials CGT stand?

10. Which American state gives its name to a famous dessert called Mud Pie?

11. The beer Stella Artois was originally brewed in which country?

12. Which herb is the central ingredient in the sauce pesto?

13. 'The Music of the Night' is a song from which stage musical?

14. In the US TV series, for what do the initials 'CSI' stand?

15. Perry Barr, Lozells, and Sparkbrook are areas of which English city?

16. Which long-running radio drama is set in the village of Ambridge?

17. Arial, gothic, and sans serif are types of what?

18. Singer Robbie Williams and darts champion Phil Taylor are both from which city?

19. The village of Cheddar, which gave its name to the famous cheese, is in which English county?
    a) Cornwall
    b) Devon
    c) Somerset

20. Which of these phrases is used to describe the government unnecessarily interfering in people's lives?
    a) granny state
    b) mummy state
    c) nanny state

Answers to Quiz 64: Sport part 2

1. Wimbledon
2. Bayern Munich
3. Middlesex
4. Golf's Open Championship
5. Wigan Athletic
6. Every two years
7. Spain
8. West Bromwich Albion
9. Bradley Wiggins
10. Tiger Woods
11. Australian
12. April
13. Blue
14. Japan
15. Blackburn Rovers
16. US PGA Championship
17. Darts
18. Uruguay
19. Blackpool
20. Australian Open

Quiz 66: Anagrams part 2

Rearrange the letters to make the name of a country.

1. Me angry

2. Mark end

3. Touch safari

4. Buxom gruel

5. Ran eating

6. Zilch creep cub

7. Hi oat pie

8. Do asinine

9. Neon lab

10. Tails aura

11. Ale zen wand

12. Maria no

13. Glib aura

14. Aid bias aura

15. Vino sale

16. Nails ark

17. Darn lie

18. Roam once

19. Lime bug

20. Handles bag

Answers to Quiz 65: Pot Luck

1. Roger Moore
2. 15
3. Only Fools and Horses
4. 14
5. 3 pm
6. Clone
7. Cheese
8. Tokyo
9. Capital Gains Tax
10. Mississippi
11. Belgium
12. Basil
13. The Phantom of the Opera
14. Crime Scene Investigation
15. Birmingham
16. The Archers
17. Fonts or typefaces
18. Stoke-on-Trent
19. Somerset
20. Nanny state

MEDIUM QUIZZES

Quiz 67: Pot Luck

1. What is the highest grossing film in UK box-office history?

2. If the counties that play in cricket's County Championship were listed alphabetically, which county would come first?

3. What is the second book in the 'Harry Potter' series?

4. Complete the proverb: 'They that sow the wind shall reap ...'

5. Which author created the children's character Tracy Beaker?

6. Jazz legend Charlie Parker played which instrument?

7. What is the first name of the title character in the classic novel 'The Great Gatsby'?

8. Darwin is the largest city in which Australian territory?

9. Who is the mother of film director Tim Burton's children?

10. Prior to launching a successful solo career, Beyoncé was a member of which band?

11. How old was Queen Elizabeth II when she acceded to the throne?

12. What are the two countries that have won football's World Cup exactly twice?

13. Jonathan Sexton plays international rugby union for which country?

14. Which best-selling author wrote the mystery and thriller novels featuring a character called Robert Langdon?

15. Which judge delivered a 2012 report into standards of the British press?

16. Sir Henry Wood founded which annual summer event, which took place for the first time in 1895?

17. 'Sure and Steadfast' is the motto of which organization?

18. Which ancient Greek philosopher and scholar said, 'I only know that I know nothing'?

19. England captain Alastair Cook plays domestic cricket for which English county?
    a) Essex
    b) Middlesex
    c) Surrey

20. To the nearest thousand, the surface area of the UK is how many square miles?
    a) 74,000
    b) 84,000
    c) 94,000

MEDIUM

Answers to Quiz 133: Pot Luck

1. The Independent
2. 18
3. Abraham
4. False
5. Wigan Athletic
6. Cheese
7. William Wordsworth
8. Haiti
9. John Keats
10. Rod Stewart
11. Farfalle
12. Henry VIII
13. The Flumps
14. Harry
15. Amelia
16. Panama
17. George Galloway
18. Tehran
19. Oxford
20. Cricket

Quiz 68: Art, Architecture, and Design

MEDIUM

1. Which controversial British artist was appointed professor of drawing at the Royal Academy in 2011?

2. Which musician was the subject of a hugely popular exhibition at the V&A in 2013?

3. Which French Impressionist was most associated with paintings of ballet dancers?

4. 'The Card Players', 'Pyramid of Skulls', and 'The Bathers' are works by which French Post-Impressionist painter?

5. Which award-winning artist directed the films 'Shame' and 'Hunger'?

6. A diptych is a piece of art containing how many painted panels?

7. Whose 'Garçon à la pipe' sold at auction for over $104m in 2004?

8. Which London art institution has hosted the annual Summer Exhibition every year since 1769?

9. 'Iron:Man', 'Another Place', and 'Event Horizon' are works by which British sculptor?

10. Which Turner Prize-winning artist said, 'It's amazing what you can do with an E in Art A-level, a twisted imagination, and a chainsaw'?

11. Sir Jonathan Ive is the lead designer at which technology company?

12. David Hockney was born in which Yorkshire city?

13. Which French Impressionist painter said, 'Colour is my day-long obsession, joy, and torment'?

14. The logo for children's TV programme 'Blue Peter' was designed by which television presenter and artist?

15. Which artist's name is used to describe a woman with a voluptuous figure?

16. 'The Treachery of Images', 'Time Transfixed', and 'The Son of Man' are paintings by which Belgian surrealist?

17. Which French artist completed many of his most famous works on the Polynesian island of Tahiti?

18. Which German artist was the court painter of Henry VIII?

19. What nationality was Frida Kahlo?
    a) Brazilian b) Mexican c) Spanish

20. Which artistic movement was chiefly pioneered by Pablo Picasso and Georges Braque?
    a) Cubism b) Futurism c) Romanticism

MEDIUM

Answers to Quiz 67: Pot Luck

1. Skyfall
2. Derbyshire
3. Harry Potter and the Chamber of Secrets
4. The whirlwind
5. Jacqueline Wilson
6. Saxophone
7. Jay
8. Northern Territory
9. Helena Bonham-Carter
10. Destiny's Child
11. 25
12. Argentina and Uruguay
13. Ireland
14. Dan Brown
15. Lord Justice Leveson
16. The Promenade Concerts
17. The Boys' Brigade
18. Socrates
19. Essex
20. 94,000

Quiz 69: Pot Luck

1. Which planet takes its name from the Roman god of agriculture?

2. What is the square root of 729?

3. Eid al-Fitr is a festival that marks the end of which month of the Muslim calendar?

4. Michael Eavis is the founder of which music festival?

5. Mount Godwin-Austen is better known by which name?

6. Which word is the official term for the end of a Parliament?

7. Which is the largest of the four main islands that make up Japan?

8. Who was the first Roman Catholic to become president of the United States?

9. In which year did Channel 4 first hit UK TV screens?

10. Who won the PDC World Darts Championship in 2011 and 2012?

11. What nationality was the 17th-century astronomer, scientist, and mathematician Christiaan Huygens?

12. Which broadcaster took over as the host of radio's 'Desert Island Discs' in 2006?

13. Which planet is named after the Roman god of the sea?

14. Which actress plays CIA agent Carrie Mathison in the acclaimed US drama 'Homeland'?

15. Roy Hodgson left which club to take up the post of manager of the England football team?

16. 'We Could Have Been Anything That We Wanted To Be', 'My Name Is Tallulah', and 'So You Want to Be a Boxer' are songs from which musical?

17. What sort of produce is traditionally sold at London's Columbia Road market?

18. Whom did Sue Barker succeed as the host of the TV quiz show 'A Question of Sport'?

19. Which of the following is a city in the US state of Florida?
    a) Moscow
    b) St Petersburg
    c) Volgograd

20. Martha Lane-Fox founded which dotcom company?
    a) Amazon.com
    b) LastMinute.com
    c) Wonga.com

MEDIUM

Answers to Quiz 68: Art, Architecture, and Design

1. Tracey Emin	11. Apple
2. David Bowie	12. Bradford
3. Edgar Degas	13. Claude Monet
4. Paul Cezanne	14. Tony Hart
5. Steve McQueen	15. Rubens (Rubenesque)
6. Two	16. Rene Magritte
7. Pablo Picasso	17. Paul Gauguin
8. Royal Academy	18. Hans Holbein the Younger
9. Anthony Gormley	19. Mexican
10. Damien Hirst	20. Cubism

Quiz 70: Barack Obama

1. In which year was Obama elected president for the first time?

2. Obama was born in which American state?

3. Prior to standing for the US presidency, Obama was a senator for which state?

4. Obama's father was from which African country?

5. Before getting married, what was Michelle Obama's maiden name?

6. Whom did Obama select as his running-mate in his first presidential election?

7. What are the names of Obama's two daughters?

8. Barack and Michelle Obama saw which film by Spike Lee on their first date?

9. True or false – Obama has won a Grammy award?

10. What was the name of Obama's 1995 memoir?

11. Obama was officially nominated as the Democratic presidential candidate for the first time in which city?

12. In the late 1960s, Obama lived for a number of years in which Asian country?

13. Obama studied law at which Ivy League university?

14. In which year was Obama awarded the Nobel Peace Prize?

15. What is the US Secret Service codename for President Obama?

16. True or false – the name Barack means 'blessed one' in Swahili?

17. Published in 2006, what was the name of Obama's second book, which outlined his vision for America?

18. Obama's 2012 campaign slogan, 'Forward' is also the motto of which English city?

19. How old was Obama when he was inaugurated as president for the first time?
    a) 47
    b) 48
    c) 49

20. What number president is Obama?
    a) 42nd
    b) 43rd
    c) 44th

MEDIUM

Answers to Quiz 69: Pot Luck

1. Saturn
2. 27
3. Ramadan
4. Glastonbury
5. K2
6. Dissolution
7. Honshu
8. John F Kennedy
9. 1982
10. Adrian Lewis
11. Dutch
12. Kirsty Young
13. Neptune
14. Claire Danes
15. West Bromwich Albion
16. Bugsy Malone
17. Flowers
18. David Coleman
19. St Petersburg
20. LastMinute.com

Quiz 71: Pot Luck

1. 'The Wrath of Khan' is the sequel to which sci-fi movie?

2. The Great Dividing Range is a mountain range in which Commonwealth country?

3. 'Cowards die many times before their deaths' is a line from which Shakespeare play?

4. Whom did Ban Ki-moon succeed as Secretary General of the United Nations?

5. Newton Heath was the original name of which Premier League football club?

6. Who played Harvey Dent in the 2008 film 'The Dark Knight'?

7. If the member states of the United Nations beginning with the letter M were listed alphabetically, which country would come first?

8. And which country would be last on the list?

9. 'The Mysterious Affair at Styles' was the first novel by which prolific crime writer?

10. Which was the last James Bond film that starred Roger Moore as 007?

11. The forint is the currency of which European country?

12. Prior to becoming president, Bill Clinton was the governor of which US state?

13. 1914's 'Making a Living' was the first film to feature which silent movie star?

14. Which name is shared by an American astronaut and an Irish leader who died in 1922?

15. Which investor from the TV show 'Dragons' Den' was the chairman of Millwall Football Club?

16. The Doge's Palace is in which European city?

17. What nationality is the tennis player Marin Čilić?

18. Doctor Emmett Lathrop Brown is a character in which famous film trilogy?

19. What is the freezing point of water in degrees Fahrenheit?
    a) 22°F
    b) 32°F
    c) 42°F

20. Billionaire American businessman Warren Buffett is known as 'The Sage of...'?
    a) Illinois
    b) Kansas
    c) Omaha

MEDIUM

Answers to Quiz 70: Barack Obama

1. 2008
2. Hawaii
3. Illinois
4. Kenya
5. Robinson
6. Joe Biden
7. Malia and Sasha
8. Do the Right Thing
9. True
10. Dreams from My Father
11. Denver
12. Indonesia
13. Harvard
14. 2009
15. Renegade
16. True
17. The Audacity of Hope
18. Birmingham
19. 47
20. 44th

Quiz 72: Films part 1

MEDIUM

1. Modern-day classic 'The Shawshank Redemption' is based on a novella by which author?

2. Who won the Cannes Film Festival's Palme d'Or at the age of 26 for 'Sex, Lies, and Videotape'?

3. Who directed 'The King's Speech', 'The Damned United', and 'Les Miserables'?

4. Which was the last James Bond film that starred Pierce Brosnan as 007?

5. 'Enter the Dragon' was the last film to feature which actor?

6. What was the occupation of the character played by Bill Murray in the 1993 comedy classic 'Groundhog Day'?

7. Which controversial Hollywood star directed the 2004 film 'The Passion of the Christ'?

8. Who played Billy The Butcher in the 2002 film 'Gangs of New York'?

9. Which British director's films include 'Dead Man's Shoes', 'A Room for Romeo Brass', and 'Made of Stone'?

10. Which star of the TV drama 'New Tricks' is the uncle of fellow-actor Ewan McGregor?

11. The famous scene where Marilyn Monroe steps over an air vent and her skirt blows up is from which 1955 film?

12. Which sport features in the films 'Any Given Sunday' and 'Remember the Titans'?

13. Which technology entrepreneur was the subject of the 2010 film 'The Social Network'?

14. What was the name of the diminutive James Bond baddie played by French actor Hervé Villechaize?

15. Which Irish actor played Oskar Schindler in the 1993 film 'Schindler's List'?

16. What nationality is the actor Viggo Mortensen?

17. Which actor played Jim Morrison in the 1991 biopic 'The Doors'?

18. In the 2006 mockumentary 'Borat', the title character was from which country?

19. In which city is the 1949 classic 'The Third Man' set?
    a) Berlin
    b) Vienna
    c) Warsaw

20. The 2007 film 'There Will Be Blood' is set in which industry?
    a) diamond mining
    b) oil
    c) railways

MEDIUM

Answers to Quiz 71: Pot Luck

1. Star Trek: The Motion Picture
2. Australia
3. Julius Caesar
4. Kofi Annan
5. Manchester United
6. Aaron Eckhart
7. Madagascar
8. Myanmar
9. Agatha Christie
10. A View to a Kill
11. Hungary
12. Arkansas
13. Charlie Chaplin
14. Michael Collins
15. Theo Paphitis
16. Venice
17. Croatian
18. The 'Back to the Future' trilogy
19. 32°F
20. Omaha

Quiz 73: Pot Luck

1. Oddjob was the bodyguard of which villain from the James Bond films?

2. In the Christian calendar, which feast is celebrated annually on 2 November?

3. Which name connects a well-known British DJ and the actor who played Captain America in the 2012 superhero film 'The Avengers'?

4. Whom did David Tennant succeed as TV's Doctor Who?

5. In North American sport, for what do the initials NHL stand?

6. Brunton Park is the home ground of which English football team?

7. 'Ode to a Nightingale' is by which English romantic poet?

8. Who was the first South American to hold the post of Secretary General of the United Nations?

9. The World Bank is based in which city?

10. By what name is the singer Park Jae-sang better known?

11. Who was the most talked about athlete on Twitter during the 2012 London Olympic Games?

12. Ted Mosby and Robin Scherbatsky are central characters in which US sitcom?

13. IPL are the initials of which cricket tournament?

14. Which British actor made his big-screen debut playing Hans Gruber in the 1988 film 'Die Hard'?

15. Dublin is in which province of Ireland?

16. 'Die Fledermaus' is an opera written by which composer?

17. Hainaut, Liège, and Namur are provinces of which European country?

18. In betting, what do the initials SP stand for?

19. What was the name of the character played by Hugo Weaving in 'The Matrix' films?
    a) Agent Jones
    b) Agent Orange
    c) Agent Smith

20. What is the national animal of India?
    a) cow
    b) snake
    c) tiger

MEDIUM

Answers to Quiz 72: Films part 1

1. Stephen King
2. Steven Soderbergh
3. Tom Hooper
4. Die Another Day
5. Bruce Lee
6. Weatherman
7. Mel Gibson
8. Daniel Day-Lewis
9. Shane Meadows
10. Denis Lawson

11. The Seven Year Itch
12. American football
13. Mark Zuckerberg
14. Nick Nack
15. Liam Neeson
16. American
17. Val Kilmer
18. Kazakhstan
19. Vienna
20. Oil

Quiz 74: Films part 2

1. British director Sam Mendes won an Oscar for his debut feature. What was the film?

2. Which actress played the title character in the 2012 film adaptation of 'Anna Karenina'?

3. Actor Michael Fassbender was born in Germany but raised in which country?

4. Which actor appeared in 'Moneyball', 'Tree of Life', and 'Happy Feet 2'?

5. Ben Kingsley played Georges Méliès, Sacha Baron Cohen played Inspector Gustave, and Ray Winstone played Claude Cabret in which 2011 drama?

6. Who played the title role in the 2012 thriller 'Jack Reacher'?

7. Which director's films include 'There Will Be Blood', 'Magnolia', and 'Boogie Nights'?

8. Which singer won the Oscar for Best Song at the 2013 ceremony?

9. Who directed the 'Godfather' trilogy?

10. Starring Bill Murray, the 2003 film 'Lost in Translation' was set in which city?

11. Who played pilot Whip Whitaker in the 2013 drama 'Flight'?

12. Who played idealistic young police officer John Blake in superhero favourite 'The Dark Knight Rises'?

13. Which 1997 film starring Mark Wahlberg was known in China as 'His Great Device Makes Him Famous'?

14. Who are the two actors who won the Best Actor Oscar for playing the same character?

15. What nationality is the controversial director Lars Von Trier?

16. Which British director won the Palme d'Or at the Cannes Film Festival in 1996 for 'Secrets and Lies'?

17. Which member of the Monty Python team directed the 1985 sci-fi fantasy film 'Brazil'?

18. What was the first film directed by Orson Welles?

19. What was the name of a 2009 sci-fi drama directed by Neill Blomkamp?
    a) District 7
    b) District 8
    c) District 9

20. Which country has won the most Oscars in the Best Foreign Film category?
    a) France
    b) Italy
    c) Spain

MEDIUM

Answers to Quiz 73: Pot Luck

1. Goldfinger
2. All Souls' Day
3. Chris Evans
4. Christopher Eccleston
5. National Hockey League
6. Carlisle United
7. John Keats
8. Javier Perez de Cuellar
9. Washington DC
10. Psy
11. Usain Bolt
12. How I Met Your Mother
13. Indian Premier League
14. Alan Rickman
15. Leinster
16. Johan Strauss II
17. Belgium
18. Starting price
19. Agent Smith
20. Tiger

Quiz 75: Pot Luck

1. Which British singer won five Grammy Awards in 2008?

2. According to the proverb, what is the thief of time?

3. Which American documentary-maker's films include 'Bowling For Columbine', 'Sicko', and 'Fahrenheit 9/11'?

4. What is the penultimate book in the Harry Potter series?

5. 'The Waste Land' is a work by which Anglo-American poet?

6. BBC sitcom 'Citizen Khan' is set in which British city?

7. What is larger, a tennis court or a basketball court?

8. 'Mrs Dalloway', 'To the Lighthouse', and 'The Waves' are works by which modernist author who died in 1941?

9. The World Health Organization is based in which European city?

10. Prior to Bradley Wiggins, who was the last cyclist to win the BBC Sports Personality of the Year award?

11. Which chemical element has the symbol Po and atomic number 84?

12. Which English Romantic poet was described as being 'mad, bad, and dangerous to know'?

13. Outside of India, which country has the largest Sikh population in the world?

14. What is the largest country in Africa?

15. 'Flatford Mill' and 'The Cornfield' are works by which English landscape painter?

16. What was the first name of the Czech composer Dvořák?

17. Bathsheba Everdene and Gabriel Oak are the central characters in which novel by Thomas Hardy?

18. What was Take That's first UK number one single?

19. What event is celebrated annually on 8 March?
    a) International Women's Day
    b) International Children's Day
    c) International Fathers' Day

20. In which year did John Paul II become Pope?
    a) 1977
    b) 1978
    c) 1979

MEDIUM

Answers to Quiz 74: Films part 2

1. American Beauty
2. Keira Knightley
3. Ireland
4. Brad Pitt
5. Hugo
6. Tom Cruise
7. Paul Thomas Anderson
8. Adele
9. Francis Ford Coppola
10. Tokyo
11. Denzel Washington
12. Joseph Gordon-Levitt
13. Boogie Nights
14. Marlon Brando and Robert De Niro (for playing Vito Corleone)
15. Danish
16. Mike Leigh
17. Terry Gilliam
18. Citizen Kane
19. District 9
20. Italy

Quiz 76: History part 1

1. Which nationalist leader was the founder and first president of the republic of Turkey?

2. Who succeeded Henry VIII as king of England?

3. In which decade of the 19th century was the American Civil War fought?

4. Prior to Bill Clinton, who was the last Democrat to win more than one US presidential election?

5. The Battle of Midway was fought in which conflict?

6. Which French monarch acceded to the throne at the age of five and reigned for 72 years?

7. Who was the emperor of Ethiopia from 1930 to 1974?

8. Who was the last Stuart monarch and the first sovereign of Great Britain?

9. Which Liberal politician was the British prime minister from 1908 until 1916?

10. In which country did the 1757 Battle of Plassey take place?

11. Helen Mirren, Joely Richardson, Vanessa Redgrave, Flora Robson, Glenda Jackson, and Cate Blanchett have all played which historical figure on screen?

12. Which English king was known as 'The Merry Monarch'?

13. Who was the mother of Queen Mary?

14. Hugh Laurie played which future English king in the classic TV comedy 'Blackadder the Third'?

15. Mafeking, the scene of a famous military siege, is in which country?

16. What nationality was the explorer Vasco da Gama?

17. In 2002, East Timor gained independence from which country?

18. Joan of Arc was burned at the stake in 1431 in which French city?

19. The 1386 Treaty of Windsor, the oldest diplomatic alliance in the world still in force, was signed between Britain and which country?
    a) France
    b) Portugal
    c) Spain

20. In which year was food rationing abolished in Britain?
    a) 1948
    b) 1950
    c) 1954

Answers to Quiz 75: Pot Luck

1. Amy Winehouse
2. Procrastination
3. Michael Moore
4. Harry Potter and the Half-Blood Prince
5. TS Eliot
6. Birmingham
7. Basketball court
8. Virginia Woolf
9. Geneva
10. Mark Cavendish in 2011
11. Polonium
12. Lord Byron
13. United Kingdom
14. Algeria
15. John Constable
16. Antonin
17. Far from the Madding Crowd
18. Pray
19. International Women's Day
20. 1978

MEDIUM

Quiz 77: Pot Luck

1. Dame Judi Dench made her debut as M in which James Bond film?

2. In which Italian city can you see Leonardo da Vinci's fresco 'The Last Supper'?

3. In which sport do teams compete for the Stanley Cup?

4. The Jorvik Viking Festival is celebrated in which English city?

5. Which English king succeeded Richard III?

6. Max Von Sydow played Reverend Father Lankester Merrin in which 1973 horror film?

7. Which country shares land borders with Papua New Guinea, East Timor, and Malaysia?

8. Which Oscar-winning actress played Jinx Johnson in the 2002 James Bond film 'Die Another Day'?

9. Which UK political party has the initials SDLP?

10. The Sikh holy site the Golden Temple is in which Indian city?

11. The Government Communications Headquarters (GCHQ) is based in which English town?

12. What is the only country on mainland South America that is a member of the Commonwealth?

13. Which actress played Nicola Murray in comedy 'The Thick of It' and DCS Innocent in 'Lewis'?

14. The bands Kaiser Chiefs and Alt-J are from which British city?

15. What are the four European Union capitals that start with the letter L?

16. A white cross on a black background is the flag of which part of Britain?

17. Who are the only father and son to have won the Formula One World Drivers' Championship?

18. Which Western European country held its first general election for over 40 years in 1977?

19. The Battle of Iwo Jima was fought in which war?
    a) World War II
    b) Korean War
    c) Vietnam War

20. In which year was the £1 coin introduced in the UK?
    a) 1981
    b) 1982
    c) 1983

MEDIUM

Answers to Quiz 76: History part 1

1. Kemal Ataturk
2. Edward VI
3. 1860s
4. Franklin D Roosevelt
5. World War II
6. Louis XIV
7. Haile Selassie
8. Queen Anne
9. Herbert Asquith
10. India
11. Elizabeth I
12. Charles II
13. Catherine of Aragon
14. George IV
15. South Africa
16. Portuguese
17. Indonesia
18. Rouen
19. Portugal
20. 1954

Quiz 78: England

1. What type of produce is sold at London's Billingsgate Market?

2. Novelist Jane Austen was born and raised in which English county?

3. Measuring 1.33 miles, the longest pleasure pier in the world is in which seaside town?

4. Which stately home was the birthplace of Winston Churchill and is the seat of the Duke of Marlborough?

5. Which midland city plays host to one of the largest Diwali celebrations outside India?

6. The Baltic Centre for Contemporary Art is in which northern English town?

7. The Ebor race meeting is run at which racecourse?

8. What range of hills straddles the England–Scotland border between Northumberland and the Scottish Borders?

9. What is the most southerly city on mainland England?

10. Which English city stands on the River Avon between the Cotswold Hills and the Mendips?

11. 'England expects that every man will do his duty' is a phrase associated with whom?

12. Broadcaster Jeremy Paxman, chef Marco Pierre-White, and actor John Simm were all born in which English city?

13. The Royal Northern College of Music is based in which city?

14. Devon shares a border with which three counties?

15. 'A New England' was a number 7 hit in 1985 for which female singer?

16. The River Severn rises in Wales and joins England in which county?

17. The Barber Institute of Fine Arts and the Cadbury World museum are in which English city?

18. The 2006 film 'This Is England' was directed by which Uttoxeter-born director?

19. US president Bill Clinton studied at which English university?
    a) Cambridge
    b) the LSE
    c) Oxford

20. Which saint was Britain's first martyr?
    a) St Alban
    b) St Anselm
    b) St Augustine

MEDIUM

Answers to Quiz 77: Pot Luck

1. Goldeneye
2. Milan
3. Ice Hockey
4. York
5. Henry VII
6. The Exorcist
7. Indonesia
8. Halle Berry
9. Social Democratic and Labour Party
10. Amritsar
11. Cheltenham
12. Guyana
13. Rebecca Front
14. Leeds
15. Lisbon, Ljubliana, London, and Luxembourg
16. Cornwall
17. Graham and Damon Hill
18. Spain
19. World War II
20. 1983

Quiz 79: Pot Luck

1. What nationality was the astronomer Nicolaus Copernicus?

2. Which actress played author Virginia Woolf in the 2002 film 'The Hours'?

3. Who are the three regular judges on TV's 'Great British Menu'?

4. 'Girl Before a Mirror', 'Three Musicians', and 'Les Demoiselles d'Avignon' are works by which prolific Spanish artist?

5. Who was the first Hanoverian king of England?

6. What is the capital city of the Canadian province of British Columbia?

7. Which name is shared by a track cycling race and the capital of the US state of Wisconsin?

8. Which British monarch started the tradition of the annual Christmas broadcast?

9. Proverbially, what are the windows of the soul?

10. The famous statue 'Manneken Pis' is a landmark in which European city?

11. What are the two tiles in Scrabble that are worth 10 points?

12. What colour is the ribbon awarded with a Victoria Cross?

13. What are the first names of TV detective duo 'Scott and Bailey'?

14. Composed by George Gershwin, the song 'Summertime' is from which opera?

15. The Webb Ellis Cup is awarded to the winners of which international sporting competition?

16. Who won the Best Actor Oscar in 2003 and 2008 for his performances in 'Mystic River' and 'Milk'?

17. What does the letter C in the economic organization OECD stand for?

18. What type of hat takes its name from the Spanish for 'shade'?

19. Which country was the first winner of the Rugby World Cup?
    a) Australia
    b) New Zealand
    c) South Africa

20. The Scandinavian crime drama 'The Killing' is set in which city?
    a) Copenhagen
    b) Oslo
    c) Stockholm

Answers to Quiz 78: England

1. Fish
2. Hampshire
3. Southend-on-Sea
4. Blenheim Palace
5. Leicester
6. Gateshead
7. York
8. The Cheviot Hills
9. Truro
10. Bath
11. Lord Nelson
12. Leeds
13. Manchester
14. Cornwall, Dorset, and Somerset
15. Kirsty MacColl
16. Shropshire
17. Birmingham
18. Shane Meadows
19. Oxford
20. St Alban

MEDIUM

Quiz 80: Famous Elizabeths

Identify the famous Elizabeths from the clues below:

1. She won Oscars for her performances in 'Butterfield 8' and 'Who's Afraid of Virginia Woolf'.

2. The protagonist of Jane Austen's 'Pride and Prejudice'.

3. The other half of Australian cricket legend Shane Warne.

4. Olympic gymnast who won bronze on the uneven bars at London 2012.

5. South African city that is home to a Test cricket ground called St George's Park.

6. 19th-century British poet whose works include 'Sonnets from the Portuguese' and 'Aurora Leigh'.

7. Bristol-born medical pioneer who was the second woman on the UK Medical Register.

8. The main character in the US TV comedy '30 Rock', played by Tina Fey.

9. Founder of one of the world's largest beauty and perfume companies.

10. US TV drama, set in the world of fashion, starring America Ferrera.

11. Character played by Beverley Callard in 'Coronation Street'.

12. UK radio's third longest serving female DJ.

13. French film, made in 1986, directed by Jean-Jacques Beineix and starring Béatrice Dalle and Jean-Hugues Anglade.

14. American actress, born in 1989, whose film credits include 'Silent House', 'Liberal Arts', and 'Martha Marcy May Marlene'?

15. Brit Award winning singer-songwriter whose albums include 'The Other Side of Daybreak', 'Trailer Park Legacy', and 'Sugaring Season'.

16. Wife of the US president who preceded Jimmy Carter.

17. Winner of the 2012 Turner Prize.

18. A member of pop group Atomic Kitten who later appeared in 'Legally Blonde: The Musical' and won 'Celebrity Masterchef'.

19. Character played by Sophie Myles in BBC spy drama 'Spooks'.

20. The lead singer with indie rockers The Gossip.

MEDIUM

Answers to Quiz 79: Pot Luck

1. Polish
2. Nicole Kidman
3. Matthew Fort, Prue Leith, and Oliver Peyton
4. Pablo Picasso
5. George I
6. Victoria
7. Madison
8. King George V
9. Eyes
10. Brussels
11. Q and Z
12. Crimson
13. Janet and Rachel
14. Porgy and Bess
15. The Rugby World Cup
16. Sean Penn
17. Co-operation
18. Sombrero
19. New Zealand
20. Copenhagen

Quiz 81: Pot Luck

1. Which city in Ukraine features in the title of a 1972 novel by Frederick Forsyth that was later turned into a film?

2. Stanley Kowalski and Blanche DuBois are the central characters in which play by Tennessee Williams?

3. Who said, 'To live is the rarest thing in the world. Most people exist, that is all'?

4. Which actress played the title character in the 2001 film 'Amelie'?

5. Mid Jutland, North Jutland, and Zealand are regions of which country?

6. In relation to illness, for what do the initials CJD stand?

7. The Great Plague and the Great Fire of London occurred during the reign of which English monarch?

8. 'If music be the food of love, play on' is a line from which play by Shakespeare?

9. Ricky Walden and Barry Hawkins are notable names in which sport?

10. Which British monarch was the subject of the 1997 film 'Mrs Brown'?

11. Which Staffordshire town is said to be the brewing capital of Britain?

12. 'Jigsaw' is the main villain in which horror-film franchise?

13. What was the first name of gardener Capability Brown?

14. Which English football team plays its home matches at the King Power Stadium?

15. 'Some Might Say' was the first number one single by which band?

16. Which event took place first – the Cricket World Cup or the Rugby World Cup?

17. In which year did the famous Woodstock Music Festival take place?

18. Which English county cricket team plays its home matches at the Riverside Ground?

19. The Altes Museum is located in which European capital?
    a) Amsterdam
    b) Berlin
    c) Prague

20. Actor Ryan Gosling was born in which country?
    a) Britain
    b) Canada
    c) New Zealand

MEDIUM

Answers to Quiz 80: Famous Elizabeths

1. Elizabeth Taylor
2. Elizabeth Bennet
3. Liz Hurley
4. Beth Tweddle
5. Port Elizabeth
6. Elizabeth Barrett Browning
7. Elizabeth Blackwell
8. Liz Lemon
9. Elizabeth Arden
10. Ugly Betty
11. Liz McDonald
12. Liz Kershaw
13. Betty Blue
14. Elizabeth Olsen
15. Beth Orton
16. Betty Ford
17. Elizabeth Price
18. Liz McClarnon
19. Beth Bailey
20. Beth Ditto

Quiz 82: Colours

1. Who lost six World Snooker Championship finals between 1984 and 1994?

2. What was the world's first national park?

3. What was the title of Taylor Swift's 2012 chart-topping album?

4. On a Scrabble board, what colour square offers a 'double letter' score?

5. Who is the actress mother of the late Natasha Richardson and Joely Richardson?

6. The 1998 novel 'Digital Fortress' was the debut book from which best-selling author?

7. 'Sciurus vulgaris' is the scientific name for which British animal?

8. Which area of Baghdad provided the title for a 2010 film directed by Paul Greengrass and starring Matt Damon?

9. Which glamorous veteran actress played Rula Romanoff in 'Coronation Street'?

10. 'It's Great When You're Straight ... Yeah' was a number one 1995 album from which Manchester band?

11. Rowan Atkinson played Inspector Raymond Fowler in which TV comedy?

12. Dating back to 1433, what is London's oldest Royal Park?

13. What was the debut album by British dance-music pioneers Massive Attack?

14. Which constituent college of the University of London is based in New Cross?

15. The 'Kansas Cannonball' is the nickname of which former sprint champion?

16. 'Black Holes and Revelations' is a 2006 album by which English rock band?

17. Poultry-processing company Venky's are the owners of which English football club?

18. Which British prime minister was preceded by the Duke of Wellington and succeeded by the Viscount Melbourne?

19. 'Come On You Reds' was a number one hit for which English football team?
    a) Arsenal
    b) Liverpool
    c) Manchester United

20. Complete the title of the 2013 Disney film: 'The Odd Life of Timothy ...'
    a) Brown
    b) Green
    c) Red

Answers to Quiz 81: Pot Luck

1. Odessa (The Odessa File)
2. A Streetcar Named Desire
3. Oscar Wilde
4. Audrey Tatou
5. Denmark
6. Creutzfeldt–Jakob disease
7. Charles II
8. Twelfth Night
9. Snooker
10. Queen Victoria
11. Burton-on-Trent
12. Saw
13. Lancelot
14. Leicester City
15. Oasis
16. The Cricket World Cup
17. 1969
18. Durham
19. Berlin
20. Canada

MEDIUM

Quiz 83: Pot Luck

1. Who plays Detective Superintendent Sandra Pullman in the police drama 'New Tricks'?

2. David Cameron is the MP for which Oxfordshire constituency?

3. Chemist Leo H Baekeland was the inventor of what type of plastic?

4. In which country was acupuncture developed?

5. Which English football team plays its home matches at the County Ground?

6. Addison Lee is a company that provides what form of transport?

7. The rainbow jersey is worn by world champions in which sport?

8. Clare, Cork, and Kerry are counties in which province of Ireland?

9. Former prime minister James Callaghan and engineer Isambard Kingdom Brunel were born in which English coastal city?

10. Who made his 800th appearance for Chelsea in their 2-0 win over Swansea in April 2013?

11. In which sport are Saeed Bin Suroor and Nicky Henderson notable names?

12. Which European football team plays its home games at a stadium called the Camp Nou?

13. Which Scandinavian novelist created the fictional character Lisbeth Salander?

14. Who is the longest serving DJ on the Radio 1 Breakfast Show?

15. Which West Yorkshire town is famed for its liquorice?

16. Huey Morgan is the front man of which New York band?

17. Who was appointed Poet Laureate in 2009?

18. Who was the Greek goddess of peace?

19. What was the surname of the character played by Clint Eastwood in the film 'Dirty Harry'?
    a) Callahan
    b) Callaway
    c) Calliope

20. Complete the title of the 2013 film starring Terence Stamp and Gemma Arterton: 'Song for ...'
    a) Marion
    b) Marjorie
    c) Marigold

MEDIUM

Answers to Quiz 82: Colours

1. Jimmy White
2. Yellowstone
3. Red
4. Light blue
5. Vanessa Redgrave
6. Dan Brown
7. Red squirrel
8. Green Zone
9. Honor Blackman
10. Black Grape
11. The Thin Blue Line
12. Greenwich Park
13. Blue Lines
14. Goldsmith's
15. Maurice Greene
16. Muse
17. Blackburn Rovers
18. Charles Grey, 2nd Earl Grey
19. Manchester United
20. Green

Quiz 84: Sport part 1

1. Which English football team has won the European Cup more times than the domestic top flight trophy?

2. Who is the only German golfer to win the US Masters?

3. Which country will host the 2019 Cricket World Cup?

4. Who is the only footballer to score for England at three World Cups?

5. Which team was promoted to the top flight of English football in 2013 after an absence of 53 years?

6. Who won both the Player of the Year and the Young Player of the Year at the 2013 Professional Footballers' Association awards?

7. Which rugby league team played its home games in 2013 at a ground called The Stoop?

8. 'The Dynamos' is the nickname of which county's one-day cricket team?

9. Which Dutchman in 2003 became the first footballer to win the Champions League with three different clubs?

10. Which racecourse hosts the race called the St Leger?

11. The King's Lynn Stars and Belle Vue Aces are teams that take part in which sport?

12. Neath RFC and Swansea RFC merged to form which Welsh rugby union team?

13. Which country won cricket's Champions Trophy in 2013?

14. What are the two teams beginning with the letter W to have won the top flight of English football?

15. Who are the three Brazilians to have won the World Formula One Drivers' Championship?

16. Which of the tennis majors did Pete Sampras fail to win?

17. Which two countries will host the 2015 Cricket World Cup?

18. Who was the captain of the American team at the 2012 Ryder Cup?

19. Which fruit appears on the badge of Worcestershire County Cricket Club?
    a) Apple
    b) Orange
    c) Pear

20. What nationality is Southampton manager Mauricio Pochettino?
    a) Argentine
    b) Italian
    c) Spanish

MEDIUM

Answers to Quiz 83: Pot Luck

1. Amanda Redman
2. Witney
3. Bakelite
4. China
5. Swindon Town
6. Taxis
7. Cycling
8. Munster
9. Portsmouth
10. Frank Lampard
11. Horse racing
12. Barcelona
13. Stieg Larsson
14. Chris Moyles
15. Pontefract
16. The Fun Lovin' Criminals
17. Carol Ann Duffy
18. Eirene
19. Callahan
20. Marion

Quiz 85: Pot Luck

1. Thames House is the HQ of which organization?

2. What are the two London boroughs that start with the letter L?

3. The Siege of Sevastopol was the last major operation of which 19th-century conflict?

4. In 2013, the British and Irish Lions rugby team toured which country?

5. Gingivitis is the inflammation of which part of the body?

6. Opium is derived from the unripe seedpods of which flower?

7. What is the tallest residential building in the European Union?

8. What are The Smiler, Oblivion, Stealth, and The Big One?

9. Who played the title character in the 2013 film version of 'The Great Gatsby'?

10. Which band have had more UK number one hit singles – the Rolling Stones or Westlife?

11. Which Beatle had a cameo role in the cult classic 'The Life of Brian'?

12. The bane of many a teenager, what is a comedo more commonly known as?

13. The 1983 novel 'The Colour of Magic' is the first book in which fantasy series created by Terry Pratchett?

14. Which medical condition has the initials DVT?

15. Ivanhoe is the middle name of which footballer who won 62 caps for England between 1999 and 2010?

16. In which Irish province are the counties of Laois, Longford, and Louth located?

17. Which amendment to the US constitution abolished slavery?

18. In relation to the internet, for what do the initials SEO stand?

19. Hollywood icon Cary Grant was born in which English city?
    a) Birmingham
    b) Bristol
    c) Liverpool

20. By what name is the British rapper, actor, and director Ben Drew more commonly known?
    a) Plan A
    b) Plan B
    c) Plan Z

Answers to Quiz 84: Sport part 1

1. Nottingham Forest
2. Bernhard Langer
3. England
4. David Beckham
5. Cardiff City
6. Gareth Bale
7. London Broncos
8. Durham
9. Clarence Seedorf
10. Doncaster
11. Speedway
12. Ospreys
13. India
14. West Bromwich Albion and Wolverhampton Wanderers
15. Emerson Fittipaldi, Nelson Piquet, and Ayrton Senna
16. French Open
17. Australia and New Zealand
18. Davis Love III
19. Pear
20. Argentine

MEDIUM

Quiz 86: Transport

1. Which London railway terminus is the home of Eurostar trains?

2. In relation to air travel, for what do the initials CAA stand?

3. On a London Underground map, what is the pink line?

4. In terms of passenger numbers, what is the third busiest airport in the UK?

5. RENFE is the national train operator of which country?

6. Michael O'Leary is the chief executive of which airline?

7. John Paul II International Airport serves which European city?

8. Which London tube line runs from Stanmore to Stratford?

9. Lightning McQueen, voiced by Owen Wilson, is the central character in which 2006 Pixar animation?

10. White City is the closest tube station to which London football club?

11. Which Swedish car manufacturer filed for bankruptcy in late 2011?

12. Etihad Airlines is the flag carrier of which country?

13. Which transport-inspired book was sold for the first time in April 1931?

14. Dulles International Airport serves which US city?

15. Atatürk International Airport serves which major city?

16. The 1979 number one 'Cars' was the only solo chart-topper by which musician?

17. What is the main motorway from London to the south coast, stretching from Sunbury-on-Thames to Southampton?

18. Which fictional policeman drove a burgundy Mk II Jaguar?

19. The A380 is an airliner made by which company?
    a) Airbus
    b) Boeing
    c) Vickers

20. Glasgow and Cardiff are both home to railway stations with what name?
    a) King Street
    b) Princess Street
    c) Queen Street

MEDIUM

Answers to Quiz 85: Pot Luck

1. The Security Service
2. Lambeth and Lewisham
3. The Crimean War
4. Australia
5. Gums
6. Poppy
7. The Shard in London
8. Roller coasters
9. Leonardo di Caprio
10. Westlife
11. George Harrison
12. A blackhead
13. Discworld
14. Deep vein thrombosis
15. Emile Heskey
16. Leinster
17. 13th
18. Search Engine Optimization
19. Bristol
20. Plan B

Quiz 87: Pot Luck

1. Tom Hanks received his first Best Actor Oscar nomination for which 1988 film?

2. The Alfred Hitchcock classic 'The 39 Steps' was based on a novel by which author?

3. The Battle of Spion Kop was fought in which war?

4. Which two countries joined the European Union on 1 January 2007?

5. In 1962, Algeria gained independence from which country?

6. Who are England's most capped footballing brothers?

7. Which pop veteran topped the album charts for the first time in 34 years in 2013 with 'Time'?

8. In finance, for what do the initials IPO stand?

9. The 1980s drama 'The Colbys' was a spin-off from which show?

10. Which British actress married James Righton of rock band Klaxons in May 2013?

11. An otoscope is a device used by doctors to look at which part of the body?

12. Giulio Andreotti, who died in May 2013, was formerly the prime minister of which European country?

13. Martin Fry was the lead singer with which 1980s band?

14. Former editor of the News of the World Rebekah Brooks was formerly married to which actor?

15. Becky Sharp is the central character in which classic 19th-century book which was subtitled 'A Novel Without a Hero'?

16. Which animal appears on the flag of the US state of California?

17. Which Hollywood acting pair are the parents of a child called Scout LaRue?

18. Who is the only female artist to have had more than ten UK number one singles?

19. Otis Lee Crenshaw is the alter ego of which British-based US comedian?
    a) Rich Hall
    b) Reginald D Hunter
    c) Scott Capuro

20. What nationality was the champion cyclist Eddy Merckx?
    a) Belgian
    b) French
    c) German

MEDIUM

Answers to Quiz 86: Transport

1. St Pancras International
2. Civil Aviation Authority
3. Hammersmith and City
4. Manchester
5. Spain
6. Ryan Air
7. Krakow
8. Jubilee line
9. Cars
10. Queens Park Rangers
11. Saab
12. The United Arab Emirates
13. The Highway Code
14. Washington DC
15. Istanbul
16. Gary Numan
17. M3
18. Inspector Morse
19. Airbus
20. Queen Street

Quiz 88: Anagrams

Rearrange the letters to make the titles of films that have won the Oscar for Best Picture since 1980:

1. Ate thirst

2. Threaded pet

3. Triad gaol

4. Lord abominably ill

5. A glider illusion mom

6. Act in it

7. Cork heel truth

8. Had gin

9. At rehab rev

10. Flea minutia bud

11. Conformed loony runt

12. Peg from rust

13. Ant pool

14. In an arm

15. Maniac tea buyer

16. A choir forfeits

17. On rung five

18. A sad emu

19. A heavers keen spoil

20. Disarm dissing ivy

Answers to Quiz 87: Pot Luck

1. Big
2. John Buchan
3. Second Boer War
4. Bulgaria and Romania
5. France
6. Gary and Phil Neville
7. Rod Stewart
8. Initial Public Offering
9. Dynasty
10. Keira Knightley
11. The ear
12. Italy
13. ABC
14. Ross Kemp
15. Vanity Fair
16. Bear
17. Demi Moore and Bruce Willis
18. Madonna
19. Rich Hall
20. Belgian

Quiz 89: Pot Luck

1. What is the Russian word for fortress?

2. Which long-running television sports programme was broadcast for the last time on 27 January 2007?

3. The battles of Lexington and Concord were initial skirmishes in which conflict?

4. Which Indonesian island is also the name of a computer programming language developed by Sun Microsystems?

5. Tim Cahill, Mark Schwarzer, and Luke Wilkshere play international football for which country?

6. Portuguese navigator Pedro Cabral is generally credited as the discoverer of which country?

7. In 2011, Michael D Higgins was elected president of which country?

8. A hysterectomy is a medical procedure to remove which part of the body?

9. The royal family of which European country live at Drottningholm Palace?

10. Who comes next on this list: Thatcher, Major, Hague, ... ?

11. What are the two London boroughs that start with the letter S?

12. In which card game can an unlucky player suffer a 'bad beat'?

13. What was the first name of the title character in the classic novel 'Gulliver's Travels'?

14. Nick Carraway is one of the central characters in which classic novel that was turned into a film in 2013?

15. In the 'Mr Men' series of books, what colour is Mr Perfect?

16. Biff Tannen is the principal baddie in which film series?

17. Huish Park is the home ground of which English football club?

18. The Union Flag appears on the flag of which American state?

19. Which of the following African countries is not landlocked?
    a) Burundi
    b) Chad
    c) Sierra Leone

20. Complete the name of the best-selling band: Noah and the ...
    a) Dolphin
    b) Shark
    c) Whale

Answers to Quiz 88: Anagrams

1. The Artist
2. The Departed
3. Gladiator
4. Million Dollar Baby
5. Slumdog Millionaire
6. Titanic
7. The Hurt Locker
8. Gandhi
9. Braveheart
10. A Beautiful Mind
11. No Country for Old Men
12. Forrest Gump
13. Platoon
14. Rain Man
15. American Beauty
16. Chariots of Fire
17. Unforgiven
18. Amadeus
19. Shakespeare in Love
20. Driving Miss Daisy

Quiz 90: Famous Pauls

Identify the famous Pauls from the clues below:

1. First black player to captain the England national football team.

2. British actor whose film credits include 'Margin Call', 'Wimbledon', and 'The Da Vinci Code'.

3. Driver of the car in which he, Dodi Fayed, and Diana, Princess of Wales were killed.

4. Sportsman who won 24 caps for New Zealand at rugby league and 6 for England at rugby union.

5. US soul singer whose hits included 'Me and Mrs Jones' and 'Only the Strong Survive'.

6. Director whose films include 'Punch Drunk Love' and 'The Master'.

7. Pioneer of the electric guitar who died in 2009.

8. Musician whose hits included the chart-topping 'Nineteen' and 'Top of the Pops' theme 'The Wizard'.

9. Dutch film director who made 'Total Recall', 'Starship Troopers', and 'Showgirls'.

10. Name shared by a character in Aussie soap 'Neighbours' and a former England goalkeeper.

11. Hollywood actor whose credits include 'Anchorman', 'The 40-Year-Old Virgin', and 'This Is 40'.

12. Australian politician dubbed 'The Lizard of Oz' by parts of the British media.

13. Nottingham-born fashion designer knighted in 2000.

14. The real name of U2 frontman Bono.

15. Veteran English musician who recorded the 2012 album 'Sonik Kicks'.

16. Canadian-born singer-songwriter who wrote the English lyrics to 'My Way'.

17. The subject of a 2013 film biopic called 'The Look of Love' starring Steve Coogan.

18. President of Germany from 1925 to 1934.

19. German footballer who scored in the 1974 and 1982 World Cup finals, noted for an impressive afro and moustache.

20. Libertarian US politician who stood as a candidate in the Republican Party presidential primaries in 2008 and 2012.

MEDIUM

Answers to Quiz 89: Pot Luck

1. Kremlin
2. Grandstand
3. The American War of Independence
4. Java
5. Australia
6. Brazil
7. The Republic of Ireland
8. Uterus
9. Sweden
10. Duncan Smith (Conservative Party leaders)
11. Southwark and Sutton
12. Poker
13. Lemuel
14. The Great Gatsby
15. Blue
16. Back to the Future
17. Yeovil Town
18. Hawaii
19. Sierra Leone
20. Whale

Quiz 91: Pot Luck

1. In computing, what is wi-fi short for?

2. Yarg cheese comes from which English county?

3. In May 2011, which former Conservative Party politician became Chairman of the BBC Trust?

4. 'Parachutes' was the debut album from which British rock band?

5. In which city is the football team Fenerbahce based?

6. Former prime minister Tony Blair was the MP for which constituency?

7. Frequently seen on clocks, what does the Latin phrase 'tempus fugit' mean in English?

8. Actress and musician Carla Bruni is married to which European politician?

9. In relation to government funding, for what do the initials PFI stand?

10. The phrase 'All work and no play makes Jack a dull boy' featured prominently in which 1980 film chiller?

11. Which British politician won the Nobel Prize for Literature in 1953?

12. What fish soup dish takes its name from the French 'chaudière' meaning stewpot?

13. What is the surname of the eponymous TV serial killer 'Dexter'?

14. Which Russian vessel was the subject of a famous 1925 silent film directed by Sergei Eisenstein?

15. Who finished second representing the United Kingdom at the 1992 Eurovision Song Contest with the song 'One Step out of Time'?

16. What type of food is pumpernickel?

17. Teriyaki is a cooking technique commonly used in the cuisine of which country?

18. Adam Clayton is the bass player with which band?

19. In which decade did Shirley Bassey have her first UK number one hit single?
    a) 1950s
    b) 1960s
    c) 1970s

20. 'Shaking the Habitual' was a 2013 album by which band?
    a) The Knife
    b) The Fork
    c) The Spoon

MEDIUM

Answers to Quiz 90: Famous Pauls

1. Paul Ince
2. Paul Bettany
3. Henri Paul
4. Henry Paul
5. Billy Paul
6. Paul Thomas Anderson
7. Les Paul
8. Paul Hardcastle
9. Paul Verhoeven
10. Paul Robinson

11. Paul Rudd
12. Paul Keating
13. Paul Smith
14. Paul Hewson
15. Paul Weller
16. Paul Anka
17. Paul Raymond
18. Paul von Hindenburg
19. Paul Breitner
20. Ron Paul

Quiz 92: Sport part 2

MEDIUM

1. Which football team claimed its first major trophy in 2013 by winning the League Cup?

2. Which bird gives its name to the feat of scoring three consecutive strikes in ten-pin bowling?

3. Which football team, despite being known as the Bluebirds, changed its colours to red after being taken over by a Malaysian consortium?

4. Which was the first sport played on the moon?

5. In which year did Scotland last qualify for the World Cup finals?

6. Which country won the Cricket World Cup for the first time in 1987?

7. What are the colours of the two rings on the bottom row of the Olympic flag?

8. The SWALEC Stadium is in which British city?

9. Which team did Chelsea face in the final of the 2013 Europa League?

10. Which country lost in the Rugby World Cup final in 1987, 1999, and 2011?

11. Who was the last Scot to win the Open Golf Championship?

12. In Olympic archery, how far in metres is the target from the archer?

13. In which year did football's European Championship first take place?

14. How many fences must a horse jump to complete the Grand National?

15. True or false – cricket was once an Olympic sport?

16. The Lance Todd Trophy is awarded in which sport?

17. Prior to managing Manchester United, Sir Alex Ferguson was in charge of which Scottish club?

18. In a Formula One grand prix, what colour flag is flown to indicate danger, such as a stranded car, ahead?

19. Both of the finalists in rugby union's 2013 Heineken Cup were from which country?
    a) England
    b) France
    c) Ireland

20. In 2013, Tai Woffinden was crowned British champion in which sport?
    a) darts
    b) speedway
    c) squash

MEDIUM

Answers to Quiz 91: Pot Luck

1.	Wireless fidelity	11.	Sir Winston Churchill
2.	Cornwall	12.	Chowder
3.	Chris Patten	13.	Morgan
4.	Coldplay	14.	Battleship Potemkin
5.	Istanbul	15.	Michael Ball
6.	Sedgefield	16.	Bread
7.	Time flies	17.	Japan
8.	Nicolas Sarkozy	18.	U2
9.	Private Finance Initiative	19.	1950s
10.	The Shining	20.	The Knife

Quiz 93: Pot Luck

1. Bob Crow is the leader of which British trade union?

2. Actors Rolf Lassgård, Krister Henriksson, and Kenneth Branagh have all played which fictional detective?

3. Which high-profile British politician was editor of 'The Spectator' magazine from 1999 to 2005?

4. Who played the title character in the 1992 film 'The Bodyguard'?

5. HNO_3 is the formula for which acid?

6. Portuguese is an official language in which Chinese Special Administrative Region?

7. What is the only London borough that begins with the letter T?

8. John Hammond, Jay Wynne, and Darren Bett present what on BBC television?

9. Ferdinand Marcos was the long-time president of which Asian country?

10. In a game of Texas hold 'em poker, how many cards does each player receive?

11. Which medical drama was set at the fictional Princeton–Plainsboro Teaching Hospital (PPTH)?

12. Tom Cruise starred as Stacee Jaxx in which heavy-metal inspired 2012 film?

13. Who plays the title character's often disappointed mother Penny in the TV sitcom 'Miranda'?

14. In imperial measures, how many yards make up a chain?

15. The style of play known as 'total football' was associated with which country?

16. In yards, what is the radius of the centre circle of a football pitch?

17. Osama bin Laden was discovered in a compound in which Pakistani city?

18. Which three British football clubs have home grounds with a capacity of over 60,000?

19. In January 2011, VAT was raised to what rate?
    a) 15%
    b) 17.5%
    c) 20%

20. Andy Murray won his first grand slam tennis title at which event?
    a) Australian Open
    b) US Open
    c) Wimbledon

MEDIUM

Answers to Quiz 92: Sport part 2

1.	Swansea City	11.	Paul Lawrie
2.	Turkey	12.	70m
3.	Cardiff City	13.	1960
4.	Golf	14.	30
5.	1998	15.	True
6.	Australia	16.	Rugby League
7.	Yellow and green	17.	Aberdeen
8.	Cardiff	18.	Yellow
9.	Benfica	19.	France
10.	France	20.	Speedway

Quiz 94: Places

1. Mexico shares a border with which four US states?

2. Mt McKinley, the highest mountain in America, is in which state?

3. Leghorn is the English name for which Italian port?

4. Port Vale football club is based in which English city?

5. Cordoba is the second largest city in which country?

6. The giant Burj Khalifa tower is in which city?

7. Which West African country was formerly known as Dahomey?

8. Which US state has borders with Washington, Oregon, Nevada, Utah, Wyoming, and Montana and the Canadian province of British Columbia?

9. The volcano Popocatépetl is in which country?

10. Which landlocked country shares borders with Azerbaijan, Georgia, Iran, and Turkey?

11. Galileo Galilei Airport serves which Italian city?

12. What was the former name of the Indian city of Chennai?

13. Monrovia is the capital city of which country?

14. Westerhope, Ouseburn, and Jesmond are areas of which English city?

15. Michigan, Ohio, Kentucky, and Illinois all have a border with which US state?

16. Actor James Bolam and singer Emeli Sande were born in which city?

17. Covering an area of 1,429 square miles, what is the smallest state in India?

18. Football club Raith Rovers are based in which Scottish town?

19. Lake Manyara is in which African country?
    a) Algeria
    b) Ethiopia
    c) Tanzania

20. Which Scandinavian city hosted the 2013 Eurovision Song Contest?
    a) Bergen
    b) Malmö
    c) Stockholm

MEDIUM

Answers to Quiz 93: Pot Luck

1. RMT
2. Kurt Wallander
3. Boris Johnson
4. Kevin Costner
5. Nitric acid
6. Macau
7. Tower Hamlets
8. Weather forecasts
9. The Philippines
10. Two
11. House
12. Rock of Ages
13. Patricia Hodge
14. 22
15. The Netherlands
16. 10
17. Abbottabad
18. Manchester United, Arsenal, and Celtic
19. 20%
20. US Open

Quiz 95: Pot Luck

1. Betty Boothroyd, Michael Martin, and John Bercow have all held which political post?

2. What title was given to the eldest sons of kings of France from 1349 until 1830?

3. The Gaelic for 'I told you I was ill' appears on the gravestone of which Anglo-Irish comedian?

4. In feet, how high is the crossbar in a football goal?

5. Which American composer and lyricist wrote the lyrics for the musical 'West Side Story'?

6. Which land animal has the heaviest brain?

7. Which Irish actor played Dr Jonathan Crane aka The Scarecrow in the film 'Batman Begins'?

8. In Japan, motorists drive on what side of the road, left or right?

9. What does the C in the acronym UNESCO stand for?

10. The bands Franz Ferdinand and Belle & Sebastian were formed in which British city?

11. Which musical instrument takes its name from the Italian for 'small flute'?

12. Which name is shared by a former Wimbledon champion and a fictional cybernetic race from the 'Star Trek' franchise?

13. Between 1982 and 2008, the Tudor rose appeared on the reverse side of which British coin?

14. Who was the first African-American to hold the post of chairman of the Joint Chiefs of Staff?

Answers – page 195

15. The renminbi is the official currency of which country?

16. Which country produces the most feature films per year?

17. Who was the oldest member of The Beatles?

18. The metatarsal is a bone found in which part of the body?

19. Which of the following was the title of a 2010 thriller starring Angelina Jolie?
    a) Pepper
    b) Salt
    c) Sugar

20. Channing Tatum starred as a male stripper in which 2012 film directed by Steven Soderbergh?
    a) 'Magic Mark'
    b) 'Magic Mike'
    c) 'Magic Miles'

MEDIUM

Answers to Quiz 94: Places

1. California, Arizona, New Mexico, and Texas
2. Alaska
3. Livorno
4. Stoke-on-Trent
5. Argentina
6. Dubai
7. Benin
8. Idaho
9. Mexico
10. Armenia
11. Pisa
12. Madras
13. Liberia
14. Newcastle upon Tyne
15. Indiana
16. Sunderland
17. Goa
18. Kirkcaldy
19. Tanzania
20. Malmö

Quiz 96: Doctors

1. Which Russian doctor wrote the plays 'The Cherry Orchard' and 'Uncle Vanya'?

2. DeForest Kelly played which well known TV and film doctor?

3. Wilko Johnson and Lee Brilleaux were members of which British pub rock band?

4. In bingo, which number has the nickname 'doctor's orders'?

5. Which Scandinavian popsters topped the charts in 1998 with 'Dr Jones'?

6. Matthew Hall is the real name of which doctor-turned-comedian?

7. Which beverage celebrated its 125th birthday in 2010?

8. Who played Dr Tinkle in the film comedy 'Carry On Doctor'?

9. Which 1965 film, directed by David Lean and starring Omar Sharif and Julie Christie, was based on a novel by Boris Pasternak?

10. The fictional Dr Jekyll was created by which Scottish author?

11. Which Nigerian-born Swedish singer had a number 2 hit in 1992 with 'It's My Life'?

12. Andre Romelle Young is the real name of which hip-hop producer and performer?

13. Which Afghan-American doctor wrote the best sellers 'The Kite Runner' and 'A Thousand Splendid Suns'?

14. Drs Cuddy, Foreman, Chase, and Taub appeared in which medical drama?

15. The 1993 song 'Two Princes' was the only UK top ten hit for which group?

16. Which Elizabethan playwright wrote, 'The Tragical History of the Life and Death of Doctor Faustus'?

17. By what name is the author Theodor Geisel more commonly known?

18. Dr Robert was the lead singer with which 1980s band?

19. Which cricketing legend was also a qualified doctor?
    a) Don Bradman
    b) Ted Dexter
    c) WG Grace

20. Which motor sport world champion is nicknamed 'The Doctor'?
    a) Lewis Hamilton
    b) Valentino Rossi
    c) Sebastian Vettel

MEDIUM

Answers to Quiz 95: Pot Luck

1. Speaker of the House of Commons
2. Dauphin
3. Spike Milligan
4. 8 feet
5. Stephen Sondheim
6. Elephant
7. Cillian Murphy
8. Left
9. Cultural
10. Glasgow
11. Piccolo
12. Borg
13. 20p
14. Colin Powell
15. China
16. India
17. Ringo Starr
18. Foot
19. Salt
20. Magic Mike

Quiz 97: Pot Luck

1. Who are the four US presidents whose first name and surname start with the same letter?

2. What was the name of the ship that brought the first group of Caribbean immigrants to Britain in 1948?

3. In imperial measurements, how many pints make a quart?

4. The words 'Murdered by a traitor and a coward whose name is not worthy to appear here' appear on the gravestone of which legendary figure from the American Wild West?

5. Who assumed the US presidency following the death of Franklin D Roosevelt?

6. Timothy McVeigh was executed in 2001 for his involvement in the bombing in 1995 of which American city?

7. What is the name of the BBC drama, written by Kay Mellor, about a group of supermarket workers who win the lottery?

8. 'Das Rheingold' is an opera by which composer?

9. Which Scottish writer was known as 'The Ploughman Poet'?

10. Who was the first manager to lead an English team to victory in football's European Cup?

11. Which British actor's autobiography was called 'My Word Is My Bond'?

12. Herbert Walker are the middle names of which US President?

13. Nicolae Ceaucescu was the long-time dictator of which country?

14. The Coptic Orthodox Church is a religious denomination largely based in which African country?

15. Which 19th-century Polish composer was sometimes known as 'The Poet of the Piano'?

16. Jean Chrétien served as the prime minister of which country from 1993 to 2003?

17. Which controversial Italian succeeded Martin O'Neill as the manager of Sunderland FC in March 2013?

18. Glaucoma is a disease that affects which part of the body?

19. What is the highest denomination banknote produced by Scottish banks?
    a) £50
    b) £100
    c) £500

20. The 19th-century French economist and politician Pierre-Joseph Proudhon is associated with which political philosophy?
    a) anarchism
    b) communism
    c) fascism

MEDIUM

Answers to Quiz 96: Doctors

1. Anton Chekhov
2. Star Trek's Dr McCoy
3. Doctor Feelgood
4. 9
5. Aqua
6. Harry Hill
7. Dr Pepper
8. Kenneth Williams
9. Dr Zhivago
10. Robert Louis Stevenson
11. Dr Alban
12. Dr Dre
13. Khaled Hosseini
14. House
15. The Spin Doctors
16. Christopher Marlowe
17. Dr Seuss
18. The Blow Monkeys
19. WG Grace
20. Valentino Rossi

Quiz 98: Natural World

1. The aardvark is native to which continent?

2. If a creature is arboreal, where does it live?

3. What type of animal is a pullet?

4. Before becoming extinct, the dodo lived on which island?

5. A squab is the young of what bird?

6. Papaveraceae refers to flowers of which family?

7. To which continent is the chinchilla native?

8. Which layer of the Earth's atmosphere lies between the troposphere and the mesosphere?

9. Which ocean is larger, the Indian or the Atlantic?

10. Mount Aconcagua is the highest mountain in which range?

11. The leveret is the name given to the young of which animal?

12. What type of creature lives in a holt?

13. A 'shrewdness' is a collective noun used to describe a group of which animal?

14. One of the deepest lakes in the world, Lake Matano is in which Asian country?

15. What is the longest river in the British Isles?

16. In January 2010, a devastating earthquake struck in which Caribbean country?

17. The Great Bear Lake, one of the largest in the world, is in which country?

18. What is the second most common gas in the earth's atmosphere?

19. What is the maximum temperature recorded in the UK?
    a) 36.5°C
    b) 37.5°C
    c) 38.5°C

20. At how many degrees north is the Arctic Circle?
    a) 62.56
    b) 66.56
    c) 70.56

MEDIUM

Answers to Quiz 97: Pot Luck

1. Woodrow Wilson, Calvin Coolidge, Herbert Hoover, and Ronald Reagan
2. Empire Windrush
3. Two
4. Jesse James
5. Harry S Truman
6. Oklahoma City
7. The Syndicate
8. Richard Wagner
9. Robert Burns
10. Sir Matt Busby
11. Roger Moore
12. George Bush, Senior
13. Romania
14. Egypt
15. Frederic Chopin
16. Canada
17. Paolo di Canio
18. The eyes
19. £100
20. Anarchism

Quiz 99: Pot Luck

1. 'Yr wyddfa' is the Welsh name for which mountain?

2. Which actor played the male title character in the TV sitcom 'Gavin and Stacey'?

3. Which fashion designer has taken time out to create a series of limited edition bottle designs for Coca Cola?

4. What are the three London boroughs that start with the letter W?

5. Which actor plays Gaius in the BBC TV drama 'Merlin'?

6. Emmelie de Forest, the winner of the 2013 Eurovision Song Contest, represented which country?

7. Former England captain Michael Vaughan played domestic cricket for which county?

8. In computing, for what do the initials LAN stand?

9. Who was the first Protestant Archbishop of Canterbury?

10. Max Rushden and Helen Chamberlain are the presenters of which Saturday morning football TV show?

11. The tiny island-nation of Tuvalu lies in which ocean?

12. What was the first Indian city to host the Commonwealth Games?

13. What is the first name of the composer Berlioz?

14. A funambulist is another name for what?

15. Suva is the capital city of which country?

16. Charles Lynton are the middle names of which former British prime minister?

17. Amongst the countries of the G8 intergovernmental organization, which has the smallest population?

18. 'Miércoles' is the Spanish for which day of the week?

19. What is the third longest river in Britain?
    a) Mersey
    b) Tay
    c) Trent

20. Which of the following countries was not described by George W Bush as being part of an 'axis of evil'?
    a) Cuba
    b) Iran
    c) North Korea

MEDIUM

Answers to Quiz 98: Natural World

1. Africa
2. In trees
3. Chicken
4. Mauritius
5. Pigeon
6. Poppy
7. South America
8. Stratosphere
9. Atlantic
10. The Andes
11. Hare
12. Otter
13. Apes
14. Indonesia
15. River Shannon
16. Haiti
17. Canada
18. Oxygen
19. 38.5°C
20. 66.56 degrees

Quiz 100: Television part 1

1. The Gallaghers, the Maguires, and the Powells are the main families in which Channel 4 drama?

2. 'That's All We've Got Time For' is a feature on which TV chat show?

3. What is the name of the character played by Derek Thompson in the medical drama 'Casualty'?

4. The TV comedy 'The Good Life' was set in which Surrey town?

5. Which boxer finished third in the 2012 series of 'I'm a Celebrity...Get Me out of Here!'?

6. Susie Dent and Rachel Riley are regulars on which TV game show?

7. Which actor and comedian plays Ollie Reeder in the political comedy 'The Thick of It'?

8. Which former star of 'Brookside' went on to play Gloria Price in 'Coronation Street'?

9. What was the name of the character played by Mackenzie Crook in 'The Office'?

10. Which Yorkshire town is also the name of the dog that won 'Britain's Got Talent' in 2012?

11. Which 'Downton Abbey' character died shortly after giving birth?

12. Who provides the acerbic commentary on Channel 4's 'Come Dine with Me'?

13. Sheridan Smith, Caroline Quentin, and Julia Sawalha have all played assistants to which TV detective?

14. Who played the title character in the Roman period drama 'I, Claudius'?

15. Jake Wood plays which East End bad boy?

16. Which alliterative newsreader appeared on the TV game show 'Treasure Hunt'?

17. Which veteran actor plays Rodney Blackstock in the TV soap 'Emmerdale'?

18. Which of the 'chasers' from the quiz show 'The Chase' is a medical doctor?

19. Who presents the TV property show 'Secret Agent'?
    a) Kirstie Allsopp
    b) Sarah Beeny
    c) Phil Spencer

20. The late Tony Gubba was a commentator on which TV talent show?
    a) Dancing On Ice
    b) Splash
    c) Strictly Come Dancing

Answers to Quiz 99: Pot Luck

1. Snowdon
2. Matthew Horne
3. Karl Lagerfeld
4. Waltham Forest, Wandsworth, and Westminster
5. Richard Wilson
6. Denmark
7. Yorkshire
8. Local Area Network
9. Thomas Cranmer
10. Soccer AM
11. Pacific Ocean
12. Delhi
13. Hector
14. Tightrope walker
15. Fiji
16. Tony Blair
17. Canada
18. Wednesday
19. Trent
20. Cuba

MEDIUM

Quiz 101: Pot Luck

1. Which British director's films include 'Swept Away', 'Revolver', and 'Sherlock Holmes'?

2. The 2012 novel 'Skagboy' is a prequel to which 1993 book by Irvine Welsh?

3. What obsolete British coin is also the name of a country in Africa?

4. 'La Brabanconne' is the national anthem of which country?

5. On which date is the Christian feast of Epiphany celebrated?

6. Which Spice Girl played Mary Magdalene in the 2013 revival of 'Jesus Christ Superstar'?

7. 'Not Just a Pretty Voice' was the title of a 2013 tour by which comedian and impressionist?

8. Who succeeded Stalin as leader of the Soviet Union?

9. The 1994 film 'The Madness of King George' was adapted from a stage play written by which author?

10. In which year did the UK join the European Economic Community?

11. The Scottish Grand National is run at which Scottish racecourse?

12. ECG machines are commonly found in hospitals. What do the initials ECG stand for?

13. Prince Harry caused controversy in 2012 after being photographed in the nude while visiting which city?

14. Gangnam is a district of which city?

Answers – page 207

15. Tony Montana is the central character in which classic 1983 crime movie?

16. Australian Trenton Oldfield disrupted which famous sporting event in April 2012?

17. The remains of King Richard III were discovered in 2012 under a car park in which city?

18. Theatre impresario Bill Kenwright is the chairman of which football club?
    a) Everton
    b) Leeds United
    c) West Ham United

19. What is the title of the award-winning musical about an Irish busker and a young Czech mother?
    a) Never
    b) Once
    c) Twice

MEDIUM

Answers to Quiz 100: Television part 1

1.	Shameless	11.	Sybil
2.	The Graham Norton Show	12.	Dave Lamb
3.	Charlie Fairhead	13.	Jonathan Creek
4.	Surbiton	14.	Derek Jacobi
5.	David Haye	15.	Max Branning
6.	Countdown	16.	Kenneth Kendall
7.	Chris Addison	17.	Patrick Mower
8.	Sue Johnston	18.	Paul Sinha
9.	Gareth Keenan	19.	Phil Spencer
10.	Pudsey	20.	Dancing On Ice

Quiz 102: Alliterative Answers

1. Which actor won an Oscar for his performance in 'A Fish Called Wanda'?

2. What 1981 romantic comedy starred John Gordon Sinclair, Clare Grogan, and Dee Hepburn?

3. Who is the alter ego of comic-book superhero The Hulk?

4. What was actor John Wayne's real name?

5. Which actor played Michael Shipman in the TV comedy 'Gavin and Stacey'?

6. 'His Dark Materials' is a fantasy trilogy by which British author?

7. 'Contagion', 'Haywire', and 'Side Effects' are films made by which American director?

8. Who was the first reggae artist to top the UK singles charts?

9. Which TV presenter hosted 'World of Sport' from 1968 until 1985?

10. Which actor, who played Tom Quinn in the TV drama 'Spooks', is married to the actress Keeley Hawes?

11. In the TV cartoon 'Wacky Races', who drove a car called the 'Turbo Terrific'?

12. Who had a number three hit in 1984 with 'What's Love Got to Do with It'?

13. Who was nominated for a Best Supporting Actor Oscar in 2013 for his performance in 'Argo'?

14. Who described herself as 'the only sex symbol Britain has produced since Lady Godiva'?

15. Who wrote the lyrics and music to the musical 'Sweeney Todd'?

16. 'The Black Velvet Gown', 'The Cinder Path', and 'The Mallen Streak' are novels by which best-selling British author?

17. Which actor played The Penguin in the 1992 film 'Batman Returns'?

18. Which British historian is best known for hosting the BBC documentary series 'A History of Britain'?

19. Who played the lead character Alex in the controversial 1971 film 'A Clockwork Orange'?

20. Blake Lively played the title character, Serena van der Woodsen, in which US TV drama?

MEDIUM

Answers to Quiz 101: Pot Luck

1. Guy Ritchie
2. Trainspotting
3. Guinea
4. Belgium
5. 6 January
6. Melanie C
7. Alistair McGowan
8. Khrushchev
9. Alan Bennett
10. 1973
11. Ayr
12. Electrocardiogram
13. Las Vegas
14. Seoul
15. Scarface
16. The Boat Race
17. Leicester
18. Everton
19. Once

Quiz 103: Pot Luck

1. The stage musical 'My Fair Lady' is based on which play by George Bernard Shaw?

2. Who is the politician husband of Labour MP Yvette Cooper?

3. What social media service was launched by Jack Dorsey in March 2006?

4. Only one country on the continent of Asia ends in the letter H. Which one?

5. Reg Presley was the lead singer with which 1960s band?

6. The Mary Peters Athletics Track is in which UK city?

7. The Blue Mosque is a famous landmark of which city?

8. Samit Patel, Ravi Bopara, and Adil Rashid have all played international cricket for which country?

9. 'The Pilgrims' is the nickname of which English football team?

10. Actress Susan Jameson, who plays Esther in 'New Tricks', is in real life married to which fellow cast member?

11. The 'Dharma Chakra' (Wheel of the Law) features on the flag of which country?

12. The 1987 hit 'Never Gonna Give You Up' was the only number one single by which artist?

13. What were the surnames of the criminal duo Bonnie and Clyde?

14. The TV sitcom 'Happy Days' was set in which American city?

15. Arsenal, Real Madrid, and Tottenham striker Emanuel Adebayor plays international football for which African country?

16. Tom Meighan, Sergio Pizzorno, Christopher Karloff, and Chris Edwards are members of which Leicester-based indie rock band?

17. The KC Stadium is in which English city?

18. In the 'Mr Men' series, what colour is Mr Mean?

19. What was the title of a 2013 film starring Matthew McConaughey?
    a) Mud
    b) Sweat
    c) Tears

20. Connage Dunlop is a cheese from which part of Britain?
    a) England
    b) Scotland
    c) Wales

MEDIUM

Answers to Quiz 102: Alliterative Answers

1.	Kevin Kline	11.	Peter Perfect
2.	Gregory's Girl	12.	Tina Turner
3.	Bruce Banner	13.	Alan Arkin
4.	Marion Morrison	14.	Diana Dors
5.	Larry Lamb	15.	Stephen Sondheim
6.	Philip Pullman	16.	Catherine Cookson
7.	Steven Soderbergh	17.	Danny DeVito
8.	Desmond Dekker	18.	Simon Schama
9.	Dickie Davies	19.	Malcolm McDowell
10.	Matthew Macfadyen	20.	Gossip Girl

Quiz 104: Numbers

1. Captain Yossarian is the central character in which 1961 novel?

2. How many possible ways are there for a batsman to be dismissed in a game of cricket?

3. Anne Hathaway played Emma Morley and Jim Sturgess played Dexter Mayhew in which 2011 film that was based on a novel by David Nicholls?

4. What was the first feature film directed by Guy Ritchie?

5. What was the only UK top five single by Canadian rockers Barenaked Ladies?

6. On a standard dartboard, which number lies between 13 and 10?

7. Who directed the 2002 horror film '28 Days Later'?

8. Valentine and Proteus are the main characters in which of Shakespeare's plays?

9. Rapper Eminem made his acting debut playing Jimmy 'B-Rabbit' Smith in which 2002 drama?

10. 'I got my head checked / By a jumbo jet / It wasn't easy / But nothing is' are lines from which 1997 hit?

11. How many sides does a 'Stop' road sign have?

12. John Travolta played train hijacker 'Ryder' in which 2009 remake of a 1974 drama?

13. The right to bear arms is enshrined in which amendment to the United States constitution?

14. RP McMurphy is the central character in which Oscar-winning 1975 film that was based on a novel by Ken Kesey?

15. Which motorway connects Birmingham with Exeter?

16. 'The Children's Crusade – A Duty-dance with Death' was the subtitle to which acclaimed novel by Kurt Vonnegut?

17. Which 1977 single was the only top five hit by the Tom Robinson Band?

18. What is the name of the game, similar to handball, that is played by two or four players in an enclosed court with a front wall and two side walls?

19. Complete the title of a 1997 film starring Brad Pitt: 'Seven Years in ...'
    a) India
    b) Nepal
    c) Tibet

20. Brian Lara holds the record for the highest score in an innings of first-class cricket. How many did he make?
    a) 401
    b) 501
    c) 601

MEDIUM

Answers to Quiz 103: Pot Luck

1. Pygmalion
2. Ed Balls MP
3. Twitter
4. Bangladesh
5. The Troggs
6. Belfast
7. Istanbul
8. England
9. Plymouth Argyle
10. James Bolam
11. India
12. Rick Astley
13. Parker and Barrow
14. Milwaukee
15. Togo
16. Kasabian
17. Hull
18. Blue
19. Mud
20. Scotland

Quiz 105: Pot Luck

1. Who succeeded Richard Nixon as president of the United States?

2. Who was president of France from 1981 until 1995?

3. In which country were the author George Orwell and the singer Cliff Richard born?

4. The name of which South African clergyman is also slang for a lower-second university degree?

5. Which billionaire unsuccessfully stood for the US presidency in 1992 and 1996?

6. Wenceslaus Square is a feature of which European capital?

7. The composer Mozart was born in which city?

8. Who succeeded his brother George IV as the British monarch in 1830?

9. Which Nepalese sherpa reached the summit of Mount Everest with Sir Edmund Hillary in 1953?

10. Aung San Suu Kyi is a political leader in which Asian country?

11. The Red Fort is a prominent building in which Asian city?

12. Prior to becoming conductor of the Berlin Symphony Orchestra, Sir Simon Rattle was the conductor of which English orchestra?

13. Karl Marx is buried in which London cemetery?

14. Which US president was associated with a series of policies known as 'The Great Society'?

15. In Shakespeare's play, which character killed Macbeth?

16. What nationality was the explorer Ferdinand Magellan?

17. Fat Sam Staccetto, Blousey Brown, and Tallulah are characters in which film musical?

18. In which country was athlete Mo Farah born?

19. Lev Bronstein was the original name of which Soviet revolutionary?
    a) Lenin
    b) Stalin
    c) Trotsky

20. Who was a co-founder of the online encyclopaedia Wikipedia?
    a) Jimmy Ireland
    b) Jimmy Scotland
    c) Jimmy Wales

MEDIUM

Answers to Quiz 104: Numbers

1. Catch-22
2. Ten
3. One Day
4. Lock, Stock, and Two Smoking Barrels
5. One Week
6. 6
7. Danny Boyle
8. Two Gentlemen of Verona
9. 8 Mile
10. 'Song 2' by Blur
11. Eight
12. The Taking of Pelham 123
13. Second
14. One Flew Over the Cuckoo's Nest
15. M5
16. Slaughterhouse-Five
17. 2-4-6-8 Motorway
18. Fives
19. Tibet
20. 501

Quiz 106: Pop Music

1. Siobhán Donaghy, Mutya Buena, and Keisha Buchanan were the original members of which British group?

2. Which member of Take That released the 2012 album 'Take the Crown'?

3. Brandon Flowers is the lead singer with which US rock band?

4. Which Canadian crooner topped the charts with albums called 'Crazy' and 'Christmas'?

5. 'Domino', the highest charting song in 2012 by British female artist, was by which singer?

6. Which female artist collaborated with Coldplay on the 2012 hit 'Princess of China'?

7. Bryan Adams' massive number one hit '(Everything I Do) I Do It for You' appeared on the soundtrack of which film?

8. What was the Beatles' last UK number one single?

9. 'Elephunk', 'The Beginning', and 'The E.N.D' are albums by which American band?

10. Which band wrote Diana Ross's 1986 number one hit 'Chain Reaction'?

11. Guy Garvey is the lead singer with which award-winning British band?

12. 'Songs in the Key of Life' is a classic 1976 album from which artist?

13. True or false – REM never had a UK number one single?

14. 'It Takes a Nation of Millions to Hold Us Back' was a 1988 album from which American rap group?

15. Kevin Rowland is the lead vocalist with which band?

16. The Mothers of Invention were the backing band for which American rock star?

17. 'Welcome to the Pleasuredome' was the debut album from which massive 1980s band?

18. Which 'X Factor' star collaborated with Flo Rida on the 2012 hit single 'Troublemaker'?

19. What nationality is the singer Carly Rae Jepsen?
    a) American
    b) Australian
    c) Canadian

20. How many months featured in the title of a 2012 album by Calvin Harris?
    a) 6 Months
    b) 12 Months
    c) 18 Months

MEDIUM

Answers to Quiz 105: Pot Luck

1. Gerald Ford
2. François Mitterand
3. India
4. Desmond Tutu (2:2)
5. Ross Perot
6. Prague
7. Salzburg
8. William IV
9. Tenzing Norgay
10. Myanmar (Burma)
11. Delhi
12. City of Birmingham Symphony Orchestra (CBSO)
13. Highgate Cemetery
14. Lyndon Johnson
15. Macduff
16. Portuguese
17. Bugsy Malone
18. Somalia
19. Trotsky
20. Jimmy Wales

Quiz 107: Pot Luck

1. Who was Britain's oldest prime minister, resigning at the age of 84 in 1894?

2. Which British author, best known for 'Brave New World', died on the same day that John F Kennedy was assassinated?

3. Sir Francis Walsingham was the principal secretary to which English monarch?

4. The Colman's Mustard Museum is in which English city?

5. The detective drama 'CSI' is set in Las Vegas but has spin-off series set in which two cities?

6. Which actor plays farmer John Middleton in the TV drama 'The Village'?

7. Which broadcaster suffered a stroke in 2013 after a particularly strenuous session on a rowing machine?

8. In spring 2013, online giants Yahoo paid $1.1bn for which microblogging site?

9. Derek Batey and Philip Schofield have hosted which TV game show?

10. Stephen Roche was the first man from which country to win cycling's Tour de France?

11. The award-winning song 'Moon River' was sung by Audrey Hepburn in which film?

12. In a mobile phone SIM card, what does the letter S stand for?

13. In which European capital will you find the Hofburg Palace?

14. Which film won eight Oscars at the 2009 Academy Awards?

15. In the film '101 Dalmatians', what sort of animal was Duchess?

16. Barbara Pierce is the wife of which former US President?

17. Which southern African city's name translates into English as 'Fountain of Flowers'?

18. John Travolta played Vincent Vega in which film?

19. In 'The Simpsons Movie', what was the name of Homer's new pet?
    a) Spider-cat
    b) Spider-dog
    c) Spider-pig

20. At which sport was an animal called Ballyregan Bob a champion?
    a) greyhound racing
    b) horse racing
    c) pigeon racing

MEDIUM

Answers to Quiz 106: Pop Music

1. Sugababes
2. Robbie Williams
3. The Killers
4. Michael Bublé
5. Jessie J
6. Rihanna
7. Robin Hood: Prince of Thieves
8. The Ballad of John and Yoko
9. The Black Eyed Peas
10. The Bee Gees
11. Elbow
12. Stevie Wonder
13. True
14. Public Enemy
15. Dexys Midnight Runners
16. Frank Zappa
17. Frankie Goes to Hollywood
18. Olly Murs
19. Canadian
20. 18 Months

Quiz 108: Olympic Games

1. At the 2012 games, which sport was hosted at Lord's cricket ground?

2. Athletes from which country traditionally lead the Olympic Opening Ceremony parade?

3. Who was the manager of the Great Britain men's football team at the 2012 games?

4. Sally Gunnell won gold in 1992 in which event?

5. What was the first Asian city to host the Summer Olympics?

6. True or false – Olympic gymnast Louis Smith once auditioned for the TV talent show the 'X Factor'?

7. The International Olympic Committee is based in which city?

8. Laser, 470, Star, and 49er are events in which Olympic sport?

9. Which British city bid to host the 1992 Olympic Games?

10. Who was the only British athlete to win a gold medal on the track at the 2008 Beijing Olympics?

11. What is the penultimate field event in an Olympic decathlon?

12. St Leo is the middle name of which Olympic legend?

13. Muhammad Ali lit the Olympic flame at the games in which city?

14. What is the most northerly city to have hosted the Summer Olympics?

15. In which event did David Hemery win gold for Britain in 1968?

16. Sam the Eagle was the mascot of the games held in which city?

17. What are the four cities whose name starts with the letter S to have hosted the Summer Olympics?

18. The Republic of Ireland won their only gold medal of the 2012 games in which sport?

19. In which city did Torvill and Dean win Winter Olympic gold in 1984?
    a) Belgrade
    b) Split
    c) Sarajevo

20. In 2012 the Jamaican men's team became the first to run the 4x100m relay in under how many seconds?
    a) 37
    b) 38
    c) 39

MEDIUM

Answers to Quiz 107: Pot Luck

1. Gladstone
2. Aldous Huxley
3. Elizabeth I
4. Norwich
5. Miami and New York
6. John Simm
7. Andrew Marr
8. Tumblr.com
9. Mr and Mrs
10. Ireland
11. Breakfast at Tiffany's
12. Subscriber
13. Vienna
14. Slumdog Millionaire
15. A cow
16. George HW Bush
17. Bloemfontein
18. Pulp Fiction
19. Spider-pig
20. Greyhound racing

Quiz 109: Pot Luck

1. Who is actress Kate Hudson's famous mother?

2. Which British composer wrote 'The Young Person's Guide to the Orchestra'?

3. Which musical set the record for the biggest day of ticket sales in West End and Broadway history after over £2.1m worth of tickets were bought on a Friday in March 2012?

4. Pervez Musharraf is the former president of which country?

5. 'When shall we three meet again? In thunder, lightning or in rain?' is the opening of which Shakespeare play?

6. 'I Saw Her Standing There' is the opening track on which album by The Beatles?

7. The Battle of Agincourt was fought in which war?

8. In 2013, the giant Trinity shopping centre opened in which British city?

9. Kenneth Branagh played which historical figure in the Opening and Closing Ceremony at the 2012 Olympics?

10. Which member of The Beatles did not make it onto the BBC's list of 100 Greatest Britons?

11. Lennard Pearce played which character in the classic sitcom 'Only Fools and Horses'?

12. What is the name of the child who owns the toys in the film trilogy 'Toy Story'?

13. Who has hosted the Oscars ceremony the most times?

14. 'Love Never Dies' is the sequel to which West End musical?

15. Who played Inspector Javert in the 2012 film 'Les Miserables'?

16. What is the only animal to appear in the title of a play by William Shakespeare?

17. Who was the last Emperor of India?

18. In which sport do teams compete for the Copa Libertadores?

19. Who succeeded Humphrey Lyttleton as the regular host of the radio programme 'I'm Sorry I Haven't a Clue'?
    a) Jack Dee
    b) Stephen Fry
    c) Hugh Laurie

20. In which country is the car manufacturer Daewoo based?
    a) China
    b) Japan
    c) South Korea

MEDIUM

Answers to Quiz 108: Olympic Games

1. Archery
2. Greece
3. Stuart Pearce
4. 400m hurdles
5. Tokyo
6. True
7. Lausanne
8. Sailing
9. Birmingham
10. Christine Ohuruogu
11. Javelin
12. Usain Bolt
13. Atlanta
14. Helsinki
15. 400m hurdles
16. Los Angeles
17. St Louis, Stockholm, Seoul, and Sydney
18. Women's boxing
19. Sarajevo
20. 37

Quiz 110: Television part 2

1. Who played PC Nick Rowan in the first series of police drama 'Heartbeat'?

2. Andy Millman, Maggie Jacobs, and Darren Lamb are the central characters in which British comedy?

3. Who are the two men to have hosted 'The Apprentice: You're Fired'?

4. Holly was the name of the ship's computer in which sci-fi series?

5. What is the name of the British sitcom starring Jo Enright and Russell Tovey set in a Midlands job centre?

6. Which form of transport was central to the 1980s drama 'Blue Thunder'?

7. The car in the 1980s drama 'Knight Rider' was called KITT. What did those initials stand for?

8. Geordi La Forge, Deanna Troi, and Tasha Yar were characters in which long-running drama?

9. Which TV chef hosted the programmes 'Simple Suppers' and 'Simple Cooking'?

10. What was the follow up series to the TV comedy 'Til Death Us Do Part'?

11. Helen Willetts, Louise Ridge, and Carol Kirkwood regularly talk about which subject on TV?

12. The Drunken Clam is the name of a bar that features in which animated comedy?

13. Who joined Karl Pilkington on the third series of 'An Idiot Abroad: The Short Way Around'?

14. 'Language, Timothy' was a catchphrase from which 1980s sitcom?

15. Gary Strang and Tony Smart were the central characters in which TV comedy?

16. Who lived at Oil Drum Lane?

17. Michael Elphick played a former firefighter turned detective in which series?

18. Which British comedy features a character called Super Hans?

19. What was the name of the priest played by Ardal O'Hanlon in classic sitcom 'Father Ted'?

20. What was the surname of 'Buffy the Vampire Slayer'?
    a) Springs b) Summers c) Winters

21. In the TV comedy 'Friends', what was Ross's occupation?
    a) architect b) doctor c) palaeontologist

MEDIUM

Answers to Quiz 109: Pot Luck

1. Goldie Hawn
2. Benjamin Britten
3. The Book of Mormon
4. Pakistan
5. Macbeth
6. Please Please Me
7. The Hundred Years' War
8. Leeds
9. Isambard Kingdom Brunel
10. Ringo Starr
11. Grandad
12. Andy Davis
13. Bob Hope
14. The Phantom of the Opera
15. Russell Crowe
16. Shrew (The Taming of the Shrew)
17. George VI
18. Football
19. Jack Dee
20. South Korea

Quiz 111: Pot Luck

1. Fran Healy is the lead singer with which band?

2. The giant Petronas Towers are in which Asian city?

3. Crystal meth dealer Walter White is the central character in which cult American drama?

4. The Chelsea Flower Show traditionally takes place in which month?

5. Who played Professor Henry Jones in the 1989 film 'Indiana Jones and the Last Crusade'?

6. Which British music impresario launched a campaign in 2013 to combat gang culture by encouraging youngsters to take up music?

7. What connects a well-known chain of hotels and a 1942 film starring Bing Crosby?

8. Wembley Stadium in London hosted the UK leg of the 1985 Live Aid concert. Which US city hosted the American leg?

9. 'The course of true love never did run smooth' is a line from which Shakespeare play?

10. Which US politician and inventor said, 'In this world, nothing can be said to be certain except death and taxes'?

11. What does the E in the acronym OPEC stand for?

12. Who succeeded Glenn Hoddle as manager of the England national football team?

13. In the Bible, which of the twelve apostles was a tax collector?

14. Which British hairdresser is best known for creating a cut called the 'wedge bob'?

15. In April 2013, Tony Hall became the director-general of which organization?

Answers – page 227

16. Timpani is a name for a set of which musical instrument?

17. Characters called Anastasia Steele and Christian Grey first appeared in which best-selling novel?

18. The Crab and Lobster is the name of the pub that features in which British drama?

19. Jack Shepherd played the title character in which 1990s TV detective drama?
    a) Inspector Alleyn
    b) Spender
    c) Wycliffe

20. What was the first of Michael Jackson's solo albums to top the UK charts?
    a) Bad
    b) Off the Wall
    c) Thriller

Answers to Quiz 110: Television part 2

1. Nick Berry
2. Extras
3. Adrian Chiles and Dara O Briain
4. Red Dwarf
5. The Job Lot
6. Helicopter
7. Knight Industries Two Thousand
8. Star Trek: The Next Generation
9. Nigel Slater
10. In Sickness and in Health
11. The weather
12. Family Guy
13. Warwick Davis
14. Sorry!
15. Men Behaving Badly
16. Steptoe and Son
17. Boon
18. Peep Show
19. Father Dougal McGuire
20. Summers
21. Palaeontologist

MEDIUM

Quiz 112: Big and Small

1. What was the real name of wrestler Big Daddy?

2. Kate Garraway and Davina McCall have both hosted which weight-loss reality TV show?

3. What was the nickname of legendary West Indian cricketer Joel Garner?

4. Which actor played Lukewarm in the TV comedy 'Porridge'?

5. Jiles Perry Richardson, Jr was the real name of which singer, songwriter, and DJ, who died in a plane crash alongside Buddy Holly and Ritchie Valens?

6. By what name was the rapper Christopher Wallace better known?

7. Which band had a number three hit single in 1984 with 'Smalltown Boy'?

8. Who directed the 2012 Oscar-nominated film 'Zero Dark Thirty'?

9. John Goodman played Walter Sobchak and Steve Buscemi played Donny Kerabatsos in which 1998 cult comedy?

10. Small Heath Alliance was the original name of which English football club?

11. Big Daddy was one of the main characters in which play by Tennessee Williams?

12. The fictional detective Philip Marlowe made his debut in which film noir?

13. Which dance duo had a number two hit in 1999 with 'Turn Around'?

14. Which Warwickshire cricketer won 17 Test caps for England and was part of the successful 1986/87 Ashes winning team?

15. 'All or Nothing' was the only number one hit single for which sixties band?

16. The Man with the Stick, Morrissey the Consumer Monkey, and Judge Nutmeg were characters in which 1990s cult comedy stage show?

17. Which 2000 film comedy starred Martin Lawrence as an FBI agent who disguises himself as an old lady to protect a federal witness and her son?

18. Which American writer and broadcaster wrote the best-selling travel book about Britain entitled 'Notes from a Small Island'?

19. What is the name of the Australian domestic Twenty20 cricket competition?
a) Big Bash b) Big Hit c) Big Slog

20. What was the title of a 2003 film starring Ewan McGregor and directed by Tim Burton?
a) Big Cats b) Big Dogs c) Big Fish

MEDIUM

Answers to Quiz 111: Pot Luck

1. Travis
2. Kuala Lumpur
3. Breaking Bad
4. May
5. Sean Connery
6. Andrew Lloyd-Webber
7. Holiday Inn
8. Philadelphia
9. A Midsummer Night's Dream
10. Benjamin Franklin
11. Exporting
12. Kevin Keegan
13. Matthew
14. Vidal Sassoon
15. The BBC
16. Kettledrums
17. Fifty Shades of Grey
18. Doc Martin
19. Wycliffe
20. Thriller

Quiz 113: Pot Luck

1. The word spa, meaning a health resort, takes its name from a town in which country?

2. What is the distance of the shortest swimming race at the Olympic Games?

3. 'Giovedi' is the Italian word for which day of the week?

4. In the TV comedy 'The Big Bang Theory' who owns the comic-book store?

5. Robin Hood Airport is situated 7 miles south-east of which English town?

6. James Grieve, George Cave, and Kempster's Pippin are varieties of which fruit?

7. Who played the title character in the 2001 film 'Bridget Jones's Diary'?

8. Osteology is the study of what?

9. The Queen's Sandringham estate is in which English county?

10. 'Shunt' was the nickname of which British Formula One driver?

11. Who are the hosts of Channel 4 cooking show 'Sunday Brunch'?

12. Purim is a festival celebrated by followers of which religion?

13. Which country in the European Union has the smallest population?

14. Which band recorded the original version of 'Love Is All Around', which went on to be a huge hit for Wet Wet Wet?

15. Which Derbyshire town is home to a 14th-century church with a crooked spire?

16. A plangonologist is a collector of what type of objects?

17. What was the last film to star Timothy Dalton as 007?

18. Derek Jacobi played which murder-solving medieval monk in a 1990s TV drama?

19. The 1987 novel 'Knots and Crosses' was the first to feature which fictional detective?
    a) Foyle
    b) Rebus
    c) Wallander

20. Who is the proprietor of the three-star Michelin restaurant in Bray called 'The Fat Duck'?
    a) Heston Blumenthal
    b) Gordon Ramsay
    c) Marco Pierre White

MEDIUM

Answers to Quiz 112: Big and Small

1. Shirley Crabtree
2. The Biggest Loser
3. Big Bird
4. Christopher Biggins
5. The Big Bopper
6. Biggie Smalls (aka Notorious B.I.G.)
7. Bronski Beat
8. Kathryn Bigelow
9. The Big Lebowski
10. Birmingham City
11. Cat on a Hot Tin Roof
12. The Big Sleep
13. Phats and Small
14. Gladstone Small
15. The Small Faces
16. Vic Reeves Big Night Out
17. Big Momma's House
18. Bill Bryson
19. Big Bash
20. Big Fish

Quiz 114: Firsts and Lasts

1. Who was the last team to win the FA Cup at the old Wembley stadium?

2. Who had a top ten hit in 1988 with 'The Last of the Famous International Playboys'?

3. Which sportsman's final words before dying were reportedly, 'I'll finally get to see Marilyn'?

4. Who was the first winner of 'The X Factor'?

5. Who was the first footballer to be sent off twice while playing for England?

6. The film character John Rambo made his debut in which film?

7. Which cricketer was the first man to win the TV talent show 'Strictly Come Dancing'?

8. What is the last word in the King James Bible?

9. Harvey Keitel played Judas Iscariot in which 1988 film directed by Martin Scorsese?

10. In video games, what genre has the initials FPS?

11. Which was the last James Bond film that starred Sean Connery as 007?

12. 'Release Me' was Engelbert Humperdinck's first number one hit single. What was his second?

13. Which team in 2002 became the first Asian country to reach the semi-final of football's World Cup?

14. What is the biggest selling single never to have reached number one in the UK?

15. What was the first 'Carry On ...' film?

16. The first woman elected to the British parliament represented which party?

17. 'Whether I shall turn out to be the hero of my own life, or whether that station will be held by anybody else, these pages must show' is the opening of which novel by Charles Dickens?

18. Which Manchester United defender was the first man to be sent off in an FA Cup final?

19. What was the title of Robin Beck's only UK hit single which topped the charts in 1988?
    a) First Dance
    b) First Love
    c) First Time

20. Which was the first British football club to take part in European competition?
    a) Celtic
    b) Hibernian
    c) Rangers

MEDIUM

Answers to Quiz 113: Pot Luck

1. Belgium
2. 50m
3. Thursday
4. Stuart
5. Doncaster
6. Apple
7. Renée Zellweger
8. Bones
9. Norfolk
10. James Hunt
11. Tim Lovejoy and Simon Rimmer
12. Judaism
13. Malta
14. The Troggs
15. Chesterfield
16. Dolls
17. Licence to Kill
18. Brother Cadfael
19. Rebus
20. Heston Blumenthal

Quiz 115: Pot Luck

1. In a mobile phone SIM card, for what does the letter I stand?

2. Which capital city was formerly known as Edo?

3. Detective Sergeant Barbara Havers is the sidekick of which fictional detective?

4. The ancient rock temples of Abu Simbel can be found in which country?

5. Which former EastEnder joined the cast of 'Hollyoaks' in 2013, playing a character called Sandy Roscoe?

6. True or false – the Tour de France cycle race always starts in Paris?

7. TV detective Inspector Morse was created by which author?

8. In publishing, what do the initials ISBN stand for?

9. Mr Rochester is a central character in which novel by Charlotte Brontë?

10. Who is the host of the long-running radio panel show 'Just a Minute'?

11. Ross Taylor, Brendon McCullum, and Tim Southee play international cricket for which country?

12. Who was the last football team from outside the top flight to win the FA Cup?

13. Who are the two bands to have had three consecutive Christmas number one singles?

14. Which British actor played eight characters in the classic 1949 comedy 'Kind Hearts and Coronets'?

15. 'Finlandia' is a symphony by which Finnish composer who died in 1957?

16. Which James Bond actor played Robin Hood in the film 'Robin and Marian'?

17. Sarah Storey is a multiple Paralympic gold medallist in which sport?

18. Which film won 11 Oscars at the 1960 Academy Awards ceremony?

19. Sir Alex Ferguson guided Manchester United to how many Premier League titles?
    a) 9
    b) 11
    c) 13

20. The logo of which European airline features an encircled stylized crane in flight?
    a) Aer Lingus
    b) KLM
    c) Lufthansa

MEDIUM

Answers to Quiz 114: Firsts and Lasts

1. Chelsea
2. Morrissey
3. Joe DiMaggio
4. Steve Brookstein
5. David Beckham
6. First Blood
7. Darren Gough
8. Amen
9. The Last Temptation of Christ
10. First-person shooter
11. Never Say Never Again
12. The Last Waltz
13. South Korea
14. 'Last Christmas' by Wham!
15. Carry On Sergeant
16. Sinn Fein
17. David Copperfield
18. Kevin Moran
19. First Time
20. Hibernian

Quiz 116: Connections part 1

1. What is the nickname of football clubs Newcastle United and Notts County?

2. Which actress played Shia Labeouf's love interest in the 2007 film blockbuster 'Transformers'?

3. Which TV presenter is the wife of Irish broadcaster and comedian Patrick Kielty?

4. Which British actor, who appeared in 'Strictly Come Dancing' in 2012, played Charles Robinson in the James Bond films 'Tomorrow Never Dies', 'The World Is Not Enough', and 'Die Another Day'?

5. What was the name of the character played by Lee Majors in the 1980s drama 'The Fall Guy'?

6. What was the title of the only number one album from indie rockers 'The White Stripes'?

7. What was the name of the character played by David Duchovny is supernatural TV drama 'The X Files'?

8. What is the nickname of the Argentine national rugby union team?

9. What was the title of the 1973 film about a plot to assassinate French president Charles de Gaulle?

10. Which British actor played the title character in the above film?

11. Calvin Broadus is the real name of which US hip-hop star?

12. Which bird featured in the title of a 1964 number one hit single by The Rolling Stones?

13. Which major film studio was founded on 31 May 1935?

14. Who was the founder of the homeless magazine 'The Big Issue'?

MEDIUM

15. Which right-wing politician, who was the Speaker of the House of Representatives from 1995 to 1998, unsuccessfully stood in the 2012 Republican presidential primary race?

16. What is the nickname of Bradford City Football Club?

17. George Clooney provided the voice of the title character in which 2009 film animation?

18. What is the nickname of the Sussex one-day cricket team?
    a) Bears
    b) Scorpions
    c) Sharks

19. Which prize is awarded to the best film at the Berlin Film Festival?
    a) Golden Bear
    b) Golden Lion
    c) Golden Shark

20. What is the connection between all the answers?

Answers to Quiz 115: Pot Luck

1. Identity
2. Tokyo
3. Inspector Lynley
4. Egypt
5. Gillian Taylforth
6. False
7. Colin Dexter
8. International Standard Book Number
9. Jane Eyre
10. Nicholas Parsons
11. New Zealand
12. West Ham United (in 1980)
13. The Beatles and The Spice Girls
14. Sir Alec Guinness
15. Sibelius
16. Sean Connery
17. Cycling (and swimming)
18. Ben-Hur
19. 13
20. Lufthansa

MEDIUM

Quiz 117: Pot Luck

1. The New Den is the home ground of which English football club?

2. Which fruit is used to make the brandy 'Calvados'?

3. Peronism was a political movement in which country?

4. Which business magnate was elected mayor of New York for the third time in 2009?

5. The 2010 film 'Brighton Rock' was based on a novel by which author?

6. Jeff Bezos was the founder of which giant online company?

7. 'Advocatus Diaboli' is the Latin name for which Roman Catholic functionary who critically examined individuals proposed for sainthood?

8. Which team overtook Manchester United as the world's most valuable football team according to a 2013 survey from 'Forbes' magazine?

9. What is the name of the green pigment contained in the leaves of plants?

10. Which Asian city was formerly known as Hanseong?

11. Hard rockers Lordi, who won the 2006 Eurovision Song Contest, represented which country?

12. Which Christian festival is celebrated nine months before Christmas?

13. HA9 0WS is the postcode of which major sporting venue?

14. Li'l Folks' was the former name of which cartoon strip?

15. What is the film-related international dialling code for Russia?

16. Mudhsuden is the real first name of which England cricketer?

17. Who is the only Swiss player to win the ladies' singles at Wimbledon?

18. Which film and TV character has been played on screen by Nichelle Nichols and most recently by Zoe Saldana?

19. Complete the title of the band: Queens of the ...
    a) Bronze Age
    b) Iron Age
    c) Stone Age

20. Which was the first British football team to win a major European trophy?
    a) Arsenal
    b) Chelsea
    c) Tottenham Hotspur

Answers to Quiz 116: Connections part 1

1. The Magpies
2. Megan Fox
3. Cat Deeley
4. Colin Salmon
5. Colt Seavers
6. Elephant
7. Fox Mulder
8. The Pumas
9. The Day of the Jackal
10. Edward Fox
11. Snoop Dogg
12. Rooster (Little Red Rooster)
13. Twentieth Century Fox
14. John Bird
15. Newt Gingrich
16. The Bantams
17. The Fantastic Mr Fox
18. Sharks
19. The Golden Bear
20. They all contain the name of an animal.

Quiz 118: Dance

1. From what country does the dance known as the cha cha cha originate?

2. The ballet 'Swan Lake' was written by which composer?

3. Led by Ashley Banjo, which dance troupe beat Susan Boyle to the 'Britain's Got Talent' title in 2009?

4. Tony Beak is the real name of which 'Strictly Come Dancing' star?

5. Which 19th-century Austrian composer was known as the 'Waltz King'?

6. Natalie Portman won her first Best Actress Oscar in 2011 for her performance in which dance-inspired 2011 film?

7. 'I Don't Wanna Dance' was a number one hit for which British pop reggae star?

8. The dance known as the 'fandango' originated in which country?

9. Who was the first winner of the TV series 'Strictly Come Dancing'?

10. The 'electric slide' is a move in what type of dancing?

11. Which dance style takes its name from a famous 1920s aviator?

12. What is the name of the American equivalent of 'Strictly Come Dancing'?

13. How many basic positions are there in ballet?

14. Which dancer and choreographer was a judge on the seventh season of 'Dancing on Ice'?

15. Which actor played the title character in the 2000 film Billy Elliot?

16. In which dance is the 'fleckerl' a common step?

17. The 'mazurka' is a traditional folk dance from which European country?

18. According to a 1992 number one hit from Snap, what 'is a dancer'?

19. Kenny Wormald played Ren McCormack, Julianne Hough played Ariel Moore and Dennis Quaid played the Rev. Shaw Moore in the 2011 remake of which film?
    a) Fame
    b) Flashdance
    c) Footloose

20. Which Latin dance is known as 'the dance of love'?
    a) rumba
    b) samba
    c) tango

Answers to Quiz 117: Pot Luck

1. Millwall
2. Apples
3. Argentina
4. Michael Bloomberg
5. Graham Greene
6. Amazon
7. Devil's advocate
8. Real Madrid
9. Chlorophyll
10. Seoul
11. Finland
12. The Annunciation
13. Wembley Stadium
14. Peanuts
15. 007
16. Monty Panesar
17. Martina Hingis
18. Lieutenant Uhura (from 'Star Trek')
19. Stone Age
20. Tottenham Hotspur

Quiz 119: Pot Luck

1. Noted for its soft, warm feathers, what type of bird is an eider?

2. From which organ of a duck or goose does the delicacy 'foie gras' come from?

3. Plumbago is another name for which mineral?

4. In ancient mythology, which winged creature had the body of a lion and the head of an eagle?

5. Wolfram is the former name of which element?

6. Who is the only player from Croatia to have won the men's singles at Wimbledon?

7. Which English football team was known as 'The Crazy Gang'?

8. Which actress won two Bafta awards in 2013 for her performances in the comedy 'Twenty Twelve' and the drama 'Accused'?

9. The Light Programme was the predecessor to which BBC radio station?

10. Which musician appeared in films including 'The Prestige', 'The Man Who Fell To Earth', and 'The Last Temptation of Christ'?

11. Which of the six main actors from the TV sitcom 'Friends' is the youngest?

12. Prior to joining the euro, what was the currency of Cyprus?

13. Which American artist had a studio called The Factory?

14. Who is the only snooker player to have won the BBC Sports Personality of the Year award?

15. The Epstein-Barr virus is the major cause of which illness?

16. Austria, Germany, Poland, and Slovakia all share a land border with which country?

17. Which was the last Scottish football team to win a European trophy?

18. Which author created the fictional boarding school Mallory Towers?

19. Who was the first winner of the FA Cup at the newly redeveloped Wembley Stadium?
    a) Arsenal
    b) Chelsea
    c) Liverpool

20. What would you do with a samisen?
    a) eat it
    b) play it
    c) wear it

Answers to Quiz 118: Dance

1. Cuba
2. Tchaikovsky
3. Diversity
4. Anton du Beke
5. Johann Strauss the Younger
6. Black Swan
7. Eddy Grant
8. Spain
9. Natasha Kaplinsky
10. Line dancing
11. The Lindy Hop (after Charles Lindbergh)
12. Dancing with the Stars
13. Five
14. Louis Spence
15. Jamie Bell
16. Viennese waltz
17. Poland
18. Rhythm
19. Footloose
20. Rumba

MEDIUM

Quiz 120: Days and Months

1. What was the name of the 1940 screwball comedy, based on a play called 'The Front Page' starring Cary Grant and Rosalind Russell?

2. On which day of the week did the September 11 terrorist attacks take place?

3. In the UK, one tax year ends and a new one begins in which month?

4. Complete the title of the Oliver Stone-directed sports movie: 'Any Given ...'

5. What is the capital of the US state of Alaska?

6. Which month is named after a two-faced Roman god of gates and doorways?

7. Which 2004 disaster movie starred Dennis Quaid as Professor Jack Hall and Jake Gyllenhaal as his son Sam Hall?

8. Complete the title of the Oscar-winning documentary about the hostage crisis at the 1972 Olympic Games: 'One Day in ...'

9. Which animal-inspired film won the award for Best Documentary at the 2006 Oscars?

10. Which month is named after the mother of the Roman god Mercury?

11. Which month provided the title of a 1981 album by U2?

12. Which politician succeeded Alan Johnson as Home Secretary in May 2010?

13. Fill in the missing word from Green Day's 2005 top ten hit: 'Wake Me Up When ... Ends'

14. In which month does the Eurovision Song Contest usually take place?

15. In which month do Antipodeans commemorate ANZAC Day?

16. What was the name of the 1990 thriller starring Sean Connery as a Soviet submarine captain who intends to defect to America?

17. Which alliterative American actress and model is best known for playing Betty Draper in 'Mad Men' and Emma Frost in 'X-Men: First Class'?

18. What was the name of the sitcom that ran from 1989 until 1994 starring Anton Rodgers as an older man having a relationship with a much younger woman?

19. What is the name of the character played by Roger Allam in the detective drama 'Endeavour'?
    a) DI Fred Monday b) DI Fred Thursday c) DI Fred Sunday

20. The Christian festival of the Ascension is always celebrated on which day of the week?
    a) Wednesday b) Thursday c) Friday

MEDIUM

Answers to Quiz 119: Pot Luck

1.	Duck	11.	Jennifer Aniston
2.	Liver	12.	Pound
3.	Graphite	13.	Andy Warhol
4.	Griffin	14.	Steve Davis
5.	Tungsten	15.	Glandular fever
6.	Goran Ivanisevic	16.	Czech Republic
7.	Wimbledon	17.	Aberdeen
8.	Olivia Colman	18.	Enid Blyton
9.	Radio 2	19.	Chelsea
10.	David Bowie	20.	Play it

Quiz 121: Pot Luck

1. William Booth was the founder of which religious organization?

2. Which precious stone was formerly known as 'Turkey-stone'?

3. In modern communications, what name is given to the symbol #?

4. Which ecclesiastical court was set up by in the 13th century by Pope Innocent III to combat heresy?

5. The International Criminal Court is based in which European city?

6. Which musician's film credits include 'Dune' and 'Quadrophenia'?

7. What type of collective farm takes its name from the Hebrew for 'gathering'?

8. Peter Griffin is a character in which animated comedy?

9. In relation to animal welfare, for what does the acronym PETA stand?

10. What is the only member of the Commonwealth that starts with the letter V?

11. In the classic western 'The Good, the Bad, and the Ugly', which actor played 'The Bad'?

12. Which Hollywood A-lister played Booker Brooks in the TV comedy 'Roseanne'?

13. The House of Keys is a representative assembly in which part of the British Isles?

14. By what name is the gas nitrous oxide also known?

15. What are names of the four London Inns of Court?

16. Richard Krajicek is the only player from which country to have won the men's singles at Wimbledon?

17. Ernest Evans was the real name of which alliterative American rock and roll star?

18. Mr Gradgrind, Mr Bounderby, and Sissy Jupe are characters in which novel by Charles Dickens?

19. England coach Andy Flower played international cricket for which country?
    a) New Zealand
    b) South Africa
    c) Zimbabwe

20. Which two-word Latin phrase means 'genuine' or 'in good faith'?
    a) bona fide
    b) de facto
    c) ex officio

MEDIUM

Answers to Quiz 120: Days and Months

1. His Girl Friday
2. Tuesday
3. April
4. Sunday
5. Juneau
6. January (after Janus)
7. The Day after Tomorrow
8. September
9. March of the Penguins
10. May (after Maia)
11. October
12. Theresa May
13. September
14. May
15. April
16. The Hunt for Red October
17. January Jones
18. May to December
19. DI Fred Thursday
20. Thursday

Quiz 122: Myth and Legend

1. Which Greek warrior was the principal character of 'The Iliad'?

2. Which 50-oared ship built for Jason was also the title of a hit 2012 film?

3. The centaur was a creature that was half man and half of which animal?

4. Hypnus was the Greek and Somnus the Roman god of what?

5. Who was the Roman equivalent of the Greek god Bacchus?

6. Which nymph offended the goddess Hera who deprived her of the power of speech except to repeat the words of others?

7. Which drink conferred immortality on the Greek gods?

8. Which major company takes its name from the Greek goddess of victory?

9. Which goddess of sexual love and beauty was the Greek equivalent of the Roman goddess Venus?

10. Which daughter of Priam and Hecuba and twin of Helenus was given the gift of prophecy by Apollo?

11. Who was the Greek god of earthquakes and later of the sea?

12. Which food gave the Olympians their immortality?

13. The name of which Roman goddess of womanhood and childbirth was also the title of a 2007 Oscar-winning film starring Ellen Page?

14. Which spirits of the wind, who take their name from the Greek for 'snatchers', carried people to their death?

15. Which Egyptian goddess is also the name of Oxford University's reserve rowing crew at the University Boat Race?

16. Which Greek god was the twin brother of Artemis?

17. The Sphinx had the head of a human and the body of which creature?

18. Who was the Roman equivalent of the Greek goddess Artemis?

19. Which sisters would lure sailors to their death with their singing?
a) The Fates b) The Muses c) The Sirens

20. Romulus and Remus were the founders of which city?
a) Athens b) Rome c) Troy

MEDIUM

Answers to Quiz 121: Pot Luck

1. The Salvation Army
2. Turquoise
3. Hashtag
4. The Inquisition
5. The Hague
6. Sting
7. Kibbutz
8. Family Guy
9. People for the Ethical Treatment of Animals
10. Vanuatu
11. Lee Van Cleef
12. George Clooney
13. Isle of Man
14. Laughing gas
15. Inner Temple, Middle Temple, Lincoln's Inn, and Gray's Inn
16. Netherlands
17. Chubby Checker
18. Hard Times
19. Zimbabwe
20. Bona fide

Quiz 123: Pot Luck

1. A shooting star is an alternative name for which celestial object?

2. Which world-famous building was built by Shah Jehan in memory of his favourite wife, who died in 1629?

3. 'Le cerveau' is the French word for which organ of the human body?

4. Which award-winning 2008 film was based on a 2005 novel called 'Q&A' by Vikas Swarup?

5. The giant Trafalgar Square Christmas tree is donated to London by the people of which city?

6. Only horses of what age are allowed to run in The Derby?

7. What is the English translation of the Greek phrase 'kyrie eleison', often heard in churches?

8. With over 4m members and responsibility for 612,000 acres of countryside and 630 properties, what is the largest conservation charity in Britain?

9. True or false – more people die each year from coconuts falling on their heads than from shark attacks?

10. Now commonly found in light bulbs, for what do the initials LED stand?

11. Which form of transport takes its name from the Japanese for 'human-powered vehicle'?

12. Which series of prayers, often said by Roman Catholics, takes its name from the Latin for 'rose garden'?

13. Over what distance is a marathon race run?

14. The alloy pewter is primarily made up of which metal?

15. Which London theatre shares its name with a rare metallic element?

16. The massive Maha Kumbh Mela is a festival celebrated by followers of which religion?

17. What nationality was Samuel Morse, the creator of Morse Code?

18. Which element takes its chemical symbol Hg from the Latin 'hydrargyrum'?

19. Sirhan Sirhan was the killer of which political leader?
    a) Robert Kennedy
    b) Malcolm X
    c) Anwar Sadat

20. The 'koto' is a traditional musical instrument from which country?
    a) India
    b) Japan
    c) Switzerland

MEDIUM

Answers to Quiz 122: Myth and Legend

1. Achilles
2. Argo
3. Horse
4. Sleep
5. Dionysus
6. Echo
7. Nectar
8. Nike
9. Aphrodite
10. Cassandra

11. Poseidon
12. Ambrosia
13. Juno
14. Harpies
15. Isis
16. Apollo
17. Lion
18. Diana
19. The Sirens
20. Rome

Quiz 124: Connections part 2

1. Whose only UK number one single was 'Great Balls of Fire'?

2. Which Indian-born 19th-century author wrote the novels 'Catherine' and 'The Luck of Barry Lyndon'?

3. By what name is the Central Criminal Court of England and Wales more commonly known?

4. What bird has the scientific name 'Erithacus rubecula'?

5. Which former peanut farmer from Georgia went on to become president of the United States?

6. Who is the lead singer with the American rock band Aerosmith?

7. What was the only UK hit single for The Knack?

8. Which actress played WPC June Ackland in cop drama 'The Bill' and Georgia Sharma in 'Emmerdale'?

9. Played by Peri Gilpin, what was the name of the title character's producer in the TV comedy 'Frasier'?

10. Which actress played Catwoman in the 2012 film 'The Dark Knight Rises'?

11. 'The Gaffer' was the nickname of which England cricketer who won 133 Test caps?

12. Which actor's first Best Actor Oscar nomination came for his performance in the 1938 gangster film 'Angels with Dirty Faces'?

13. Which Northern Irish racing driver won five Formula One grand prix between 1976 and 1983?

14. Who was the Roman god of wine?

15. Which TV smoothie played Lewis Archer in the TV soap 'Coronation Street'?

16. What is the name of the fictional actor who often hosts infomercials and educational films in animated comedy 'The Simpsons'?

17. Which East Sussex seaside town is home to an annual International Chess Congress?

18. Which American folk hero was known as the 'King of the Wild Frontier'?

19. Which female TV chef finished sixth in the 2012 series of 'I'm a Celebrity … Get Me out of Here!'?

20. What is the connection between all the answers?

MEDIUM

Answers to Quiz 123: Pot Luck

1. Meteor
2. Taj Mahal
3. Brain
4. Slumdog Millionaire
5. Oslo
6. Three years
7. Lord, have mercy
8. The National Trust
9. True
10. Light Emitting Diode
11. Rickshaw
12. Rosary
13. 26 miles 385 yards
14. Tin
15. Palladium
16. Hinduism
17. American
18. Mercury
19. Robert Kennedy
20. Japan

Quiz 125: Pot Luck

1. In 'The Simpsons', what is Mr Burns' first name?

2. Which British-born Aussie comedian wrote the music and lyrics to the hit musical 'Matilda'?

3. In relation to electoral systems, for what do the initials AV stand?

4. In 2011, Recep Tayyip Erdogan was reelected as the prime minister of which country?

5. The Walloons are the French-speaking population of which country?

6. In a mobile phone SIM card, for what does the letter M stand?

7. The Joshua Tree National Park is situated in which American state?

8. Which song acted as a daily alarm call for Bill Murray in the 1993 film comedy 'Groundhog Day?

9. On a standard dartboard, what colour is the outer portion of the bullseye?

10. Which business guru hosts an annual shareholder meeting known as 'Woodstock for capitalists'?

11. ASOS is an internet fashion retailer. For what do the initials ASOS stand?

12. Robert Robinson, Barry Took, Anne Robinson, Terry Wogan, and Jeremy Vine have all hosted which TV programme?

13. In the 'Back to the Future' film trilogy, what is the name of Marty McFly's father?

14. Which three colours appear on the flag of Estonia?

15. Who is the all-time leading goal-scorer for the England national football team?

16. Which four colours are the balls used in a game of croquet?

17. Which Spice Girl is the mother of a daughter called Bluebell Madonna?

18. Which religious leader gained his 7 millionth Twitter follower in July 2013?

19. Kate Bliss, Jonty Hearnden, and David Harper are experts on TV on what subject?
    a) antiques
    b) food
    c) property

20. 'Prunus armeniaca' is the scientific name for which fruit?
    a) apricot
    b) kiwi fruit
    c) tangerine

MEDIUM

Answers to Quiz 124: Connections part 2

1. Jerry Lee Lewis
2. William Makepeace Thackeray
3. The Old Bailey
4. Robin
5. Jimmy Carter
6. Steve Tyler
7. My Sharona
8. Trudie Goodwin
9. Roz Doyle
10. Anne Hathaway
11. Alec Stewart
12. James Cagney
13. John Watson
14. Bacchus
15. Nigel Havers
16. Troy McClure
17. Hastings
18. Davy Crockett
19. Rosemary Shrager
20. They all contain the name of a sidekick or partner of a fictional detective

Quiz 126: Sport part 3

1. Which team won rugby's Six Nations Championship in both 2012 and 2013?

2. Over how many laps is a speedway race run?

3. Which team has won the Formula One constructors' title the most times?

4. 'The Cobra' is the nickname of which Nottingham-based world super-middleweight champion boxer?

5. In which town will you find a rugby league team called the Vikings?

6. Which Irish province won rugby union's Heineken Cup in 2009, 2011, and 2012?

7. Which Australian won the World Snooker Championship in 2010?

8. Which American lost in the final of the men's singles at Wimbledon in 2004, 2005, and 2009?

9. A series of holes known as Amen Corner is a feature of which famous golf course?

10. Welford Road is the home ground of which English rugby union team?

11. Who are the two Irish rugby union players to have made over 130 international appearances?

12. In which sport do teams compete for the Mosconi Cup?

13. True or false – neither John McEnroe nor Bjorn Borg won the Australian Open?

14. Darth Maple is the nickname of which darts player?

15. England internationals Joe Root and Jonny Bairstow play domestic cricket for which county?

16. Who is the only player from the Republic of Ireland to have won the World Snooker championship?

17. Who are the two English football teams to have won the European Cup / Champions League exactly once?

18. Which nickname is shared by the football clubs Luton Town and Stockport County?

19. In 2012, England's cricketers completed their first Test series win since 1984/85 in which country?
    a) India
    b) Pakistan
    c) Sri Lanka

20. Whom did Sam Allardyce succeed as manager of West Ham United?
    a) Alan Curbishley
    b) Avram Grant
    c) Gianfranco Zola

MEDIUM

Answers to Quiz 125: Pot Luck

1. Montgomery
2. Tim Minchin
3. Alternative Vote
4. Turkey
5. Belgium
6. Module
7. California
8. 'I Got You Babe' by Sonny and Cher
9. Green
10. Warren Buffett
11. As Seen On Screen
12. Points of View
13. George
14. White, blue, and black
15. Sir Bobby Charlton
16. Black, blue, red, and yellow
17. Geri Halliwell
18. Pope Francis
19. Antiques
20. Apricot

Quiz 127: Connections part 3

1. Who received his first Best Actor Oscar nomination in 2013 for 'Silver Linings Playbook'?

2. Who was the coach of the England cricket team that won the Ashes in 2005?

3. What is the real name of DJ Fatboy Slim?

4. Pierce Brosnan played Andy Osnard in which 2001 adaptation of a John Le Carré novel?

5. What was the name of the actress who played Betty Williams (Turpin) in the TV soap 'Coronation Street'?

6. Who is the arch-nemesis of international man of mystery, Austin Powers?

7. Who was the first black player to play Test cricket for England?

8. 'Dear Sir or Madam, will you read my book? / It took me years to write, will you take a look?' are lines from which song by The Beatles?

9. Which long-standing character in Aussie TV soap 'Neighbours' is played by Tom Oliver?

10. What is the name of the character played by John Hamm in the TV drama 'Mad Men'?

11. Michelle Pfeiffer received her first Best Actress Oscar nomination for her performance in which 1989 film?

12. What 1946 film noir starring Lana Turner and John Garfield was remade in 1981 with Jack Nicholson and Jessica Lange in the lead roles?

13. Who won the fifth series of 'I'm a Celebrity ... Get Me out of Here!'?

14. Mick Hucknall had a number 13 hit in 1997 with a cover of which Gregory Isaacs reggae classic?

15. The 1975 number one 'January' was the only UK chart topper from which Scottish band?

16. 'The Artist' is the nickname of which professional darts player?

17. Released in 1989, what was the title of singer Martika's only UK top five single?

18. What was the name of the covert White House investigations unit established during the presidency of Richard Nixon to stop the leaking of classified information to the media?
    a) The Carpenters b) The Plumbers c) The Pilots

19. What was Petula Clark's first number one hit single?
    a) Sailor b) Soldier c) Spy

20. What is the connection between all the answers?

MEDIUM

Answers to Quiz 126: Sport part 3

1. Wales
2. Four
3. Ferrari
4. Carl Froch
5. Widnes
6. Leinster
7. Neil Robertson
8. Andy Roddick
9. Augusta National
10. Leicester Tigers
11. Ronan O'Gara and Brian O'Driscoll
12. Pool
13. True
14. John Part
15. Yorkshire
16. Ken Doherty
17. Aston Villa and Chelsea
18. The Hatters
19. India
20. Avram Grant

Quiz 128: History part 2

1. Who was the British prime minister from 1964 to 1970 and then from 1974 until 1976?

2. Which royal dynasty ruled Great Britain and Ireland from 1714 until 1901?

3. Which wars ended with the death of King Richard III at Bosworth Field?

4. In 1956, Tunisia gained independence from which country?

5. The Peterloo Massacre took place in which English city?

6. Who was the first English monarch from the House of Tudor?

7. Gallipoli, the scene of a major First World War battle, is in which modern day country?

8. Which German word describes the political union of Austria with Germany following Hitler's annexation of Austria in 1938?

9. Gaius Octavius was the original name of which Roman Emperor?

10. Which organization was founded in 1920 with the object of promoting international peace and security?

11. In which decade was the first credit card introduced?

12. Which US President coined the phrase the 'Four Freedoms'?

13. The first Communist government in the world was established in which country?

14. Who was the British prime minister at the end of the First World War?

15. In which European country was a tax on beards introduced in the early 18th century?

16. Which British politician delivered the controversial 1968 'Rivers of Blood' speech?

17. Who was Britain's first Labour prime minister?

18. What was the military codename given to the Allied invasion of Normandy on 6 June 1944?

19. What was the name of the Commission that investigated the assassination of US President John F Kennedy?
a) Wallace Commission
b) Walter Commission
c) Warren Commission

20. The Arab Spring demonstrations of 2010 started in which country?
a) Egypt
b) Libya
c) Tunisia

Answers to Quiz 127: Connections part 3

1. Bradley Cooper
2. Duncan Fletcher
3. Norman Cook
4. The Tailor of Panama
5. Betty Driver
6. Doctor Evil
7. Roland Butcher
8. Paperback Writer
9. Lou Carpenter
10. Don Draper
11. The Fabulous Baker Boys
12. The Postman Always Rings Twice
13. Carol Thatcher
14. Night Nurse
15. Pilot
16. Kevin Painter
17. Toy Soldiers
18. The Plumbers
19. Sailor
20. They all contain a job or occupation

Quiz 129: Pot Luck

1. Which objects would you find in an ossuary?

2. From what is the alcoholic drink sake made?

3. In a pack of standard playing cards, which is the only king that does not sport a moustache?

4. Who is the only rugby union player to win the BBC Sports Personality of the Year Award?

5. Which technology company was founded by internet entrepreneurs Niklas Zennström from Sweden and Janus Friis from Denmark?

6. Which beach provided Martha and the Muffins with their only top ten hit?

7. Benjamin Braddock is the central character in which novel by Charles Webb that was later turned into a 1967 Oscar-winning film?

8. In 2013, Nawaz Sharif was elected prime minister of which country?

9. In newspapers, what are provided by Templegate, Newsboy, and Marlborough?

10. Which major British airport was originally known as Elmdon Airport?

11. Which film director is the godfather of both Gwyneth Paltrow and Drew Barrymore?

12. The award-winning restaurant Noma is located in which European capital?

13. In which month does the St Leger horse race take place?

14. Created by CS Forester, what is the first name of the fictional Napoleonic-era sailor Hornblower?

15. Abuja is the capital city of what country?

16. The detective drama 'Zen' was set in which country?

17. How old was Michael Jackson when he died?

18. Which Hollywood couple first appeared on screen together in the 2005 film 'Mr & Mrs Smith'?

19. Pierre Hardy is a famous designer of what?
    a) hats
    b) jewellery
    c) shoes

20. What is the nickname of the Kent one-day cricket team?
    a) Concordes
    b) Hurricanes
    c) Spitfires

MEDIUM

Answers to Quiz 128: History part 2

1. Harold Wilson
2. The Hanoverians
3. The Wars of the Roses
4. France
5. Manchester
6. Henry VII
7. Turkey
8. Anschluss
9. Augustus
10. The League of Nations
11. 1950s
12. Franklin D Roosevelt
13. Russia
14. David Lloyd George
15. Russia
16. Enoch Powell
17. Ramsay MacDonald
18. Operation Overlord
19. Warren Commission
20. Tunisia

Quiz 130: The Name Is James

1. Which author created the fictional detective Cordelia Gray?

2. Who played the title character in the 1970s detective drama 'The Rockford Files'?

3. TV drama 'All Creatures Great and Small' was based on a collection of books by which author?

4. Which British fighter won gold in the 2008 Olympic middleweight boxing tournament?

5. Which veteran actor played Jack Halford in the TV drama 'New Tricks'?

6. Which cultural critic, poet, journalist, and broadcaster wrote the autobiographical collection 'Unreliable Memoirs'?

7. The Famous Flames were the backing band for which singer?

8. Which Formula One World Champion was an amateur budgie breeder?

9. Which director collaborated with Ismail Merchant on the films 'A Room with a View' and 'The Remains of the Day'?

10. Which actor won his only Best Actor Oscar in 1941 for his performance in 'The Philadelphia Story'?

11. Which acclaimed Hollywood director's films include 'Terminator', 'Aliens', and 'True Lies'?

12. What name is shared by a cricketer who made his England Test debut in 2012 and a singer-songwriter who recorded the album 'Mud Slide Slim and the Blue Horizon'?

13. The 1956 film 'Giant' was the last film starring which Hollywood icon?

14. Solomon Joel Cohen was the birth name of which South-African-born comic actor who died in 1976?

15. Who was the fourth President of the United States?

16. Which English singer-songwriter, who topped the album charts with 'Undiscovered' and 'The Awakening', was named Best British Male at the 2007 Brit Awards?

17. Which actor played undercover cop Tommy Murphy in detective drama 'Murphy's Law'?

18. Who was hanged at Bedford jail in 1962 after being found guilty of the so-called 'A6 Murder'?

19. Which actor played the title character in 'Dawson's Creek' and appears as himself in 'Don't Trust the B---- in Apartment 23'?

20. Which British motorcyclist won the World Superbikes Championship in 2004 and 2007?
    a) James Eyeland
    b) James Kneeland
    c) James Toseland

MEDIUM

Answers to Quiz 129: Pot Luck

1. Human bones
2. Fermented rice
3. King of hearts
4. Jonny Wilkinson
5. Skype
6. Echo Beach
7. The Graduate
8. Pakistan
9. Horse racing tips
10. Birmingham
11. Steven Spielberg
12. Copenhagen
13. September
14. Horatio
15. Nigeria
16. Italy
17. 50
18. Brad Pitt and Angelina Jolie
19. Shoes
20. Spitfires

Quiz 131: Pot Luck

1. 'On the Street Where You Live' and 'With a Little Bit of Luck' are songs from which musical?

2. What nationality was the abstract artist Piet Mondrian?

3. Mary Ann Evans was the real name of which 19th-century author?

4. Which actor played the antiques dealer Lovejoy in the TV series of the same name?

5. True or false – in 1990 there was a British sitcom based on Hitler called 'Heil Honey, I'm Home!'?

6. Car manufacturer Kia is based in which country?

7. Which sport was the subject of the 2007 film comedy 'Blades of Glory'?

8. Malt whisky is made primarily from which malted cereal?

9. Elinor and Marianne Dashwood are the central characters in which classic novel?

10. Oran is the second largest city in which Arab country?

11. The Order of Isabella the Catholic is an honour awarded by which country?

12. 'The War Requiem' is a piece of music written by which 20th-century British composer?

13. True or false – Van Morrison has never had a UK top ten single?

14. Which medical TV drama is centred on a health centre called The Mill?

15. Sue Cleaver plays which long-serving character in the TV soap 'Coronation Street'?

16. In the TV drama 'Minder', who succeeded Terry McCann as Arthur Daley's minder?

17. Mamie Doud was the wife of which US president?

18. Which singer's gravestone features the words 'The Best Is Yet to Come'?

19. What is the name of the conceptual artist who won the Turner Prize in 2004?
    a) Jeremy Deller
    b) Keith Deller
    c) Mark Deller

20. Which version of the Windows computer operating system was launched in October 2012?
    a) Windows 7
    b) Windows 8
    c) Windows Vista

MEDIUM

Answers to Quiz 130: The Name Is James

1. PD James
2. James Garner
3. James Herriott
4. James DeGale
5. James Bolam
6. Clive James
7. James Brown
8. James Hunt
9. James Ivory
10. James Stewart
11. James Cameron
12. James Taylor
13. James Dean
14. Sid James
15. James Madison
16. James Morrison
17. James Nesbitt
18. James Hanratty
19. James Van Der Beek
20. James Toseland

Quiz 132: Famous Toms

Identify the famous Toms and Thomases from the clues below:

1. Liverpool-born actor who played TV's 'Dr Who' from 1974 until 1981.

2. President of the United States of America from 1801 to 1809.

3. British actor whose film credits include 'Inception', 'The Dark Knight Rises', and 'Bronson'.

4. Welsh rugby player who won 100 caps and has the nickname 'Alfie'.

5. Fashion designer turned film director who received an Oscar nomination for the 2009 drama 'A Single Man'.

6. Name shared by a multiple major winning golfer and a Labour MP who wrote the book 'Dial M for Murdoch'.

7. British playwright who was born in 1937 as Tomáš Straussler.

8. 18th-century British artist whose works include 'Mr and Mrs Robert Andrews' and 'Colonel John Bullock'.

9. Actor whose real surname is Mapother.

10. Comedian who hosted TV shows 'Name That Tune' and 'Crosswits'.

11. Matthew Macfadyen played this character in the long-running TV drama 'Spooks'.

12. German Nobel Prize winning author whose works include 'Death In Venice' and 'The Magic Mountain'.

13. British actor nominated for Oscars for his performances in 'Michael Clayton' and 'In the Bedroom'.

MEDIUM

Answers – page 269

14. Anglo-American political philosopher who wrote the influential 'Common Sense'.

15. British author best known for his 'Confessions of an English Opium-Eater'.

16. English philosopher, who died in 1679, whose best known work is 'Leviathan'.

17. Commonly heard at sports events, it was the only top ten single for The Piranhas.

18. Author whose novels include 'A Man in Full', 'I Am Charlotte Simmons', and 'Back to Blood'.

19. Actor who won his first Oscar for his performance in the 1993 thriller 'The Fugitive'.

20. British singer who had a number 4 hit in 1991 with 'Thinking About Your Love'.

MEDIUM

Answers to Quiz 131: Pot Luck

1. My Fair Lady
2. Dutch
3. George Eliot
4. Ian McShane
5. True
6. South Korea
7. Ice skating
8. Barley
9. Sense and Sensibility
10. Algeria
11. Spain
12. Benjamin Britten
13. True
14. Doctors
15. Eileen Grimshaw
16. Ray Daley
17. Dwight Eisenhower
18. Frank Sinatra
19. Jeremy Deller
20. Windows 8

Quiz 133: Pot Luck

1. 'Bridget Jones' Diary' first appeared in 1995 as a column in which newspaper?

2. Which number lies between 1 and 4 on a standard dartboard?

3. In 'The Simpsons', what is the name of Homer Simpson's father?

4. True or false – former Premier League referee Dermot Gallagher is the father of Oasis brothers Noel and Liam Gallagher?

5. Which is the only football team to have won the FA Cup and been relegated from the top flight of English football in the same season?

6. What type of food is Stinking Bishop?

7. Which English poet lived at Dove Cottage in Grasmere?

8. The Tontons Macoutes were a paramilitary organization in which Caribbean country?

9. A manuscript of a poem written by which English Romantic poet was sold at auction for £181,250 in April 2013?

10. Before finding fame as a pop star, which singer had a job measuring plots at Highgate Cemetery?

11. Which type of pasta takes its name from the Italian for butterfly?

12. Which English monarch was known as 'Bluff King Hal'?

13. Posie, Perkin, and Pootle were characters in which children's TV show?

14. What was the most popular name for a baby boy in 2012?

15. And what was the most popular name for a baby girl in 2012?

16. Manuel Noriega was the leader of which central American country from 1983 until 1989?

17. Who was the first sitting Member of Parliament to appear on a reality TV show?

18. War leaders Churchill, Roosevelt, and Stalin first met at a conference in which Middle Eastern capital?

19. Headington and Cowley are areas of which English city?
    a) Cambridge
    b) Hull
    c) Oxford

20. Which sport is played at the St Lawrence Ground?
    a) cricket
    b) football
    c) rugby union

MEDIUM

Answers to Quiz 132: Famous Toms

1. Tom Baker
2. Thomas Jefferson
3. Tom Hardy
4. Gareth Thomas
5. Tom Ford
6. Tom Watson
7. Tom Stoppard
8. Thomas Gainsborough
9. Tom Cruise
10. Tom O'Connor
11. Tom Quinn
12. Thomas Mann
13. Tom Wilkinson
14. Thomas Paine
15. Thomas de Quincey
16. Thomas Hobbes
17. Tom Hark
18. Tom Wolfe
19. Tommy Lee Jones
20. Kenny Thomas

DIFFICULT QUIZZES

Quiz 134: Pot Luck

1. What creature is mentioned in the title of the final book of Stieg Larsson's 'Millennium' trilogy?

2. Which rock guitarist, best known for playing with Black Sabbath, penned the 2013 Eurovision entry for Armenia?

3. Who is the only current EastEnders character who appeared in the first ever episode of the BBC soap?

4. Which actor played Q in the 2012 Bond film 'Skyfall'?

5. Which singer said, 'If more men were homosexual, there would be no wars, because homosexual men would never kill other men, whereas heterosexual men love killing other men'?

6. Which politician was awarded the 2007 Nobel Peace Prize?

7. Prior to Benedict XVI, who was the last pope to resign from office?

8. What is the final book in 'The Chronicles of Narnia' series?

9. Which name connects a British pop band from the 1980s and an Italian political movement led by by comedian-turned-activist Beppe Grillo?

10. The highest paid political leader in the world is the prime minister of which small Asian country?

11. Erika Mann, the daughter of the German novelist Thomas Mann, was married to which English poet?

12. What was the name of the former Russian spy who died in London in 2006 after being poisoned with radioactive polonium-210?

13. Which trilogy of science fiction novels are set in the nation of Panem?

14. Which Dutch-born abstract impressionist's 1953 painting 'Woman III' sold for $137.5m in 2006?

15. Which member of the royal family was born Katherine Lucy Mary Worsley in 1933?

16. What is Austria's second city?

17. Which Australian is the founder of the Wikileaks website?

18. Which military and political leader, born in the 12th century, had the given name Temujin?

19. Briton Luke Campbell won gold at the 2012 Olympics in which sport?
    a) boxing
    b) canoeing
    c) cycling

20. Chef Yotam Ottolenghi's best-selling 2012 recipe book is named after which city?
    a) Jerusalem
    b) Marrakech
    c) Tehran

Answers to Quiz 200: Pot Luck

1. The ear
2. Atlantic City
3. Cat Stevens
4. Lisa Kudrow
5. Mark Williams
6. Erika
7. Israel
8. One Man, Two Guvnors
9. Charles Foster
10. San Francisco
11. New Zealander
12. Ann Cleeves
13. Poetry
14. Nine
15. San Francisco
16. Aston Villa
17. Anita Dobson
18. Iggy Pop
19. Bookmaker
20. Hall

DIFFICULT

Quiz 135: Places part 1

1. The Canadian province of Manitoba has borders with which two American states?

2. Mount Townsend and Mount Twynham are mountains in which country?

3. Huang He is the local name for which river?

4. What is the southernmost island of the Caribbean?

5. What are the only two landlocked countries in South America?

6. What is the only country that passes through the equator as well as the tropics of Cancer and Capricorn?

7. The major archaeological site of Angkor, home to a series of monuments, is in which country?

8. Retired in 1997, the Royal Yacht Britannia is currently moored in which city?

9. The headquarters of the RNLI are in which town?

10. The massive Mammoth Cave National Park is in which US state?

11. Often used to distinguish between the north and south of the USA, the Mason-Dixon Line originally marked the boundary between which two states?

12. Hoping to cover some 200 square miles, the new National Forest will be created in which three English counties?

13. Stretching some 297 miles across the Nullabar Plain, the straightest stretch of railway in the world is in which country?

14. The ancient city of Carthage is in which modern-day country?

15. Which four countries make up the area known as the Horn of Africa?

16. The 'Ndrangheta is an organized-crime group based in which region of Italy?

17. Which two Central American countries were involved in the so-called 'Soccer War'?

18. The Gellért Baths are in which European capital?

19. The Southern Alps are in which country?
    a) Australia
    b) New Zealand
    c) South Africa

20. The Groeningemuseum is in which city?
    a) Amsterdam
    b) Bruges
    c) Brussels

Answers to Quiz 134: Pot Luck

1. Hornet
2. Tony Iommi
3. Ian Beale
4. Ben Whishaw
5. Morrissey
6. Al Gore
7. Pope Gregory XII
8. The Last Battle
9. Five Star
10. Singapore
11. WH Auden
12. Alexander Litvinenko
13. The Hunger Games
14. Willem de Kooning
15. The Duchess of Kent
16. Graz
17. Julian Assange
18. Genghis Khan
19. Boxing
20. Jerusalem

DIFFICULT

Quiz 136: Pot Luck

1. Which Hollywood actor co-wrote and directed the 2011 political thriller 'The Ides of March'?

2. 'Reputation is an idle and very false burden, often got without merit and lost without being deserved' is a line from which Shakespeare play?

3. Chaitra is a month in the calendar of which religion?

4. The 2001 hit 'Chase the Sun' by Planet Funk is regularly heard at events in which sport?

5. In relation to technology and education, for what does the acronym MOOC stand?

6. What nationality is the tennis champion Juan Martin del Potro?

7. Which actor and film director said, 'I hate television. I hate it as much as peanuts. But I can't stop eating peanuts'?

8. Which Austrian daredevil jumped from a capsule 24 miles above the earth in October 2012?

9. Which fictional detective made his debut in a novel called 'Faceless Killers'?

10. What is the only London borough that begins with the letter M?

11. The Lodge is the official residence of the prime minister of which country?

12. Michelangelo died in the same year that Shakespeare was born. What was the year?

13. In 2010, Mohamed al Fayed sold Harrods to an investment company run by the royal family of which country?

14. Which US president had the Secret Service codename Lancer?

15. What connects the course that hosts golf's European PGA Championship and Aussie TV drama 'Prisoner: Cell Block H'?

16. Which three politicians served as Chancellor of the Exchequer under Margaret Thatcher?

17. In 2013, Chuck Hagel succeeded Leon Panetta in which American political position?

18. In which year was the smoking ban introduced in England and Wales?

19. What is celebrated each year on 11 March?
    a) Commonwealth Day b) Europe Day c) Coronation Day

20. Which Eastern European capital city hosted the 2013 World Track Cycling Championships?
    a) Kiev b) Minsk c) Tallinn

Answers to Quiz 135: Places part 1

1. Minnesota and North Dakota
2. Australia
3. Yellow River
4. Trinidad
5. Bolivia and Paraguay
6. Brazil
7. Cambodia
8. Edinburgh
9. Poole
10. Kentucky
11. Maryland and Pennsylvania
12. Derbyshire, Leicestershire, and Staffordshire
13. Australia
14. Tunisia
15. Djibouti, Eritrea, Ethiopia, and Somalia
16. Calabria
17. Honduras and El Salvador
18. Budapest
19. New Zealand
20. Bruges

DIFFICULT

Quiz 137: Art, Architecture, and Design

1. 'Après le déjeuner', the most expensive painting sold at auction by a female artist was by which Russian painter?

2. The award-winning architect Dame Zaha Hadid was born in which country?

3. Which contemporary artist's balloon sculpture 'Tulips' was sold at auction for over $33m in November 2012?

4. The 1956 film 'Lust for Life' starred Kirk Douglas as which painter?

5. Which German-American architect was the director of the famous Bauhaus school of design from 1919 to 1928?

6. Who was the founder of the school of painting known as the Vienna Sezession?

7. Which Chinese dissident artist designed the Beijing National Stadium which hosted the 2008 Olympics?

8. Which British designer and retailer founded The Design Museum?

9. Which Indian-born sculptor designed the giant ArcelorMittal Orbit at the London Olympic Park?

10. What nationality was the artist Paul Klee?

11. Which art school is mentioned in the Pulp song 'Common People'?

12. What is the name of the German professor who exhibits human cadavers?

13. Who painted 'Bal du Moulin de la Galette' which was sold at auction for $78.1m in 1990?

14. Which renaissance painter's most famous works include 'The Taking of Christ' and 'The Calling of St Matthew'?

15. Which European city gives its name to a famous tubular-steel chair designed by Mies van der Rohe?

16. The National Gallery of Art is in which American city?

17. Which Russian-born abstract painter founded the Munich group 'Der Blaue Reiter' (The Blue Rider)?

18. British artist Tracey Emin grew up in which seaside resort?

19. David Hockney lives in which seaside town?
    a) Bridlington b) Scarborough c) Whitby

20. Which area of London gave its name to a group of early 20th-century Post-Impressionists including Walter Sickert and Augustus John?
    a) Camden Town b) Kentish Town c) Canning Town

Answers to Quiz 136: Pot Luck

1. George Clooney
2. Othello
3. Hinduism
4. Darts
5. Massive Online Open Course
6. Argentine
7. Orson Welles
8. Felix Baumgartner
9. Kurt Wallander
10. Merton
11. Australia
12. 1564
13. Qatar
14. John F Kennedy
15. Wentworth
16. Geoffrey Howe, Nigel Lawson, and John Major
17. Secretary of Defense
18. 2007
19. Commonwealth Day
20. Minsk

DIFFICULT

Quiz 138: Pot Luck

1. The four Roman Catholic Archbishops of England are based in which dioceses?

2. Which nickname is shared by a London football team and an NBA basketball franchise in San Antonio?

3. Which member of the royal family celebrates a birthday on 14 November?

4. Caaguazu, Itapua, and Neembucu are departments of which South American country?

5. In the poker game pot-limit Omaha, how many cards does a player start with?

6. In 2013 Canadian Mark Carney became the governor of which organisation?

7. In which field of the arts is Sergei Polunin a notable name?

8. Which German writer, born in Frankfurt in 1749, said, 'Doubt grows with knowledge'?

9. Which British artist's 1952 work, 'Boy's Head', a small portrait of his neighbour Charlie Lumley, sold at auction for £3.2m in 2011?

10. Which double Oscar-nominated actress plays the title character in ITV detective drama 'Vera'?

11. The Iranian prophet Zarathustra is the founder of which religion?

12. Which military and political leader said, 'To do all that one is able to do, is to be a man; to do all that one would like to do, is to be a god'?

13. Which Irish actor starred alongside Colin Farrell in the 2008 drama 'In Bruges'?

14. Tugela Falls, the largest waterfall in Africa and the second largest in the world is in which country?

15. Who played the title character's wife in the 2013 film biopic 'Hitchcock'?

16. True or false – Bill Clinton, George W Bush, and Barack Obama are all left-handed?

17. 24 Sussex Drive is the official residence of the prime minister of which country?

18. Which Hollywood superstar appeared in the short-lived British soap opera 'Families'?

19. Prior to becoming Archbishop of Canterbury, Justin Welby was bishop of which diocese?
    a) Birmingham b) Durham c) York

20. The TV crime drama 'Spiral' is set in which country?
    a) Denmark b) Germany c) France

Answers to Quiz 137: Art, Architecture, and Design

1. Natalia Goncharova
2. Iraq
3. Jeff Koons
4. Vincent van Gogh
5. Walter Gropius
6. Gustav Klimt
7. Ai Weiwei
8. Terence Conran
9. Anish Kapoor
10. Swiss
11. St Martins College of Art and Design
12. Gunther von Hagens
13. Pierre-Auguste Renoir
14. Caravaggio
15. Barcelona
16. Washington DC
17. Wassily Kandinsky
18. Margate
19. Bridlington
20. Camden Town

DIFFICULT

Quiz 139: Sports Governing Bodies

Identify the sport which is governed by the body with the following initials:

1. ITTF

2. FINA

3. FIBA

4. UCI

5. FISA

6. FIH

7. IIHF

8. ICC

9. FIDE

10. GAA

11. FIL

12. MLB

13. FIM

14. BSPA

15. IJF

16. The R&A

17. IWF

18. GBGB

19. FIA

20. BHA

Answers to Quiz 138: Pot Luck

1. Westminster, Birmingham, Liverpool, and Southwark
2. Spurs
3. Prince Charles
4. Paraguay
5. Four
6. The Bank of England
7. Ballet
8. Johann Wolfgang von Goethe
9. Lucian Freud
10. Brenda Blethyn
11. Zoroastrianism
12. Napoleon Bonaparte
13. Brendan Gleeson
14. South Africa
15. Helen Mirren
16. False – Clinton and Obama are left-handed. George W Bush isn't, but father George HW Bush is.
17. Canada
18. Jude Law
19. Durham
20. France

DIFFICULT

Quiz 140: Pot Luck

1. 'Volver' and 'The Skin I Live In' are films by which Spanish director?

2. The Royal Academy was founded by which British monarch?

3. Who said, 'Painting is just another way to keep a diary'?

4. Which Christian feast is celebrated each year on 6 August?

5. Tom Brady, Peyton Manning, and Joe Flacco are notable names in which sport?

6. Who was the first British monarch who was also a qualified pilot?

7. Commonly used in relation to the internet, for what do the initials URL stand?

8. What is the most westerly bridge over the River Thames in London?

9. Searchlight was the Secret Service codename of which US president?

10. Our Lady of Peace Basilica, the third largest church in the world is in which African country?

11. The most votes received by a political party in a UK general election is 14.092m. Who was the leader of the party that achieved that massive vote?

12. Which actor played Dr Watson alongside Robert Downey Jr in the 2009 film 'Sherlock Holmes'?

13. Which former prime minister later served as foreign secretary under Edward Heath?

14. What type of coffee takes its name from the white cowl worn by an order of Catholic friars?

15. The provinces of A Coruña, Lugo, Ourense, and Pontevedra make up which autonomous region of Spain?

Answers – page 287

16. Which British artist was appointed a member of the Order of Merit in January 2012?

17. Which unit of measurement is equal to 3.26 light years?

18. Corfe Castle is in which English county?

19. What was the name of the NASA rover that landed on Mars in 2012?
    a) Curiosity
    b) Inquisitor
    c) Sightseer

20. The coronet of which rank of the peerage features eight strawberry leaves?
    a) Baron
    b) Duke
    c) Marquis

Answers to Quiz 139: Sports Governing Bodies

1. Table tennis
2. Aquatics (swimming and diving)
3. Basketball
4. Cycling
5. Rowing
6. Hockey
7. Ice hockey
8. Cricket
9. Chess
10. Gaelic sports (football and hurling)
11. Lacrosse
12. Baseball
13. Motorcycling
14. Speedway
15. Judo
16. Golf
17. Weightlifting
18. Greyhound racing
19. Autosports
20. Horse racing

DIFFICULT

Quiz 141: Films part 1

1. What was the 1955 sequel to 'Gentlemen Prefer Blondes'?

2. Martin Scorsese won his only Best Director Oscar for which film?

3. What 1951 film is the only one to win three of the four acting categories at the same Oscars ceremony?

4. Which actor, who starred in the TV comedy 'Cheers', provides the voice of Hamm in the 'Toy Story' films?

5. Complete the title of the 2012 film starring Kristen Stewart: 'Snow White and the ...'

6. What was the last film directed by Alfred Hitchcock?

7. Film composer Jonny Greenwood is also a member of which best-selling British rock group?

8. Which Australian actress received a Best Supporting Actress Oscar nomination in 2013 for her performance in 'Silver Linings Playbook'?

9. According to 'Forbes' magazine, who was the highest earning actor of 2012?

10. Prior to 'Argo', which was the last film to win the Oscar for Best Picture without being nominated in the Best Director category?

11. Who won back-to-back Best Actor Oscars in 1993 and 1994?

12. In 2007, which British actor was awarded the French 'Chevalier des Arts et des Lettres' medal?

13. Who holds the record for the most Oscar nominations in the Best Actress category with 14?

14. Which Paul Verhoven film holds the record for the most Razzie nominations with 13?

15. 'The Bourne Identity' and its sequels are centred on a character created by which thriller writer?

16. Who won the 2001 Oscar for Best Actor for his performance in 'Training Day'?

17. Who played the president's wife in the 2012 biopic 'Lincoln'?

18. Which British city was the subject of Terence Davies' 2008 film 'Of Time and the City'?

19. Roger Thornhill is the name name of the lead character in which Hitchcock classic?
    a) 'North by Northwest' b) 'Psycho' c) 'Vertigo'

20. What is the minimum length a film needs to be in order to be eligible for the Best Picture Oscar?
    a) 30 minutes b) 40 minutes c) 50 minutes

Answers to Quiz 140: Pot Luck

1. Pedro Almodovar
2. George III
3. Pablo Picasso
4. Transfiguration
5. American football
6. King Edward VIII
7. Uniform Resource Locator
8. Hampton Court Bridge
9. Richard Nixon
10. Cote d'Ivoire
11. John Major
12. Jude Law
13. Sir Alec Douglas-Home
14. Cappuccino (from the Cappuchin Order)
15. Galicia
16. David Hockney
17. Parsec
18. Dorset
19. Curiosity
20. Duke

DIFFICULT

Quiz 142: Pot Luck

1. Los Pinos is the official residence of the president of which country?

2. Novelist Nick Hornby is the brother-in-law of which British thriller writer?

3. What does the J in JD Salinger stand for?

4. Which Asian monarch lives at Chitralada Palace?

5. Which English town was known as Glevum in Roman times?

6. Which actor won both the Worst Actor and Worst Actress awards at the 2012 Razzies?

7. How old were both Tony Blair and David Cameron when they became prime minister?

8. Oviedo is the capital city of which autonomous community in the north-west of Spain?

9. Jim Bolger, Helen Clark, and Jenny Shipley have all been prime minister of which country?

10. Which sport was featured in the 2009 film 'The Blind Side'?

11. Kara Zor-El is the alter ego of which comic-book superhero?

12. 'I'd like to have some milk. Please, please give me some more' were the final words of which famous person, who died in 2009?

13. What are the two London boroughs that start with the letter R?

14. Which are the two teams to have won football's Champions League the year after losing in the final?

15. Steve Harris and Nicko McBrain are members of which heavy-metal band?

Answers – page 291

16. Which US president had the Secret Service codename Rawhide?

17. In 2000, who became the first person to be nominated for the Best Director Oscar for two different films in the same year?

18. What were the two films?

19. The 1966 film about a rebellion against French colonial forces was called The Battle of ...
    a) Algiers
    b) Cairo
    c) Marrakech

20. How many letters are there in the Welsh alphabet?
    a) 26
    b) 28
    c) 30

Answers to Quiz 141: Films part 1

1. Gentlemen Marry Brunettes
2. The Departed
3. A Streetcar Named Desire
4. John Ratzenberger
5. Huntsman
6. Family Plot
7. Radiohead
8. Jacki Weaver
9. Tom Cruise
10. Driving Miss Daisy
11. Tom Hanks
12. Jude Law
13. Meryl Streep
14. Showgirls
15. Robert Ludlum
16. Denzel Washington
17. Sally Field
18. Liverpool
19. North by Northwest
20. 40 minutes

DIFFICULT

Quiz 143: Natural World

1. Mount Kosciuszko is the highest mountain in which country?

2. The cyclamen is the national flower of which European country?

3. 'Struthio camelus' is the scientific name of which animal?

4. What is the only mammal that doesn't have teeth?

5. Eas a' Chual Aluinn is Britain's highest what?

6. The active volcano Sabancaya is in which South American country?

7. Which country is home to the most mammal species?

8. Indian, Javan, and Sumatran are types of which creature?

9. Egyptian ichneumon and Indian grey are species of which mammal?

10. The Iguaçu Falls sit at the border of which two South American countries?

11. The island of Borneo is divided between which three countries?

12. What type of animal is the dik-dik?

13. 'Pandion haliaetus' is the scientific name for which bird?

14. The golden wattle is the national flower of which Commonwealth country?

15. What is the only coastal national park in Britain?

16. The kea is a species of parrot native to which country?

17. Lake Assal, the lowest point in Africa at 515ft below sea level, is in which tiny East African country?

18. What type of creature is an avocet?

19. Kerepakupai Merú is the indigenous name for what?
    a) Angel Falls
    b) Ayers Rock
    c) Amazon River

20. What is the outermost region of a planet's atmosphere?
    a) chromosphere
    b) exosphere
    c) troposphere

Answers to Quiz 142: Pot Luck

1. Mexico
2. Robert Harris
3. Jerome
4. The King of Thailand
5. Gloucester
6. Adam Sandler (for 'Jack and Jill')
7. 43
8. Asturias
9. New Zealand
10. American football
11. Supergirl
12. Michael Jackson
13. Redbridge and Richmond upon Thames
14. AC Milan and Bayern Munich
15. Iron Maiden
16. Ronald Reagan
17. Steven Soderbergh
18. 'Erin Brockovich' and 'Traffic'
19. Algiers
20. 28

DIFFICULT

Quiz 144: Pot Luck

1. Which space shuttle, which shares its name with the Christian name of a British fictional detective, took its last flight in 2012?

2. In 2013, Holly Bleasdale became Britain's first European indoor athletics champion in which field event?

3. In computing, for what do the initials HTTP stand?

4. James Roderick Moir is the real name of which English comedian?

5. Which US president, who was elected in 1836, was the first man to hold the post who was not born a British subject?

6. Lake Victoria is divided between which three African countries?

7. In which year did the first James Bond film appear in UK cinemas?

8. Gunpowder, Russian Caravan, and Twankay are varieties of what drink?

9. 'Murphy', 'Molloy', and 'Malone Dies' are novels by which Irish author, who died in 1989?

10. Which word describes giving human characteristics to non-human entities?

11. What is the largest national park in England?

12. Bangui is the capital of which country, beloved of 'Pointless' host Richard Osman?

13. Which Manchester United midfielder was the first Asian player to score a hat-trick in the Premier League?

14. Which media mogul made a donation of $1 billion to the United Nations in 1997?

15. Christopher Tietjens is the central character in which series of novels by Ford Madox Ford which were adapted for TV in 2012?

16. The Royal Concertgebouw Orchestra is based in which European city?

17. What is the most visited museum in the world?

18. Costing some $65,000 per night, the most expensive hotel room in the world is in which European city?

19. In London, what are informally known as 'The Magnificent Seven'?
    a) cemeteries
    b) markets
    c) prisons

20. In which of these Alfred Hitchcock films did James Stewart not appear?
    a) North by Northwest
    b) Rear Window
    c) Vertigo

Answers to Quiz 143: Natural World

1. Australia
2. Cyprus
3. Ostrich
4. Anteater
5. Waterfall
6. Peru
7. Indonesia
8. Rhinoceros
9. Mongoose
10. Argentina and Brazil
11. Brunei, Indonesia,
    and Malaysia
12. Antelope
13. Osprey
14. Australia
15. Pembrokeshire Coast National Park
16. New Zealand
17. Djibouti
18. Bird
19. Angel Falls
20. Exosphere

DIFFICULT

Quiz 145: Ologies

Of what subjects are the following -ologies the field of study?

1. Neurology

2. Virology

3. Eremology

4. Apiology

5. Limnology

6. Myology

7. Angiology

8. Cytology

9. Gerontology

10. Balneology

11. Metrology

12. Nosology

13. Mycology

14. Histology

15. Nephology

16. Osteology

17. Pedology

18. Oology

19. Phycology

20. Odontology

Answers to Quiz 144: Pot Luck

1. Endeavour
2. Pole vault
3. HyperText Transfer Protocol
4. Vic Reeves
5. Martin Van Buren
6. Uganda, Tanzania, and Kenya
7. 1962
8. Tea
9. Samuel Beckett
10. Anthropomorphism
11. Lake District
12. Central African Republic
13. Shinji Kagawa
14. Ted Turner
15. Parade's End
16. Amsterdam
17. The Louvre
18. Geneva
19. Cemeteries
20. North by Northwest

DIFFICULT

Quiz 146: Pot Luck

1. In which European city will you find the Mariinsky Theatre?

2. Which quiz show celebrated its 1,000th episode in March 2013?

3. Which British naval commander, who shares a surname with a former England cricketer, was Horatio Nelson's second in command at the Battle of Trafalgar?

4. Mount Elbrus is the highest peak in which range of mountains?

5. The president of which Middle Eastern country lives at the Baabda Palace?

6. Which Northamptonshire town, which is the home of a racecourse, was known as Lactodorum in Roman times?

7. Richard Seddon was the longest serving prime minister of which country?

8. The Oscar-winning film 'Brokeback Mountain' was based on a short story by which author?

9. Which comedian performed a 25-hour stand-up marathon in 2013 to raise money for Comic Relief?

10. In relation to aviation, for what do the initials VTOL stand?

11. The massive Salt Lake Stadium, the second largest football venue in the world, is in which country?

12. 'Honest: My Story So Far' is the 2013 autobiography of which British pop star and reality TV judge?

13. Sir Anthony Hopkins played which author in the 1993 film 'Shadowlands'?

14. Iapetus, Tethys, and Dione are moons of which planet of the Solar System?

15. What is the second longest bone in the human body?

16. Which fictional detective was given an obituary in the New York Times after being killed off in 1975?

17. Awarded the OBE in 2012, fashion designer Barbara Halanicki was the founder of which iconic 1960s clothes store?

18. The first US presidential inauguration held in Washington DC saw which president sworn in?

19. Wilhelm is the middle name of which Hollywood superstar?
    a) Leonardo DiCaprio
    b) Sylvester Stallone
    c) Bruce Willis

20. How many Welsh MPs are elected to the UK parliament?
    a) 30
    b) 40
    c) 50

Answers to Quiz 145: Ologies

1. Nervous system
2. Viruses
3. Deserts
4. Bees
5. Lakes
6. Muscles
7. Blood and vascular medicine
8. Cells
9. Ageing
10. Treatment of diseases using baths and bathing
11. Measurement
12. Classification of diseases
13. Fungi
14. Tissues (in organisms)
15. Clouds
16. Bones
17. Soil
18. Eggs
19. Algae
20. Teeth

DIFFICULT

Quiz 147: Sport part 1

1. Which track hosts horse racing's King George VI Chase?

2. Sir Alex Ferguson's last game in charge of Manchester United was a 5-5 draw against which team?

3. Who is the youngest player to score a goal for the England football team?

4. Arnold Raymond Cream was the original name of which world heavyweight boxing champion who held the title in the 1950s until beaten by Rocky Marciano?

5. How many matches must a player win in order to become the World Snooker champion?

6. Which was the first Olympic Games that featured competitors from all five continents?

7. The final of both the BDO and PDC World Darts Championship is played over the best of how many sets?

8. Which three football clubs were founder members of both the Football League and the Premier League?

9. 'The Flea' is the nickname of which world-renowned footballer?

10. What is the only team to have won the Football League play offs in all three divisions?

11. Who is the only Englishman to win European football's Golden Boot Award?

12. Who smashed an unbeaten 170 from just 66 balls for Royal Challengers Bangalore in a 2013 IPL cricket match?

13. Who in 2013 became the first player from outside the UK and Ireland to make 500 Premier League appearances?

14. The Stadium of Light, home ground of Sunderland, is also the name of the ground of which Portuguese club?

15. Max Whitlock is an international medal-winner in which sport?

16. '36' is the nickname of which English rugby union international who plays at centre or fly-half?

17. Which is the only team to reach the last four of Champions League in six successive seasons?

18. In 2001, who became the last Englishman to be named European Footballer of the Year?

19. How much was the annual salary cap in rugby's Aviva Premiership for the 2012/13 season?
    a) £4m b) 4.5m c) 5m

20. Who was the first person to manage a British team to victory in the European Cup?
    a) Matt Busby b) Bill Shankly c) Jock Stein

Answers to Quiz 146: Pot Luck

1. St Petersburg
2. A Question of Sport
3. Cuthbert Collingwood
4. Caucasus
5. Lebanon
6. Towcester
7. New Zealand
8. Annie Proulx
9. Mark Watson
10. Vertical Take Off and Landing
11. India
12. Tulisa Contostavlos
13. CS Lewis
14. Saturn
15. Tibia
16. Hercule Poirot
17. Biba
18. Thomas Jefferson
19. Leonardo DiCaprio
20. 40

DIFFICULT

Quiz 148: Pot Luck

1. In relation to elections, for what do the initials AMS stand?

2. Which former Coronation Street actor is now an artisan cheese maker?

3. Philip Seymour Hoffman won a Best Actor Oscar in 2005 for his portrayal of which author?

4. Which is the only province of Canada that is officially bilingual?

5. Which TV soap celebrated its 40th anniversary in 2012 with a live episode that featured two weddings, two births, and a death?

6. The classic French horse race the Prix de l'Arc de Triomphe is held at which course?

7. By what name is the 17th-century author Jean-Baptiste Poquelin more commonly known?

8. The longest suspension bridge in Europe, the Great Belt, is in which country?

9. Which country left the Commonwealth in 2003?

10. Briton Robbie Grabarz won Olympic bronze at the 2012 games in which athletics event?

11. Who was the first African to hold the post of Secretary General of the United Nations?

12. 'Being and Time' is the best known work of which German philosopher, who was born in Baden in 1889?

13. Novelists Catherine O'Flynn, Jonathan Coe, and Mike Gayle are from which English city?

14. Prior to Bradley Wiggins in 2012, who was the last English winner of the BBC Sports Personality of the Year award?

15. In 2006, Evo Morales became the first indigenous president of which South American country?

16. Which former Orient and West Bromwich Albion winger was the first English player to play for Real Madrid?

17. 'The Rock' is the nickname of which professional wrestler turned Hollywood star?

18. Racing drivers Roland Ratzenberger and Ayrton Senna lost their lives driving at which circuit in 1994?

19. The song 'Keep Right On to the End of the Road' is sung by supporters of which football club?
    a) Birmingham City
    b) Coventry City
    c) Manchester City

20. Wally Pfister is associated with which area of film-making?
    a) cinematography
    b) costume design
    c) soundtracks

Answers to Quiz 147: Sport part 1

1. Kempton Park
2. West Bromwich Albion
3. Wayne Rooney
4. Jersey Joe Walcott
5. Five
6. Stockholm 1912
7. 13
8. Aston Villa, Blackburn Rovers, and Everton
9. Lionel Messi
10. Blackpool
11. Kevin Phillips
12. Chris Gayle
13. Mark Schwarzer
14. Sporting Lisbon
15. Gymnastics
16. Billy Twelvetrees
17. Barcelona
18. Michael Owen
19. £4.5m
20. Jock Stein

DIFFICULT

Quiz 149: Alliterative Answers

1. Ben Stiller wrote, produced, directed, and starred in which 2008 action comedy about a group of actors making a Vietnam war film?

2. The Blackhearts were the banking band for which female, American rock guitarist?

3. Which sprinter is the only Namibian to win an Olympic medal?

4. Which Academy Award winning British film maker directed the films 'Red Road', 'Fish Tank', and 'Wuthering Heights'?

5. What was the only UK hit single for The Archies?

6. 'Lyrical Ballads' is a collection by Samuel Taylor Coleridge and what other Romantic poet?

7. Michael Douglas won his first Best Actor Oscar for playing which character in the film 'Wall Street'?

8. Which Democrat lost to Richard Nixon in the 1968 US presidential election?

9. Currently serving a life sentence in an American jail, what is the real name of the man nicknamed the 'Shoe Bomber'?

10. Which Scottish-born musician and artist briefly played bass with The Beatles?

11. Which British playwright's works include 'Absurd Person Singular', 'The Norman Conquests', and 'Private Fears in Public Places'?

12. Which economist was appointed Chairman of the US Federal Reserve in 2006?

13. Barbara Vine is the pseudonym of which British author?

14. Which sitcom starred Kathy Burke as Linda La Hughes and James Dreyfus as Tom Farrell?

15. Which politician came second behind Michael Dukakis in the race to become the Democratic Party presidential nominee in 1988?

16. Which 2003 body-switch family comedy starred Jamie Lee Curtis and Lindsay Lohan?

17. Which rank outsider won the 1986 World Snooker Championship?

18. Who was the lead singer with Scottish rock band Deacon Blue?

19. Which son of a British prime minister directed the films 'The Winslow Boy' in 1948 and 'The Browning Version' in 1951?

20. What was the name of the Australian speech therapist played by Geoffrey Rush in the 2010 film 'The King's Speech'?

Answers to Quiz 148: Pot Luck

1. Additional Member System
2. Sean Wilson (Martin Platt)
3. Truman Capote
4. New Brunswick
5. Emmerdale
6. Longchamp
7. Molière
8. Denmark
9. Zimbabwe
10. High jump
11. Boutros Boutros-Ghali
12. Martin Heidegger
13. Birmingham
14. Zara Phillips
15. Bolivia
16. Laurie Cunningham
17. Dwayne Johnson
18. Monza
19. Birmingham City
20. Cinematography

DIFFICULT

Quiz 150: Pot Luck

1. The members of which New York band ran a garbage-truck business called DiFontaine's Carting & Asbestos Removal Company?

2. True or false – Bernard Manning once appeared as a guest on the TV quiz 'A Question of Sport'?

3. Who was the British Foreign Secretary immediately prior to William Hague?

4. Bute House is the official residence of which British politician?

5. At just 12m, Bath Hills is the highest point in which British National Park?

6. Infantile paralysis is another name for which disease?

7. Who is older – Matt Damon or Leonardo DiCaprio?

8. What nationality is Jacques Rogge, the head of the International Olympic Committee?

9. Which information service, beloved of football fans looking for scores, disappeared from TV screens in October 2012?

10. WL Mackenzie King was the longest serving prime minister of which country?

11. Which British Olympian was asked, 'Haven't you run before?' by a TV interviewer after winning the New Orleans half marathon in 2013?

12. In the 'Batman' comics and films, what is the first name of Commissioner Gordon?

13. Which former spy chief went on to join the judging panel for literature's Booker Prize?

14. In which South American country will you see football teams called Newell's Old Boys, Boca Juniors, and Estudiantes?

15. A thoroughbred horse race called The Caulfield Cup is run in which country?

16. In December 2012, Sally Humphreys became the third wife of which veteran rocker?

17. The Red Lichties is the nickname of which Scottish football club?

18. Attracting more than 5.5m visitors per year, what is Britain's most popular tourist attraction?

19. 'Portraying Life' was the title of a blockbuster 2013 exhibition at the Royal Academy featuring the works of which French painter?
    a) Edgar Degas b) Édouard Manet c) Claude Monet

20. Which American basketball star made an unlikely visit to North Korea in 2013 to meet President Kim Jong-un?
    a) Magic Johnson b) Michael Jordan c) Dennis Rodman

Answers to Quiz 149: Alliterative Answers

1.	Tropic Thunder	11.	Alan Ayckbourn
2.	Joan Jett	12.	Ben Bernanke
3.	Frankie Fredericks	13.	Ruth Rendell
4.	Andrea Arnold	14.	Gimme, Gimme, Gimme
5.	Sugar Sugar	15.	Jesse Jackson
6.	William Wordsworth	16.	Freaky Friday
7.	Gordon Gekko	17.	Joe Johnson
8.	Hubert Humphrey	18.	Ricky Ross
9.	Richard Reid	19.	Anthony Asquith
10.	Stuart Sutcliffe	20.	Lionel Logue

DIFFICULT

Quiz 151: Politics

1. Margaret Thatcher was the MP for which constituency from 1959 until 1992?

2. In April 2012, Joyce Banda became the president of which African country?

3. Eric Williams was the first prime minister of which independent Caribbean country?

4. Who was Britain's first female home secretary?

5. By what name is the veteran politician Lord Bannside better known?

6. Pierre Trudeau is a former prime minister of which country?

7. In April 2013, Uhuru Kenyatta was sworn in as president of which African country?

8. UNESCO is based in which European city?

9. Laura Cinchilla, the first female president in Central America, was elected in 2010 in which country?

10. Whom did José Manuel Barroso succeed as President of the European Commission?

11. Which UK politician was an MP at the age of 21, chancellor at 23, and prime minister at 24?

12. In February 2010, Viktor Yanukovych became the president of which former Soviet republic?

13. Which German politician won the Nobel Peace Prize in 1971?

14. Sirimavo RD Bandaranaike, the world's first female prime minister, was elected in which country?

15. Who was the only politician to hold the offices of President of the United States (1909-1913) and Chief Justice of the US Supreme Court?

16. Who was the first US president to be impeached?

17. 'A View from the Foothills' is an award-winning diary by which former Labour MP?

18. Which US president was the last to be born under British rule and the first to die in office, after just a month in the position?

19. How old was Margaret Thatcher when she died?
    a) 85
    b) 86
    c) 87

20. Up to and including 2012, how many parliamentary seats had not changed hands between parties since the end of World War II?
    a) 32
    b) 132
    c) 232

Answers to Quiz 150: Pot Luck

1. Fun Lovin' Criminals
2. True
3. David Miliband
4. The First Minister of Scotland
5. Norfolk Broads
6. Polio
7. Matt Damon
8. Belgian
9. Ceefax
10. Canada
11. Mo Farah
12. James
13. Dame Stella Rimington
14. Argentina
15. Australia
16. Ronnie Wood
17. Arbroath
18. The British Museum
19. Édouard Manet
20. Dennis Rodman

DIFFICULT

Quiz 152: Pot Luck

1. Which British female singer shaved her head in 2013 to raise money for Comic Relief?

2. In 1957, who became the first British composer to win an Oscar, for his score to 'The Bridge on the River Kwai'?

3. Elected in 1995, Jean-Claude Juncker is the long-serving prime minister of which country?

4. Which American spoken-word musician and poet who died in 2012 recorded 'The Revolution Will Not Be Televised' and 'The Bottle'?

5. '@Rustyrockets' is the Twitter handle of which English actor and comedian?

6. The Cuming Museum, The Hunterian Museum, and The Fan Museum are in which English city?

7. Who was President of Russia from May 2008 to May 2012?

8. Excluding Oxbridge colleges, which educational institution has won the TV quiz 'University Challenge' the most times?

9. 'Vauxhall and I', 'Ringleader of the Tormentors', and 'Years of Refusal' are albums by which controversial British singer?

10. Who succeeded Hirohito as emperor of Japan in 1989?

11. Whom did Jacques Rogge succeed as President of the International Olympic Committee?

12. 'Upfront and Personal' was the 2009 autobiography from which singer turned 'Loose Woman'?

13. The headquarters of social media giant Twitter are in which US city?

14. Ishtar Terra and Aphrodite Terra are areas of which planet of the Solar System?

15. President Zine al-Abidine Ben Ali fled which African country after the so-called Arab Spring uprising?

16. Who succeeded Tiberius as Roman Emperor?

17. Which Chinese dissident was awarded the Nobel Peace Prize in December 2010?

18. Which Shakespearean character said, 'This above all: to thine own self be true, And it must follow, as the night the day, Thou canst not then be false to any man'?

19. Hugh Porter was a long-time BBC commentator on which sport?
    a) cycling
    b) golf
    c) snooker

20. How many members sit in the Welsh Assembly?
    a) 50
    b) 60
    c) 70

Answers to Quiz 151: Politics

1. Finchley
2. Malawi
3. Trinidad and Tobago
4. Jacqui Smith
5. The Reverend Ian Paisley
6. Canada
7. Kenya
8. Paris
9. Costa Rica
10. Romano Prodi
11. William Pitt the Younger
12. Ukraine
13. Willy Brandt
14. Sri Lanka
15. William Taft
16. Andrew Johnson
17. Chris Mullin
18. William Henry Harrison
19. 87
20. 232

DIFFICULT

Quiz 153: Connections

1. Which female cyclist won gold at the 2012 Olympics in the Team Pursuit and Omnium events?

2. Which English actor, satirist, writer, and comedian played 'The Impressive Clergyman' in the cult adventure film 'The Princess Bride'?

3. 'Rushmore', 'The Darjeeling Limited', and 'Moonrise Kingdom' are films from which American director?

4. Who is the lead singer with synth-pop duo Erasure?

5. Who won a Best Supporting Actor Oscar in 2005 for his performance in 'Million Dollar Baby'?

6. Which German composer's works include 'Der Rosenkavalier', 'Salome', and 'Till Eulenspiegel's Merry Pranks'?

7. Who is the lead singer with Antipodean pop group Crowded House?

8. Gaz Schofield, Dave Horsefall, Lomper, Horse, and Guy were characters in which 1997 film comedy?

9. 'The Magpies' is the nickname of which Australian Rules Football team?

10. Which British actor played Sonny Kapoor in the 2011 film 'The Best Exotic Marigold Hotel'?

11. What was the only UK hit single for the legendary soul band Booker T & the MGs?

12. Who was the first presenter of popular Radio 5 panel show 'Fighting Talk'?

13. What was the name of the central family in the TV sitcom 'Desmond's'?

14. Located in Chertsey, Surrey, what is the second most visited theme park in Britain?

15. Michael C Hall plays the title character in which US detective drama?

16. Which team, which plays its home games at the Broadfield Stadium, was promoted to the Football League at the end of the 2010/11 season?

17. What is the second most populous county of the Irish Republic after Dublin?

18. What was the name of the character played by British actor Anthony Head in the fantasy drama 'Buffy the Vampire Slayer'?
    a) Cedric Giles b) Rupert Giles c) Tarquin Giles

19. The debut studio album from controversial US rappers NWA was called 'Straight Outta ...'?
    a) Brooklyn b) Compton c) Watts

20. What is the connection between all the answers?

Answers to Quiz 152: Pot Luck

1. Jessie J
2. Sir Malcolm Arnold
3. Luxembourg
4. Gil Scott Heron
5. Russell Brand
6. London
7. Dmitry Medvedev
8. Manchester
9. Morrissey
10. Akihito
11. Juan Antonio Samaranch
12. Coleen Nolan
13. San Francisco
14. Venus
15. Tunisia
16. Caligula
17. Liu Xiaobo
18. Polonius (in 'Hamlet')
19. Cycling
20. 60

DIFFICULT

Quiz 154: Pot Luck

1. Kim Campbell was the first woman to become prime minister of which country?

2. 'A Star Called Henry' and 'The Woman Who Walked Into Doors' are by which Irish author?

3. 'Now, fair Hippolyta, our nuptial hour / Draws on apace' is the opening of which Shakespeare play?

4. The first Winter Olympic Games were held in which country?

5. Which footballer has the most followers on Twitter?

6. Ascraeus Mons, Arsia Mons, and Pavonis Mons are volcanoes on which planet of the Solar System?

7. Poet Tomas Tranströmer, who was awarded the Nobel Prize for Literature in 2011, is from which country?

8. The giant Gateway Arch, the tallest man-made monument in America, is in which city?

9. Who was the longest serving presenter on children's TV favourite 'Blue Peter'?

10. 'Live and Laughing' and 'Hello Wembley' are the titles of best-selling DVDs from which stand up comedian?

11. Which best-selling author wrote the 2013 novel 'Long Live the King'?

12. If all the member states of the United Nations beginning with the letter S were listed alphabetically, which country would come first?

13. 'All the Fun of the Fair' is a jukebox musical based on the songs of which performer?

14. The first female elected head of state in Africa, Ellen Johnson Sirleaf, was president of which country?

15. In computing, what is a PDA?

16. Who directed the 1997 Oscar-winning film 'Good Will Hunting'?

17. The headquarters of the Mormon Church are in which American city?

18. The title of which James Bond film is also a colloquial name for people from the county of Wiltshire?

19. Which British dance act directed the music at the 2012 Olympic Games opening ceremony?
    a) Orbital
    b) The Prodigy
    c) Underworld

20. What is the name of the award-winning 2012 documentary about a 23-year-old French Algerian who convinced a Texan family that he was their missing 16-year-old boy?
    a) The Faker
    b) The Fraudster
    c) The Imposter

Answers to Quiz 153: Connections

1. Laura Trott
2. Peter Cook
3. Wes Anderson
4. Andy Bell
5. Morgan Freeman
6. Richard Strauss
7. Tim Finn
8. The Full Monty
9. Collingwood
10. Dev Patel
11. Green Onions
12. Johnny Vaughan
13. Ambrose
14. Thorpe Park
15. Dexter
16. Crawley Town
17. Cork
18. Rupert Giles
19. Compton
20. They all contain the name of an England cricketer

DIFFICULT

Quiz 155: Television part 1

1. 'Woodentop' was the original name of which long-running TV drama?

2. Keith Barron and Gwen Taylor starred in which Spanish-set sitcom?

3. Two people hosted the TV game show 'The Crystal Maze'. Richard O'Brien was one, who was the other?

4. Which UK sketch show was broadcast in America under the name 'Brilliant!'?

5. In the comedy 'The Big Bang Theory', what is Sheldon Cooper's middle name?

6. Ten Forward was the name of a bar in which science-fiction series?

7. Which actress plays Sister Julienne in period drama 'Call the Midwife'?

8. Which 1980s detectives were the owners of a Löwchen dog called 'Freeway'?

9. Music impresario Andrew Lloyd-Webber made his acting debut in which TV soap?

10. Which TV detective lived in the guest house of a beachfront estate, known as Robin's Nest?

11. Which award-winning American drama is based on the Israeli series 'Hatufim' (Prisoners of War)?

12. What is the name of the comic-book store in 'The Simpsons'?

13. Which BBC comedy was set in a Manchester pub called The Grapes?

14. In EastEnders, which comedian played a fake registrar at the wedding of Alfie Moon and Kat Slater?

15. Phil Gallagher plays the title role in which CBeebies programme?

16. Which supernatural drama featured a trio of flatmates who were in fact a ghost, a werewolf, and a vampire?

17. Which US TV comedy featured a bar called McGinty's?

18. Paul Whitehouse played voiceover artist Danny Spencer in which bittersweet BBC comedy?

19. What is the name of the school bully played by Henry Lloyd-Hughes in 'The Inbetweeners'?
a) Mark Dearden b) Mark Donovan c) Mark Durden

20. What is the name of the host of financial makeover show 'SuperScrimpers'?
a) Mrs Moneypenny b) Mrs Saver c) Mrs Thrift

Answers to Quiz 154: Pot Luck

1. Canada
2. Roddy Doyle
3. A Midsummer Night's Dream
4. France
5. Cristiano Ronaldo
6. Mars
7. Sweden
8. St Louis
9. John Noakes
10. Michael McIntyre
11. Fay Weldon
12. Saint Kitts and Nevis
13. David Essex
14. Liberia
15. Personal Digital Assistant
16. Gus Van Sant
17. Salt Lake City
18. Moonraker
19. Underworld
20. The Imposter

DIFFICULT

Quiz 156: Pot Luck

1. Which sporting event was hosted in Wales for the first time at Sophia Gardens, Cardiff in 2009?

2. Watches in most watch adverts show what time?

3. The flag of South Africa is made up of how many colours?

4. Former boxing world champion Nigel Benn is a cousin of which former England football captain?

5. Which 2012 film starring Mark Wahlberg featured a pot-smoking, foul-mouthed, sex-obsessed cuddly toy?

6. Which DJ and film critic host a movie-review programme called 'Wittertainment'?

7. In the 'Batman' films, what is the surname of the butler, Alfred?

8. Scleritis is a disease that affects which part of the body?

9. 'Jarhead', 'Revolutionary Road', and 'Road to Perdition' were directed by which British film maker?

10. Which three European football teams won the European Cup, Cup Winners' Cup, and the old UEFA Cup?

11. In a game of backgammon, each player starts with how many checkers?

12. The 2018 Winter Olympic Games will be held in which country?

13. In medicine, a CT scan is a type of X-ray. For what do the initials CT stand?

14. The Coen Brothers film 'No Country for Old Men' is based on a novel by which author?

15. A skyscraper called the Nakatomi Plaza is the setting for which classic 1988 action film?

16. US vice-president Joe Biden was a senator in which state?

17. Enceladus and Mimas are moons of which planet?

18. The giant Hassan II mosque, the tallest religious building in the world, is in which country?

19. Which Premier League football club was originally known as St Domingo's?
    a) Everton
    b) Liverpool
    c) Southampton

20. Which Soviet-era film director's works include 'Solaris', 'The Mirror', 'Stalker', and 'Nostalghia'?
    a) Sergei Eisenstein
    b) Aleksei German
    c) Andrei Tarkovsky

Answers to Quiz 155: Television part 1

1. The Bill
2. Duty Free
3. Ed Tudor-Pole
4. The Fast Show
5. Lee
6. Star Trek: The Next Generation
7. Jenny Agutter
8. Jonathan and Jennifer Hart (in 'Hart to Hart')
9. Hollyoaks
10. Magnum PI
11. Homeland
12. The Android's Dungeon and Baseball Card Shop
13. Early Doors
14. David Walliams
15. Mr Maker
16. Being Human
17. Frasier
18. Happiness
19. Mark Donovan
20. Mrs Moneypenny

DIFFICULT

Quiz 157: Pop Music part 1

1. 'I Created Disco' was the debut album from which Scottish DJ and producer?

2. Which two female singers appeared on 'Time' magazine's list of the world's 100 most influential people in 2012?

3. What is the UK's biggest selling album of all time that is not a compilation?

4. What is the stage name of the Honolulu-born singer Peter Gene Hernandez, who topped the charts with 'Unorthodox Jukebox'?

5. Which veteran singer and comedy team recorded the first Comic Relief single?

6. The 2013 album 'Old Sock' is the 20th album from which veteran rock guitarist?

7. What was The Beatles' biggest selling single?

8. Who was the first rapper to have a million-selling single in the UK?

9. 'English Electric' was a 2013 album by which veteran synth popsters?

10. 'Ta Dah' and 'Magic Hour' are albums by which American group?

11. Which duo received an award for Outstanding Contribution to Music at the 2009 Brit Awards?

12. Celine Dion had two million-selling singles in the UK. 'My Heart Will Go On' was one, what was the other?

13. Which pair of actors were responsible for the ninth biggest selling UK single of all time?

14. In December 2012, Adele's '21' became the fourth biggest selling album of all time. Which 1995 album did she overtake to reach fourth place?

15. Which Briton is the only man to be inducted into the Rock and Roll Hall of Fame three times, twice with bands and finally, in 2000, as a solo artist?

16. Which two girl groups collaborated on the 2007 Comic Relief single 'Walk This Way'?

17. The famous Woodstock music festival was held in which American state?

18. Who is the youngest member of Take That?

19. In 2013, who became the first DJ to play a set at the Houses of Parliament?
a) Fatboy Slim b) Calvin Harris c) Gilles Peterson

20. 'Krypton Factor' host Gordon Burns is a cousin of which Brit Award winning artist?
a) Noel Gallagher b) Adele c) Ed Sheeran

Answers to Quiz 156: Pot Luck

1. An Ashes Test match between England and Australia
2. 10 past 10
3. Six
4. Paul Ince
5. Ted
6. Simon Mayo and Mark Kermode
7. Pennyworth
8. The eye
9. Sam Mendes
10. Juventus, Ajax, and Bayern Munich
11. 15
12. South Korea
13. Computed tomography
14. Cormac McCarthy
15. Die Hard
16. Delaware
17. Saturn
18. Morocco
19. Everton
20. Andrei Tarkovsky

DIFFICULT

Quiz 158: Pot Luck

1. Situated in Drury Lane, what is London's oldest theatre?

2. Which contemporary American comedian said, 'The whole object of comedy is to be yourself, and the closer you get to that, the funnier you will be'?

3. Which controversial British broadcaster penned the 2009 book 'I'm Only Being Honest'?

4. Authors Roald Dahl and Ken Follett were born in which British city?

5. The tangerine-flavoured liqueur Van Der Hum is produced in which country?

6. What is the only London borough that begins with the letter N?

7. Which classic gangster movie was based on a 1986 book by Nicholas Pileggi called 'Wiseguy'?

8. 'Going to Sea in a Sieve' was a 2012 autobiography by which broadcaster?

9. Who was the US vice-president from 1989 until 1993?

10. Which country is home to the most Arabic speakers?

11. Phil Silvers, best known for playing Sergeant Bilko, appeared in a Carry On film. Which one?

12. In which year did The Beatles release their debut album, 'Please Please Me'?

13. If all of Shakespeare's plays were listed alphabetically, which play would be first on the list?

14. When was the last time that both the Summer and Winter Olympics were held in the same year?

15. St Magnus Cathedral, the most northerly cathedral in Britain, is in which town on the Orkney Islands?

16. How many of the eight starters in the men's 100m at the 2012 Olympics finished in a time of under 10 seconds?

17. The Rungrado May Day Stadium, the largest sporting arena in the world, is in which city?

18. Who was the Republican Party's vice-presidential candidate in the 2012 US election?

19. Valery Gergiev is a notable name in which field?
    a) classical music
    b) fashion design
    c) sculpture

20. Which country is home to more castles per square mile than any other in the world?
    a) Ireland
    b) Scotland
    c) Wales

Answers to Quiz 157: Pop Music part 1

1. Calvin Harris
2. Adele and Rihanna
3. Sergeant Pepper's Lonely Hearts Club Band
4. Bruno Mars
5. Cliff Richard and The Young Ones
6. Eric Clapton
7. She Loves You
8. Coolio (with 'Gangster's Paradise')
9. OMD
10. Scissor Sisters
11. The Pet Shop Boys
12. Think Twice
13. Robson Green and Jerome Flynn
14. 'What's the Story Morning Glory' by Oasis
15. Eric Clapton
16. Girls Aloud and Sugababes
17. New York
18. Robbie Williams
19. Fatboy Slim
20. Ed Sheeran

DIFFICULT

Quiz 159: Transport part 1

1. In which English city will you find stations called St David's, Central, and St Thomas?

2. Colin Chapman was the founder of which motor manufacturer?

3. Eglinton Airport serves which city in the UK?

4. Which organization is responsible for the tracks, bridges, tunnels, level crossings, viaducts, and 18 mainline stations on the British railways?

5. Which transport initiative was introduced in London on 17 February 2003?

6. Serving 82 million passengers annually, what is the busiest London Underground station?

7. The best-selling car of all time is made by which company?

8. The M69 links Coventry and which other midland city?

9. The busiest airport in the world serves which city?

10. Which London Underground line serves the most stations?

11. In which year was the M25 officially opened?

12. One of the busiest in the world, Soekarno–Hatta International Airport is in which country?

13. In which decade was the 70mph speed limit for British motorways introduced?

14. Which central London tube station, which is also the title of a top five UK single, has the most platforms, with 10?

15. Which capital city is served by airports called Suvarnabhumi Airport and Don Mueang International Airport?

16. The underground railway network in which city serves the most stations?

17. With regards to British railways, for what do the initials ATOC stand?

18. McCarran International Airport serves which American city?

19. What is the average speed of a London Underground train?
    a) 16.5mph
    b) 20.5mph
    c) 24.5mph

20. How many miles of motorway are there in Britain?
    a) 1,219
    b) 2,219
    c) 3,219

DIFFICULT

Quiz 160: Pot Luck

1. What are the three countries to have hosted both the Summer and Winter Olympics in the same year?

2. Who was the last player to win the World Snooker Championship on his debut appearance in the tournament?

3. Which political leader was named 'Time' magazine's Person of the Year in 1939 and 1942?

4. Which actor, who starred in the cult comedy 'This Is Spinal Tap', was formerly the holder of a hereditary peerage?

5. In which English city will you find an athletics venue called the Alexander Stadium?

6. Actress Kyra Sedgwick, best known for her starring role in the TV drama 'The Closer', is married to which Hollywood star?

7. Purchased for £45m in 2012, 'Diana and Callisto' was painted by which Venetian artist?

8. Arthur Kipps is the central character in which Susan Hill book, which was turned into a film in 2012?

9. Writer and critic Charlie Brooker, director Sam Mendes, and actress Kate Winslet were all born in which English town?

10. Clint Eastwood has won Best Director Oscars for which two films?

11. Which island state in the Indian Ocean is a member of the Arab League?

12. Which music producer, best known for his work with Amy Winehouse, is a distant relative of Tory politicians Malcolm Rifkind and Leon Brittan?

13. Which Oscar-winning actress married Ned Rocknroll in 2012?

14. Which long-serving Director General of the BBC stepped down in 2012 to take a job at the New York Times?

15. Which American rock star's microphone was switched off after a 2012 concert at Hyde Park overran?

16. The Battle of Appomattox was fought in which war?

17. Lapangan Merdeka, the largest city square in the world, is in which Asian capital?

18. Who starred as President Aladeen of the fictional Republic of Wadiya in a 2012 film?

19. How tall is London landmark The Shard?
    a) 300m
    b) 310m
    c) 320m

20. How much is the annual salary paid to the president of the USA?
    a) $300,000
    b) $400,000
    c) $500,000

Answers to Quiz 159: Transport part 1

1. Exeter
2. Lotus
3. Derry (Londonderry)
4. Network Rail
5. The Congestion Charge
6. Waterloo
7. Toyota (Corolla)
8. Leicester
9. Atlanta
10. District Line (with 60)
11. 1986
12. Indonesia
13. 1960s
14. Baker Street
15. Bangkok
16. New York
17. Association of Train Operating Companies
18. Las Vegas
19. 20.5mph
20. 2,219 miles

DIFFICULT

Quiz 161: History

1. In 1973, the son of which espionage author succeeded Eamon de Valera as president of the Republic of Ireland?

2. Notorious in the 1970s and 1980s, by what name is Ilich Ramírez Sánchez better known?

3. Suharto was the president of which country from 1967 to 1998?

4. Who was Britain's first black Cabinet minister?

5. Michael Manley served three terms as prime minister of which country?

6. Who became emperor of Rome following the murder of Caligula?

7. In 1998, Frenchman Benoit Lecomte became the first person to swim which body of water?

8. Who was the president of the Confederate States when the American Civil War broke out?

9. What was the name of the Russian nuclear submarine that sank in the Barents Sea in August 2000?

10. In which year was Margaret Thatcher elected leader of the Conservative Party?

11. Which politician shared the Nobel Peace Prize with Nelson Mandela in 1993?

12. Which French politician was President of the European Commission from 1985 until 1995?

13. In which year were pubs in England and Wales allowed to open all day on a Sunday for the first time?

14. In which decade was did the Crimean War take place?

15. Which four countries were involved in the 19th-century conflict known as the Peninsular War?

16. Between 1990 and 2000 Alberto Fujimora was the president of which country?

17. Jacques de Molay was the last grand master of which military order?

18. Which two countries signed the 1922 Treaty of Rapallo?

19. What was the name of the group of engineers, inventors, scientists, and thinkers that met in Birmingham between 1765 and 1813?
    a) Eclipse Society
    b) Lunar Society
    c) Solar Society

20. Rosalynn was the first name of the wife of which US President?
    a) Eisenhower
    b) Ford
    c) Carter

Answers to Quiz 160: Pot Luck

1. France, USA, and Germany
2. Terry Griffiths
3. Josef Stalin
4. Christopher Guest
5. Birmingham
6. Kevin Bacon
7. Titian
8. The Woman In Black
9. Reading
10. Unforgiven and Million Dollar Baby
11. Comoros
12. Mark Ronson
13. Kate Winslet
14. Mark Thompson
15. Bruce Springsteen
16. The American Civil War
17. Jakarta
18. Sacha Baron Cohen
19. 310m
20. $400,000

DIFFICULT

327

Quiz 162: Pot Luck

1. In computing, what do the initials FTP stand for?

2. Which Italian brandy-and-orange liqueur takes its name from the Latin word for gold?

3. Film director Stanley Kubrick, actress Sienna Miller, and politician Boris Johnson were all born in which city?

4. A UK album is certified as having gone gold after it has sold how many copies?

5. Who played Sergeant Carter in the 2012 film remake of 'The Sweeney'?

6. Esch-sur-Alzette is the second largest city of which European country?

7. 'MF Dnes', 'Blesk', and 'Lidové noviny' are newspapers published in which European country?

8. What celestial object derives its name from the Greek for 'hairy one'?

9. Which James Bond villain had a third nipple?

10. 'Pro tanto quid retribuamus' (What shall we give in return for so much) is the motto of which UK city?

11. Joseph Smith was the founder of which religious movement?

12. In 2013, Andrew Parker succeeded Sir Jonathan Evans as the director-general of which organization?

13. Which entrepreneur from the TV show 'Dragons' Den' bought and relaunched the camera shop brand Jessops?

14. 'The Rachel Papers' was the debut novel by which British author?

15. Which actor played the sadistic Don Logan in the British crime classic 'Sexy Beast'?

16. In which year did the Channel Tunnel officially open?

17. Born in 1624 in Leicestershire, George Fox was the founder of which religious movement?

18. Which planet was named after the son and husband of Gaea in Greek mythology?

19. In which year was the Battle of Gettysburg fought?
    a) 1863
    b) 1864
    c) 1865

20. In terms of stations served, the largest underground railway network in Europe is in which city?
    a) London
    b) Madrid
    c) Paris

Answers to Quiz 161: History

1. Erskine Childers
2. Carlos the Jackal
3. Indonesia
4. Paul Boateng
5. Jamaica
6. Claudius
7. Atlantic Ocean
8. Jefferson Davis
9. Kursk
10. 1975
11. FW De Klerk
12. Jacques Delors
13. 1995
14. 1850s
15. Britain, France, Spain, and Portugal
16. Peru
17. The Knights Templar
18. Germany and the Soviet Union
19. Lunar Society
20. Carter

DIFFICULT

Quiz 163: Pop Music part 2

1. Which British pop star was the subject of a documentary called 'Madman Across the Water'?

2. 'Didn't It Rain' was a 2013 album from which British actor-turned-musician?

3. Danny, Noel, Kym, Suzanne, and Myleene were members of which band, created from a TV talent show?

4. Robyn Fenty is the real name of which singer?

5. Which British actor and comedian was a member of a 1980s new-wave band called Seona Dancing?

6. Who had a Christmas number one in 2003 with a cover of the Tears for Fears hit 'Mad World'?

7. Which was the first football team to release a record upon reaching the final of the FA Cup?

8. 'Survival', the official anthem of the London 2012 Olympics, was by which band?

9. The 1994 chart topper 'Beck to Bedlam' was the debut album from which singer-songwriter?

10. Barcelona and Spain footballer Gerard Piqué is the partner of which pop star?

11. Which debut album has spent the most consecutive weeks in the top ten of the UK album charts?

12. 'Funeral' was an acclaimed 2004 album by which Canadian band?

13. Which 1960s duo originally performed under the names Caesar and Cleo?

14. Who succeeded Reggie Yates as the host of the Official Chart Show on BBC Radio 1 in January 2013?

15. What was legendary rock and roller Chuck Berry's only UK number one single?

16. Footballer Ashley Cole is a distant relation of which American diva?

17. Which veteran indie rockers released the 2013 album 'More Light'?

18. What is the stage name of Natasha Khan, who recorded the Mercury Prize nominated albums 'Fur and Gold' and 'Two Suns'?

19. What unusual arrivals joined Paul McCartney on stage at a concert in Brazil in May 2013?
    a) an errant pair of sheep b) a swarm of grasshoppers
    c) a flock of seagulls

20. What is the real first name of pop star Emeli Sande?
    a) Adele b) Britney c) Cristina

Answers to Quiz 162: Pot Luck

1. File Transfer Protocol
2. Aurum
3. New York
4. 100,000
5. Plan B (Ben Drew)
6. Luxembourg
7. Czech Republic
8. Comet
9. Francisco Scaramanga
10. Belfast
11. Church of Jesus Christ of Latter-day Saints
(Mormons)
12. MI5
13. Peter Jones
14. Martin Amis
15. Ben Kingsley
16. 1994
17. Society of Friends (Quakers)
18. Uranus
19. 1863
20. Paris

DIFFICULT

Quiz 164: Pot Luck

1. Mr and Mrs Wormwood, Miss Honey, and Miss Trunchbull are characters in which children's story by Roald Dahl?

2. Valued at £3.5m, a pure gold replica of which footballer's left foot was unveiled in Tokyo in 2013?

3. The 1971 film 'Play Misty for Me' was which actor's directorial debut?

4. Sonatrach, the largest company in Africa, is based in which country?

5. How many copies must a UK album sell in order to be classified as platinum?

6. Which number sits between 18 and 13 on a standard dartboard?

7. Who played the title character in the 2012 comic-book adaptation 'Dredd'?

8. In which part of the human body will you find the orbicularis oculi muscle?

9. In astronomy, what are Haumea, Makemake, and Eris?

10. Hazen is the middle name of which contemporary British stand-up comedian?

11. Which BBC drama is set in the fictional midlands town of Letherbridge?

12. The Roskilde music festival takes place in which country?

13. Which British musician won the Oscar for Best Original Song in 1999 for 'You'll Be in My Heart' from the film 'Tarzan'?

14. Which comedian wrote the Rod-Stewart-inspired musical 'Tonight's the Night'?

15. Sir Edmund Barton was the first prime minister of which country?

16. Who provided the voice of Puss in Boots in the 'Shrek' films?

17. The coach carrying the football team from which country was attacked by gunmen at the 2009 Africa Cup of Nations?

18. 'Go, bid the soldiers shoot' is the closing line of which Shakespeare play?

19. In 1975, a Japanese woman named Junko Tabei became the first woman to do what?
    a) climb Everest
    b) single-handedly sail around the world
    c) swim the English Channel

20. How many members make up the London Assembly?
    a) 20
    b) 25
    c) 30

Answers to Quiz 163: Pop Music part 2

1. Elton John
2. Hugh Laurie
3. Hear'Say
4. Rihanna
5. Ricky Gervais
6. Gary Jules
7. Arsenal (with 'Good Old Arsenal' in 1971)
8. Muse
9. James Blunt
10. Shakira
11. 'Our Version of Events' by Emeli Sande
12. Arcade Fire
13. Sonny and Cher
14. Jameela Jamil
15. My Ding-a-Ling
16. Mariah Carey
17. Primal Scream
18. Bat for Lashes
19. A swarm of grasshoppers
20. Adele

DIFFICULT

333

Quiz 165: Anagrams

Rearrange the letters to make a Brit Award winning singer or band.

1. Nearly dale

2. Call dopy

3. Annex el nino

4. Sticky romance

5. Earl well up

6. New yak set

7. Down rehab

8. Thy lake becks

9. A catchers pert ermines

10. No can freak

11. Seared hen

12. Fogies froth

13. Encode intro

14. Cone lee erg

15. Besot shy pop

16. Leathers lift

17. Submarine jet kilt

18. Note throb

19. Howlers Cry

20. Snooty email

Answers to Quiz 164: Pot Luck

1. Matilda
2. Lionel Messi
3. Clint Eastwood
4. Algeria
5. 300,000
6. 4
7. Karl Urban
8. The eye
9. Dwarf planets
10. Michael McIntyre
11. Doctors
12. Denmark
13. Phil Collins
14. Ben Elton
15. Australia
16. Antonio Banderas
17. Togo
18. Hamlet
19. Climb Everest
20. 25

DIFFICULT

Quiz 166: Pot Luck

1. 'Badlands', 'Days of Heaven', and 'Tree of Life' are films from which American director?

2. What is the only racecourse in the county of Lincolnshire?

3. The Sahitya Akademi Award is a literary prize awarded in which country?

4. What was the name of the US Navy's first nuclear-powered submarine?

5. In the 2012 film 'John Carter', the title character finds himself transported to which planet?

6. Who was the US vice-president during the presidency of Gerald Ford?

7. The hit musical 'Hairspray' is set in which American city?

8. The steel-toothed baddie Jaws appeared in which two James Bond films?

9. Hugh Jackman played which member of the 'X-Men' in the superhero-inspired film franchise?

10. In 2013, which country allowed privately owned newspapers to operate for the first time in almost 50 years?

11. True or false – there are no London Underground stations outside the M25?

12. Who stood down as chairman of broadcaster BSkyB in April 2012?

13. St John's is the capital city of which Commonwealth country?

14. Which film character said, 'I do wish we could chat longer, but I'm having an old friend for dinner'?

15. 'The Only Way Is Epic' was a 2013 stage show from which patriotic stand-up comedian?

16. Nigel Havers and the late Richard Griffiths are the godfathers of which actor and comedian?

17. The CIA's Operation Neptune Spear resulted in death of which person?

18. By what name are members of the religious Order of the Reformed Cistercians of the Strict Observance better known?

19. Which actor was awarded the Freedom of the City of London in March 2013?
    a) Michael Caine
    b) Bob Hoskins
    c) Ray Winstone

20. In what field of the arts is Akram Khan a notable name?
    a) dance
    b) photography
    c) sculpture

Answers to Quiz 165: Anagrams

1. Lana Del Rey
2. Coldplay
3. Annie Lennox
4. Arctic Monkeys
5. Paul Weller
6. Kanye West
7. Ben Howard
8. The Black Keys
9. Manic Street Preachers
10. Frank Ocean
11. Ed Sheeran
12. Foo Fighters
13. One Direction
14. Cee Lo Green
15. Pet Shop Boys
16. The Fratellis
17. Justin Timberlake
18. Beth Orton
19. Sheryl Crow
20. Alison Moyet

DIFFICULT

Quiz 167: Food and Drink

1. Who is the wine expert on the revived TV show 'Food and Drink'?

2. Which country is the world's leading producer of tea?

3. In Jewish cuisine, what type of fish is known as 'lox'?

4. Which Christmas cake takes it name from the German word for 'tunnel'?

5. The caipirinha is the national cocktail of which country?

6. By what name is the fish called the Cornish sardine also known?

7. The brand of beer called Trooper takes its name from a song by which heavy-metal band?

8. Which popular curry dish takes its name from the Bengali for 'twice onions'?

9. 'Ipomoea batatas' is the scientific name for which vegetable which is commonly used in Caribbean cuisine?

10. The Granny Smith apple originated in which country?

11. Bamia and bhindi are alternative names for which vegetable?

12. Which vegetable is the main ingredient in the soup dish Erwtensoep?

13. The name of which spirit derives from the Gaelic for 'the drink that satisfies'?

14. Bento is a packed-lunch meal popular in the cuisine of which country?

15. Which Italian dessert, made from sponge biscuits, means 'pick me up' in English?

DIFFICULT

16. The meat and sauerkraut stew Bigos is the national dish of which country?

17. What German liqueur's name translates into English as 'master hunter'?

18. What vegetable is the central ingredient in the Moroccan dish Zaalouk?

19. Which TV presenter was the co-founder of a restaurant called 'Fishy Fishy'?
    a) Ant McPartlin
    b) Dermot O'Leary
    c) Kate Thornton

20. The cheese Blacksticks Blue is from which English county?
    a) Devon
    b) Lancashire
    c) Somerset

Answers to Quiz 166: Pot Luck

1. Terrence Malick
2. Market Rasen
3. India
4. USS Nautilus
5. Mars
6. Nelson A Rockefeller
7. Baltimore
8. 'The Spy Who Loved Me' and 'Moonraker'
9. Wolverine
10. Myanmar (Burma)
11. False
12. James Murdoch
13. Antigua and Barbuda
14. Hannibal Lecter
15. Al Murray
16. Jack Whitehall
17. Osama bin Laden
18. Trappists
19. Michael Caine
20. Dance

DIFFICULT

Quiz 168: Pot Luck

1. In April 2013, a prize pool of $1m was awarded in the first world championship of which video game?

2. Which American thoroughfare is especially associated with the advertising industry?

3. Which British broadcaster wrote the 2008 book, 'Why Do I Say These Things?'?

4. How did 23-year-old Ryan Mania make the news in April 2013?

5. What does the J in the name of the author JM Coetzee stand for?

6. Which 19th-century author, who wrote the poem 'The Hunting of the Snark', was a lecturer in mathematics at Oxford?

7. Which saint, who died on Iona in 597, is credited with founding Christianity in Scotland?

8. Which playwright's works include 'The Doll's House', 'The Master Builder', and 'Hedda Gabler'?

9. What does the D in the comedian Reginald D Hunter's name stand for?

10. 'Odes', 'Isabella', and 'The Eve of St Agnes' are works by which English poet?

11. Which German philosopher's works include 'Critique of Pure Reason' and 'Critique of Practical Reason'?

12. Turned into a 1976 film starring Sissy Spacek, what was author Stephen King's first novel?

13. Which Roman poet who died around 140AD is best known for his 'Satires'?

14. Bandar Seri Begawan is the capital city of which Commonwealth nation?

15. Who is Claudia Winkleman's co-host on the BBC's 'Film 2013' programme?

16. Which musical, which opened in London in 1985, celebrated its 10,000th performance in January 2010?

17. Justine Roberts and Carrie Longton are the co-founders of which influential parenting discussion website?

18. The Basin Reserve is a sporting venue in which capital city?

19. The world's tallest hotel, the JW Marriott Marquis, is in which city?
    a) Dubai
    b) Shanghai
    c) Singapore

20. Which of the following is not a political party that has fielded a candidate in a US presidential election?
    a) The Free Soil Party
    b) The Know-Nothing Party
    c) The Capitalist Party

Answers to Quiz 167: Food and Drink

1. Kate Goodman
2. India
3. Smoked salmon
4. Stollen
5. Brazil
6. Pilchard
7. Iron Maiden
8. Dopiaza
9. Sweet potato
10. Australia
11. Okra
12. Pea
13. Drambuie
14. Japan
15. Tiramisu
16. Poland
17. Jägermeister
18. Aubergine
19. Dermot O'Leary
20. Lancashire

DIFFICULT

Quiz 169: Films part 2

1. The 2013 thriller 'Welcome to the Punch' was set in which city?

2. Which British actor played Emperor Palpatine in the 'Star Wars' films?

3. Who is the only child of two Oscar winners to win an Oscar herself?

4. Who played the title character in the 2013 comedy 'Burt Wonderstone'?

5. Sir Hugo Drax is a villain in which James Bond film?

6. Which 2000 film, starring Guy Pearce, was Christopher Nolan's debut feature film?

7. Which British actress won a Best Supporting Actress Oscar for her performance in 'The Constant Gardener'?

8. The 1957 Kurosawa film 'Throne of Blood' was based on which Shakespeare play?

9. Which actor played James Rhodes aka War Machine in 'Iron Man 3'?

10. Who provided the voice of the title character in the 2012 comedy 'Ted'?

11. Which 1977 Woody Allen classic was titled 'Urban Neurotic' in Germany?

12. Who won a Best Supporting Actor Oscar in 2002 for his performance in 'Iris'?

13. Who was the female lead in the Hitchcock classic 'Vertigo'?

14. 'May the odds be ever in your favour' is a quote from which 2012 film?

15. Which Scottish film maker directed the cult classic 'Local Hero'?

16. Which record by Oasis is also the title of a 2008 romcom starring Ryan Reynolds and Abigail Breslin?

17. Mrs Wilberforce, Professor Marcus, Major Courtney, and 'One-Round' Lawson are characters in which classic film comedy?

18. Who played the eponymous hero in the 2004 comedy 'The Life Aquatic with Steve Zissou'?

19. Who provided the voice of caveman Grug Crood in the 2013 film 'The Croods'?
    a) Nicolas Cage
    b) Tom Cruise
    c) Bill Murray

20. Which Hollywood actress provided the voice of the witch in the 2012 animation 'Room on the Broom'?
    a) Gillian Anderson
    b) Natalie Portman
    c) Julia Roberts

Answers to Quiz 168: Pot Luck

1. Call of Duty
2. Madison Avenue
3. Jonathan Ross
4. He rode the winning horse in the Grand National
5. John
6. Lewis Carroll
7. St Columba
8. Henrik Ibsen
9. Darnell
10. John Keats
11. Immanuel Kant
12. Carrie
13. Juvenal
14. Brunei
15. Danny Leigh
16. Les Miserables
17. Mumsnet
18. Wellington, New Zealand
19. Dubai
20. The Capitalist Party

DIFFICULT

Quiz 170: Pot Luck

1. Which British supermodel raised £200,000 for Comic Relief in 2013 by reading a chapter of 'Fifty Shades of Grey' on Radio 1?

2. What nationality is women's Olympic 10,000m gold medallist Tirunesh Dibaba?

3. In terms of fleet size and passenger numbers, what is Europe's largest airline?

4. Alben W Barkley was vice-president to which US president?

5. If all of the member states of the United Nations beginning with the letter T were listed alphabetically, which country would come first?

6. And what country would be last on that list?

7. Which American actor and singer co-founded the fashion label 'William Rast'?

8. 'Prepared' is the motto of which English football club?

9. What nationality is the best-selling conductor and violinist Andre Rieu?

10. The US TV drama 'Treme' is set in which city?

11. The Pope delivers an address at Christmas and Easter called 'Urbi et Orbi'. What does 'Urbi et Orbi' mean in English?

12. Port-Vila is the capital city of which Commonwealth country?

13. In 2009, which team became the first to win a trophy at Wembley and get relegated from the Football League in the same season?

14. Which Anglo-Irish poet wrote mystery stories under the pseudonym of Nicholas Blake?

15. What is the last opera in Wagner's 'Ring Cycle'?

16. Holly Golightly was the heroine of which novel and film?

17. 'The Out Out Tour' was a stand-up show from which London comic?

18. Influential midfielder Mesut Özil plays international football for which country?

19. Which British comedian is an honorary member of the Society of Crematorium Organists?
    a) Bill Bailey
    b) Jack Dee
    c) Vic Reeves

20. The 2013 album 'What About Now' was by which veteran American rock band?
    a) Aerosmith
    b) Bon Jovi
    c) Kiss

Answers to Quiz 169: Films part 2

1.	London	11.	Annie Hall
2.	Ian McDiarmid	12.	Jim Broadbent
3.	Liza Minnelli	13.	Kim Novak
4.	Steve Carell	14.	The Hunger Games
5.	Moonraker	15.	Bill Forsyth
6.	Memento	16.	Definitely, Maybe
7.	Rachel Weisz	17.	The Ladykillers
8.	Macbeth	18.	Bill Murray
9.	Don Cheadle	19.	Nicolas Cage
10.	Seth MacFarlane	20.	Gillian Anderson

DIFFICULT

Quiz 171: Television part 2

1. 23 Meteor Street was the setting for which TV comedy starring Simon Pegg and Jessica Stevenson?

2. Sid Snot, Gizzard Puke, and Cupid Stunt were characters created by which comedian?

3. Which actor, who went on to play a popular fictional TV detective, played Tiberius in the Roman period drama 'I, Claudius'?

4. David Haig played the title character in which TV comedy which was revived in 2013?

5. Which Aussie comedian hosts comedy chat show 'The Last Leg'?

6. Sharona Fleming and Natalie Teeger were assistants of which obsessive TV detective?

7. Which actor's credits include Mr Stink, Pontius Pilate, and Ian Fletcher?

8. Nurse Kim Wilde, Dr Pippa Moore, and Sister Den Flixter are characters in which hospital-set comedy?

9. Which former 'Coronation Street' star played Twiggy's girlfriend in the comedy 'The Royle Family'?

10. Connections, Sequences, Connecting Wall, and Missing Vowels are rounds in which TV quiz show?

11. Which actor and comedian provided the voice of Mr Smith in 'The Sarah Jane Adventures'?

12. Which TV drama is set on the Chatsworth Estate?

13. Who played motor-mouthed agent Ari Gold in 'Entourage' and the title character in the British drama 'Mr Selfridge'?

14. Maddie Magellan, Carla Borrego, and Joey Ross are characters from which detective drama?

15. Who were the original team captains on the panel show 'Shooting Stars'?

16. In the classic comedy 'Rising Damp', what was the name of Rigsby's cat?

17. Which TV quiz show host was named 'Heat' magazine's 'Weird Crush of the Year' in 2012?

18. Which Olympian won the first series of the celebrity diving show 'Splash'?

19. Who is the host of the BBC3 comedy show 'Good News'?
    a) Russell Brand b) Russell Howard c) Russell Kane

20. In the TV comedy 'Flight of the Conchords', what is the name of the band's manager?
    a) Malcolm b) Mitchell c) Murray

Answers to Quiz 170: Pot Luck

1. Kate Moss
2. Ethiopian
3. Lufthansa
4. Harry Truman
5. Tajikistan
6. Tuvalu
7. Justin Timberlake
8. Aston Villa
9. Dutch
10. New Orleans
11. To the city and to the world
12. Vanuatu
13. Luton Town
14. Cecil Day-Lewis
15. Götterdämmerung (Twilight of the Gods)
16. Breakfast at Tiffany's
17. Micky Flanagan
18. Germany
19. Bill Bailey
20. Bon Jovi

DIFFICULT

Quiz 172: Pot Luck

1. Which TV comedy star wrote the acclaimed young adult horror books 'The Enemy', 'The Dead', and 'The Fear'?

2. In 1863, which South American country became the first to abolish capital punishment for all crimes?

3. By what name is the pop star Jessica Cornish better known?

4. The Isambard Kingdom Brunel designed ocean liner SS Great Britain is docked in which port?

5. Which author's previously unpublished first novel, 'The Narrative of John Smith', was finally released in 2011?

6. Alexander Dubcek was the first secretary of the Communist Party in which country?

7. The bustard is the official bird of which English county?

8. The Amhara and the Oromo are the two biggest ethnic groups in which African country?

9. In 2010, Stella English won which reality TV show?

10. What nationality was the composer Franz Liszt?

11. 'Eugene Onegin' and 'The Queen of Spades' are operas by which Russian composer?

12. Which surname is shared by the authors who created Napoleonic-era rifleman Richard Sharpe and forensic investigator Kay Scarpetta?

13. In 2012, Frances O'Grady succeeded Brendon Barber as the general secretary of which organization?

14. Whom did Nick Clegg narrowly beat in the vote to become the leader of the Liberal Democrats?

15. Wangari Maathai, the first African woman to be awarded the Nobel Peace Prize, was from which country?

16. 'Homage to Gaia', 'The Revenge of Gaia', and 'The Vanishing Case of Gaia' are works by which British scientist?

17. Which Paralympic sport is also known as 'murderball'?

18. Who was the first woman to be appointed Poet Laureate?

19. Miller was the maiden name of which best-selling crime writer?
    a) Agatha Christie
    b) Daphne du Maurier
    c) PD James

20. Which actress starred in the Hitchcock classic 'The Birds'?
    a) Tippi Hedren
    b) Kim Novak
    c) Eva Marie Saint

Answers to Quiz 171: Television part 2

1. Spaced
2. Kenny Everett
3. George Baker
4. Yes, Prime Minister
5. Adam Hills
6. Adrian Monk
7. Hugh Bonneville
8. Getting On
9. Sally Lindsay
10. Only Connect
11. Alexander Armstrong
12. Shameless
13. Jeremy Piven
14. Jonathan Creek
15. Ulrika Johnson and Mark Lamarr
16. Vienna
17. Richard Osman
18. Eddie 'The Eagle' Edwards
19. Russell Howard
20. Murray

DIFFICULT

Quiz 173: Olympic Games

1. What were the names of the two official mascots of the 2012 Olympics?

2. Who was the last Canadian sprinter to win the men's Olympic 100m race?

3. Prior to Rebecca Adlington in 2008, who was the last British swimmer to win an Olympic gold medal?

4. Which fashion designer created the 2012 British Olympic team kit?

5. Ryan Lochte won five medals, including two golds, at the 2012 games in which sport?

6. What is the penultimate event of an Olympic heptathlon competition?

7. Which British woman won silver in rowing at the 2004 games and gold in cycling four years later?

8. Waldi the Dachshund, the first Olympic mascot, was created for the games in which city?

9. Sean Kerly, Ian Taylor, and Imran Sherwani won gold medals for Britain in 1988 in which sport?

10. What was the first city to host the Summer Olympics more than once?

11. Missy Franklin was a multiple medal winner at the 2012 games in which sport?

12. Which French resort town hosted the first Winter Olympics?

13. China was the leading Asian country at the 2012 games with 38 golds. Which Asian country was next with 13?

14. What are the five sports to have featured in every modern Olympics?

15. The Dominican Republic's Felix Sanchez is a double Olympic champion (and double World Champion) at which athletics event?

16. Rugby sevens is one of two new sports added to the 2016 Olympic programme. What is the other?

17. Kirani James won which tiny Caribbean country's first Olympic medal after winning the men's 400m at the 2012 games?

18. Amy Williams won Winter Olympic gold for Britain in 2010 in which sport?

19. How many different sports were featured in the 2012 Olympic Games?
    a) 26 b) 28 c) 30

20. In 2012, judo player Wojdan Shaherkani became the first woman from which country to compete at the Olympic Games?
    a) Iran b) North Korea c) Saudi Arabia

Answers to Quiz 172: Pot Luck

1. Charlie Higson
2. Venezuela
3. Jessie J
4. Bristol
5. Sir Arthur Conan Doyle
6. Czechoslovakia
7. Wiltshire
8. Ethiopia
9. The Apprentice
10. Hungarian
11. Tchaikovsky
12. Cornwell
13. The Trades Union Congress
14. Chris Huhne
15. Kenya
16. James Lovelock
17. Wheelchair rugby
18. Carol Ann Duffy
19. Agatha Christie
20. Tippi Hedren

DIFFICULT

Quiz 174: Pot Luck

1. The 1980s cult classic 'Ferris Bueller's Day Off' is set in which city?

2. The first name of the 21st President of the USA is also the name of which city in England?

3. Which US president said, 'I believe that banking institutions are more dangerous to our liberties than standing armies'?

4. Which former Formula One driver won gold in the hand-cycling events at the 2012 Paralympic Games?

5. What was the largest country by population that didn't win a gold medal at the 2012 Olympics?

6. The Welsh Grand National is run at which racecourse?

7. In March 2013, Joseph Muscat was elected prime minister of which European country?

8. 'Hugh the Drover' and 'Riders to the Sea' are works by which composer?

9. The house where Samuel Johnson was born is in which Midlands town?

10. The ancient Inca ruin Machu Picchu is in which country?

11. Which letter comes between sigma and upsilon in the Greek alphabet?

12. Which sport is played by a team called Plymouth Albion?

13. The baht is the currency of which Asian country?

14. Which electronic toy, which is also known as a cyberpet, takes its name from the Japanese word for egg?

15. Hertfordshire Mavericks, Loughborough Lightning, and Surrey Storm are teams that play which sport?

Answers – page 355

16. The title of which children's television programme was also the name given to the act of making men join the Navy by force?

17. Tarawa is the capital city of which Commonwealth country?

18. In 1965, amateur Tommy Smith became the first American to win which staple of the sporting calendar?
a) The British Grand Prix b) The Derby
c) The Grand National

19. Lake Volta, one of the largest man-made lakes in the world, is in which African country?
a) Ghana b) Kenya c) Tanzania

20. The 2013 film 'One Mile Away' was about a truce between gangs in which British city?
a) Birmingham b) Glasgow c) Manchester

Answers to Quiz 173: Olympic Games

1. Wenlock and Mandeville
2. Donovan Bailey
3. Adrian Moorhouse
4. Stella McCartney
5. Swimming
6. Javelin
7. Rebecca Romero
8. Munich (1972)
9. Hockey
10. Paris
11. Swimming
12. Chamonix
13. South Korea
14. Athletics, cycling, fencing, gymnastics, and swimming
15. 400m hurdles
16. Golf
17. Grenada
18. Skeleton
19. 26
20. Saudi Arabia

DIFFICULT

Quiz 175: Anatomy and Medicine

1. Which organ of the body is responsible for the disease diabetes mellitus?

2. Cholecystitis is the inflammation of which organ of the body?

3. By what name is acetaminophen more commonly known?

4. An ostectomy is a surgical procedure that involves removing what from the body?

5. Also known as Chronic Fatigue Syndrome, for what do the initials ME stand?

6. The Wassermann test is used to diagnose which disease?

7. By what name is the drug lysergic acid diethylamide more commonly known?

8. Trachoma is a disease that afflicts which part of the body?

9. What is the most common sexually transmitted disease in the UK?

10. Which part of the body is affected by plantar fasciitis?

11. A human vertebral column is usually made up of how many bones?

12. A ganglion cyst most commonly affects which part of the body?

13. By what name is the eye condition strabismus better known?

14. Louis Washkansky was the first person to undergo which medical procedure?

15. The Schick test is used to determine susceptibility to which disease?

16. Sometimes known as shock therapy, for what do the initials ECT stand?

17. What does the acronym SARS stand for in relation to the flu-like disease?

18. What disease, sometimes known as king's evil, was believed to be curable if touched by a member of a royal family?

19. Glossitis is the inflammation of what?
    a) eyes
    b) liver
    c) tongue

20. Which kidney condition is also known as nephritis?
    a) Bright's disease
    b) Salako's disease
    c) Wright's disease

Answers to Quiz 174: Pot Luck

1. Chicago
2. Chester
3. Thomas Jefferson
4. Alex Zanardi
5. India
6. Chepstow
7. Malta
8. Ralph Vaughan Williams
9. Lichfield
10. Peru
11. Tau
12. Rugby union
13. Thailand
14. Tamagotchi
15. Netball
16. Press Gang
17. Kiribati
18. The Grand National
19. Ghana
20. Birmingham

DIFFICULT

Quiz 176: Pot Luck

1. Which name is shared by a US politician who served as vice-president under Thomas Jefferson and James Madison and an American funk musician?

2. 'Victoria concordia crescit' is the motto of which Premier League football club?

3. What is the only team to win Football League play-off finals at four different venues?

4. Herpetology is the scientific study of?

5. Which pair of industrialists appear on the £50 note?

6. Robin Windsor, Pasha Kovalev, and Kristina Rihanoff are regulars on which TV show?

7. 'Faggot' is the German word for which musical instrument?

8. What nationality was the composer Gustav Mahler?

9. Which comic actress wrote the Spice Girls musical 'Viva Forever'?

10. Sir Stanley Matthews played football for which two English league clubs?

11. What are the Christian names of 'Winnie the Pooh' creator AA Milne?

12. What nationality was the influential architect Oscar Niemeyer?

13. 'Locked On', 'Against All Enemies', and 'Threat Vector' are novels by which thriller writer?

14. In 2009, whom did Vincent Nichols succeed as the Roman Catholic Archbishop of Westminster?

DIFFICULT

15. In which year was the British £2 coin launched?

16. How many strings are there on a balalaika?

17. In relation to digital communication, for what do the initials ADSL stand?

18. Henry Sewell was the first prime minister of which country?

19. How many tiles are in an English language version of Scrabble?
    a) 100
    b) 110
    c) 120

20. The Pitti Palace is in which Italian city?
    a) Florence
    b) Rome
    c) Venice

Answers to Quiz 175: Anatomy and Medicine

1. Pancreas
2. Gall bladder
3. Paracetamol
4. A bone
5. Myalgic Encephalomylitis
6. Syphilis
7. LSD
8. The eye
9. Chlamydia
10. The foot
11. 33
12. The wrist
13. A squint
14. Heart transplant
15. Diphtheria
16. Electroconvulsive Therapy
17. Severe Acute Respiratory Syndrome
18. Scrofula
19. Tongue
20. Bright's disease

DIFFICULT

Quiz 177: Sport part 2

DIFFICULT

1. England rugby international Ben Foden is married to a member of which popular girl band?

2. Who was the first Yorkshireman to score his maiden Test century on his home ground?

3. Coventry Bees, Peterborough Panthers, and Wolverhampton Wolves compete in which sport?

4. In which city will you find a venue called the Wankhede Stadium?

5. Denny Hulme is the only driver from which country to have won the Formula One World Drivers' Championship?

6. Which stadium has hosted football's European Cup / Champions League final the most times?

7. Who is the youngest driver to have won the Formula One Drivers' Championship?

8. Which Dutchman did Phil Taylor beat to claim the 2013 PDC World Professional Darts Championship?

9. Which British rider finished in second place in the 2012 Tour de France?

10. Craven Park is the home ground of which rugby league team?

11. The film 'Chariots of Fire' features the Olympic Games set in which city?

12. Which New Zealander is the all-time leading points scorer in international rugby union?

13. The wife of which famous show jumper trained the winner of the 2013 Grand National?

14. The Akmal brothers play international cricket for which country?

15. 'The Wall' was the nickname of which obdurate Indian batsman who retired from Test cricket in 2012?

16. Sakhir is the venue for the Formula One grand prix in which country?

17. With 54 games in charge, who has captained the England cricket team in the most Test matches?

18. Who was the only Scot on Europe's successful 2012 Ryder Cup team?

19. Which county has won the All-Ireland Senior Football Championship the most times?
    a) Cork b) Kerry c) Mayo

20. Arsenal footballer Carl Jenkinson played international football at youth level for which country?
    a) Denmark b) Finland c) Norway

Answers to Quiz 176: Pot Luck

1. George Clinton
2. Arsenal
3. Crystal Palace
4. Amphibians and reptiles
5. Matthew Boulton and James Watt
6. Strictly Come Dancing
7. Bassoon
8. Austrian
9. Jennifer Saunders
10. Stoke City and Blackpool
11. Alan Alexander
12. Brazilian
13. Tom Clancy
14. Cormac Murphy-O'Connor
15. 1998
16. Three
17. Asymmetric Digital Subscriber Line
18. New Zealand
19. 100
20. Florence

DIFFICULT

Quiz 178: Pot Luck

1. The first budget speech to be televised was in 1990. Which Chancellor delivered that speech?

2. Milton Obote was twice the president of which African country?

3. 'Atlas Shrugged' and 'The Fountainhead' are novels by which Russian-born American novelist who died in 1982?

4. The Greyhound Derby is hosted at which track?

5. St Willibrord is the patron saint of which European country?

6. David Karp was the founder of which microblogging social media site?

7. In 2002, who became the first man to make a solo, non-stop, circle of the earth in a balloon?

8. 'Bastinado' is a form of punishment that involves hitting which part of the body with a pliable cane?

9. Of what is speleology the study?

10. According to the title of the 2013 Palme d'Or winning film, what 'is the Warmest Colour'?

11. Which British rock band premiered their new single, 'End of the Beginning' on the season 13 finale of 'CSI: Crime Scene Investigation'?

12. What type of fish was the star of the hit film 'Finding Nemo'?

13. In April 2013, Nicolas Maduro was elected president of which South American country?

14. What is the name of the parliaments of both Spain and Portugal?

15. What name is given to the full moon that occurs closest to the autumn equinox in September?

16. Tincal is an alternative name for which light, colourless crystalline substance?

17. +353 is the international dialling code for which European country?

18. In which field of the arts is Vasily Petrenko a notable name?

19. 'Ars gratia artis' (Art for art's sake) is the motto of which film studio?
    a) Disney
    b) Fox
    c) MGM

20. The Rock and Roll Hall of Fame is located in which American city?
    a) Cincinnati
    b) Cleveland
    c) Pittsburgh

Answers to Quiz 177: Sport part 2

1. The Saturdays
2. Joe Root
3. Speedway
4. Mumbai
5. New Zealand
6. Wembley
7. Sebastian Vettel
8. Michael Van Gerwen
9. Chris Froome
10. Hull Kingston Rovers
11. Paris
12. Dan Carter
13. Harvey Smith (Sue Smith)
14. Pakistan
15. Rahul Dravid
16. Bahrain
17. Michael Atherton
18. Paul Lawrie
19. Kerry
20. Finland

DIFFICULT

Quiz 179: Places part 2

1. Kitty Hawk, scene of the first flight by the Wright Brothers, is in which US state?

2. Excluding America, which country is home to the most McDonalds restaurants?

3. Bulmer's, the world's biggest cider producer, is based in which city?

4. What are the four UNESCO World Heritage Sites in London?

5. Formula Rossa, the world's fastest roller coaster, can be found in the Ferrari World theme park in which city?

6. Stari Most, which translates into English as 'Old Bridge', is a famous landmark in which central European city?

7. Narita Airport serves which Asian city?

8. The first Odeon cinema in the UK opened in 1930 in which English city?

9. The composer Gustav Holst was born in which town?

10. Which African country has borders with Angola, Botswana, South Africa, and Zambia?

11. The motoring organization the AA is based in which Hampshire town?

12. Which American city is home to sports teams called the Royals and Chiefs?

13. Which country is home to the largest Japanese community in the world outside of Japan?

14. Which central American country is known as 'The Land of Lakes and Volcanoes'?

15. Actor and comedian Rowan Atkinson and the best-selling author Jack Higgins were born in which English city?

16. Which country was formerly known as the Trucial States?

17. SE11 5SS is the postcode of which British sporting venue?

18. Tartu is the second largest city in which European country?

19. The bear and the madrone tree is the official symbol of which European capital?
    a) Amsterdam
    b) Madrid
    c) Paris

20. The village of Gotham is in which English county?
    a) Lancashire
    b) Nottinghamshire
    c) Warwickshire

Answers to Quiz 178: Pot Luck

1. John Major
2. Uganda
3. Ayn Rand
4. Wimbledon
5. The Netherlands
6. Tumblr.com
7. Steve Fossett
8. The feet
9. Caves
10. Blue
11. Black Sabbath
12. Clownfish
13. Venezuela
14. Cortes
15. Harvest moon
16. Borax
17. Republic of Ireland
18. Classical music (conductor)
19. MGM
20. Cleveland

DIFFICULT

Quiz 180: Pot Luck

1. The Latin phrase 'Consectatio excellentiae' appears on the crest of which English football club?

2. European pop band The Knife are from which country?

3. Which English monarch started the Hundred Years' War?

4. The greyhound-racing track at Monmore Green is in which English city?

5. Which Oscar-winning British actress slept in a fitted glass box as part of a 2013 exhibition at the Museum of Modern Art, New York?

6. António de Oliveira Salazar was the long-time dictator of which country?

7. Which Nobel Prize winning American novelist's works include 'Humboldt's Gift' and 'The Adventures of Augie March'?

8. Who in 2005 became the UK's first black archbishop?

9. Who was the Member of Parliament for Huntingdon from 1979 until 2001?

10. What is the maximum number of horses that can take part in the Grand National?

11. 'Madness and Civilization' and 'Discipline and Punish' are works by which controversial 20th-century French philosopher?

12. Bill Murray played which US president in the 2012 film 'Hyde Park on the Hudson'?

13. 'The Staggies' is the nickname of which Scottish football club?

14. Which band was the subject of the documentary 'Oil City Confidential'?

15. Apia is the capital city of which Commonwealth country?

16. The Aran Islands lie off the coast of which Irish county?

17. Which author created the fictional location 'Totleigh Towers'?

18. The English National Cricket Academy is in which Leicestershire town?

19. Magnus Carlsen is a world-class player of which game?
    a) chess
    b) poker
    c) Tetris

20. British composer Arthur Sullivan, German philosopher Friedrich Nietzsche, and Irish wit Oscar Wilde all died in the same year. Which one?
    a) 1899
    b) 1900
    c) 1901

Answers to Quiz 179: Places part 2

1. North Carolina
2. Japan
3. Hereford
4. Tower of London, Maritime Greenwich, Westminster Palace, Kew's Royal Botanical Gardens
5. Abu Dhabi
6. Mostar
7. Tokyo
8. Birmingham
9. Cheltenham
10. Namibia
11. Basingstoke
12. Kansas City
13. Brazil
14. Nicaragua
15. Newcastle
16. The United Arab Emirates
17. The Oval cricket ground
18. Estonia
19. Madrid
20. Nottinghamshire

DIFFICULT

Quiz 181: Television part 3

1. What is the most frequently nominated British television series in the history of the Emmy Awards?

2. What was the name of the PR company run by Siobhan Sharpe in the BBC comedy 'Twenty Twelve'?

3. Which 'X Factor' singer won 'Celebrity Big Brother' in January 2013?

4. Jack Rimmer was the original head teacher of which school?

5. Which actress played Sophie in 'Peep Show', Alex Smallbone in 'Rev', and Sally Owen in 'Twenty Twelve'?

6. Who is the host of the TV quiz show 'Tipping Point'?

7. Which member of the King family was killed off in a special live episode marking 'Emmerdale's' 40th anniversary?

8. What is the first name of the neurosurgeon played by James Nesbitt in the medical drama 'Monroe'?

9. Who plays the lead character in the US TV comedy 'Anger Management'?

10. Who were the original team captains on the TV panel show '8 out of 10 Cats'?

11. What is the name of the actor who plays Martin 'Ash' Ashford in medical drama 'Casualty'?

12. Which Hollywood star played Frank Gallagher in the US version of the Channel 4 show 'Shameless'?

13. Which Coronation Street star won 'Let's Dance for Comic Relief' in 2013?

14. Brian Badonde, Aziz Azizzi, and Dufrais Constantinople are characters in which TV comedy?

15. Edd Kimber, Joanne Wheatley, and John Whaite have all won which TV talent show?

Answers – page 369

16. Which controversial critic is the host of 'How TV Ruined Your Life'?

17. Which series is set in the fictional realm of Westeros?

18. Which 'Coronation Street' character attempted to fake his own death in the Lake District in 2010 but accidentally fell in and drowned?

19. Which actress played Sandra's mother in the cop drama 'New Tricks'?
    a) Sheila Hancock
    b) Judi Dench
    c) June Whitfield

20. Who played the title character in the 2013 drama 'Wodehouse in Exile'?
    a) Tim Pigott-Smith
    b) Timothy Spall
    c) Tom Conti

Answers to Quiz 180: Pot Luck

1. Sunderland
2. Sweden
3. Edward III
4. Wolverhampton
5. Tilda Swinton
6. Portugal
7. Saul Bellow
8. John Sentamu
9. John Major
10. 40
11. Michel Foucault
12. Franklin D Roosevelt
13. Ross County
14. Dr Feelgood
15. Samoa
16. Galway
17. PG Wodehouse
18. Loughborough
19. Chess
20. 1900

DIFFICULT

Quiz 182: Pot Luck

1. Gay Meadow is the former ground of which English football club?

2. 'Per ardua ad astra' (Through adversity to the stars) is the motto of which British organization?

3. The Tagus River flows through which European capital?

4. Easter Island is a dependency of which South American country?

5. Singer-turned-actress Billie Piper is married to which actor?

6. In which country will you find an international cricket venue called the Kensington Oval?

7. Taller than a double decker bus, the world's biggest deckchair was a 2012 feature on the beach at which English resort?

8. Which comedienne provided the voice of Dory in the 2003 film 'Finding Nemo'?

9. Dens Park is the home ground of which Scottish football club?

10. Welsh leader Owen Glendower features in which Shakespeare play?

11. Who is the oldest member of the Monty Python comedy team?

12. Roger Saul was the founder of which fashion company, noted for its handbags?

13. Conductor Sir Charles Hallé, founder of the famous orchestra that bears his name, was also a noted player of which instrument?

14. Marc Randolph and Reed Hastings were the founders of which video-streaming service?

15. What was the first name of Hansard, after whom reports of UK parliamentary debates are named?

16. Of all British Formula One drivers, who has won the most grand prix races?

17. If all the countries of the Commonwealth were listed alphabetically, which would be first on the list?

18. And which country would be last?

19. What game was the subject of the 1998 film 'Rounders'?
    a) chess
    b) poker
    c) Scrabble

20. The American remake of Scandinavian drama 'The Killing' was set in which city?
    a) Baltimore
    b) Cleveland
    c) Seattle

Answers to Quiz 181: Television part 3

1. Downton Abbey
2. Perfect Curve
3. Rylan Clark
4. Waterloo Road
5. Olivia Colman
6. Ben Shephard
7. Carl King
8. Gabriel
9. Charlie Sheen
10. Sean Lock and Dave Spikey
11. Patrick Robinson
12. William H Macy
13. Anthony Cotton
14. Facejacker
15. The Great British Bake Off
16. Charlie Brooker
17. Game of Thrones
18. Joe McIntyre
19. Sheila Hancock
20. Tim Pigott-Smith

DIFFICULT

Quiz 183: Firsts and Lasts

1. Which was the first city from outside Europe to host the Olympic Games?

2. In which year did the last branch of Woolworths in the UK close?

3. Who was the first cricketer to captain his country in 100 Test matches?

4. Sir Alexander Bustamente was the first prime minister of which country?

5. In which year did Concorde make its last commercial flight?

6. Which cricketer was the first man to take 800 Test match wickets?

7. Which German footballer scored the last goal at the old Wembley stadium before it was redeveloped in 2000?

8. In which decade did the first regular radio broadcasts from Parliament take place?

9. The first British motor racing Grand Prix took place in 1926 at which circuit?

10. In which year was the first iPhone released?

11. In 1929, Margaret Bondfield became the first woman to serve as what?

12. Canadian diplomat Arnold Cantwell Smith was the first secretary-general of which organization?

13. Opened in 1976, what was Britain's first out-of-town shopping centre?

14. What was Michael Jackson's first solo UK number one hit single?

15. Who were the first sponsors of football's League Cup?

16. 1974's 'Aunts Aren't Gentlemen' was the last novel to feature which comic duo?

17. In which month does the Last Night of the Proms usually take place?

18. In 1981, Dr Gro Harlem Brundtland became the first female prime minister of which European country?

19. Which film was released first?
    a) The Bourne Identity
    b) The Bourne Supremacy
    c) The Bourne Ultimatum

20. What was the name of the doctor who pioneered the technique that made the world's first test-tube baby possible?
    a) Patrick Fawlty
    b) Patrick Steptoe
    c) Patrick Trotter

Answers to Quiz 182: Pot Luck

1.	Shrewsbury Town	11.	John Cleese
2.	The RAF	12.	Mulberry
3.	Lisbon	13.	Piano
4.	Chile	14.	Netflix
5.	Laurence Fox	15.	Luke
6.	Barbados	16.	Nigel Mansell
7.	Bournemouth	17.	Antigua and Barbuda
8.	Ellen DeGeneres	18.	Zambia
9.	Dundee	19.	Poker
10.	Henry IV, Part 1	20.	Seattle

DIFFICULT

Quiz 184: Pot Luck

1. In which British city will you find Portobello Beach?

2. Who played the American president in the 1996 film 'Mars Attacks!'?

3. 'Reincarnated' is a 2013 documetary about which rapper who has converted to Rastafarianism?

4. What is the minimum age at which horses can run in the Grand National?

5. What was the first feature film directed by Danny Boyle?

6. Dave Harris was the landlord of which fictional drinking den?

7. Which British comedian and broadcaster wrote the 2008 memoir 'Look Who It Is'?

8. Juan d'Arienzo, Anibal Troilo, and Osvaldo Pugliese are associated with which style of dance?

9. Which French actress played 007's love interest, Vesper Lynd, in the 2006 film 'Casino Royale'?

10. Which popular puzzle derives from the 'Latin Squares' idea developed by the 18th-century Swiss mathematician Leonard Euler?

11. +49 is the international dialling code for which European country?

12. Paul Allen was the co-founder of which technology company?

13. The 1941 film 'The Maltese Falcon' was the first film from which director?

14. The Caro-Kann Defence and the Pirc's Defence are strategies employed in which game?

15. In which European city will you find a sporting venue called the Allianz Arena?

16. The genre of dance music known as 'house' originated in which American city?

17. Fede Alvarez, the director of the 2013 film 'Evil Dead', is from which South American country?

18. Who, in 1974 and 1979, became the first American director to win the Palme d'Or at the Cannes film festival more than once?

19. 'Borgen' is the title of a popular Danish TV drama shown on the BBC. What does 'Borgen' mean?
    a) bridge
    b) castle
    c) barracks

20. The subject of a 2012 film, New Yorker Bill Cunningham is a notable name in which field of the arts?
    a) painting
    b) photography
    c) sculpture

Answers to Quiz 183: Firsts and Lasts

1. St Louis
2. 2009
3. South Africa's Graeme Smith
4. Jamaica
5. 2003
6. Muttiah Muralitharan
7. Dietmar Hamman
8. 1970s
9. Brooklands
10. 2007
11. A British Cabinet minister
12. The Commonwealth
13. Brent Cross
14. One Day in Your Life
15. The Milk Marketing Board (The Milk Cup)
16. Jeeves and Wooster
17. September
18. Norway
19. The Bourne Identity
20. Patrick Steptoe

DIFFICULT

Quiz 185: Sport part 3

1. Sandy Park is the home ground of which Premiership rugby union team?

2. Who are the three Englishmen to have won the World Snooker Championship since 2000?

3. Since 1981, only four men have been British jump racing's champion jockey. Name the quartet.

4. Broadhall Way is the home ground of which English Football League club?

5. Which British tennis player partnered Denmark's Frederik Nielsen to the Wimbledon men's doubles title in 2012?

6. Which was the first team from Eastern Europe to win football's European Cup?

7. What nationality is the Formula One driver Valtteri Bottas?

8. The Cambridgeshire Handicap is a horse race run at which course?

9. How many players start the tournament in the men's singles at Wimbledon?

10. In Formula One, the flying of which colour flag warns of unsporting behaviour?

11. The football club Ferencvaros is based in which European capital city?

12. Ivan Mauger and Tony Rickardsson have been world champion multiple times in which sport?

13. With six titles, which team has won American football's Super Bowl the most times?

14. Between 2000 and 2012, only three players without the surname Williams won the ladies' singles at Wimbledon. Which three?

15. Which country surprisingly won the women's football World Cup in 2011?

16. The Nottingham Panthers, Belfast Giants, and Cardiff Devils are teams that play which sport?

17. Which country beat Burkino Faso 1-0 in the 2013 final to win their third Africa Cup of Nations title?

18. Which British world champion boxer also has a degree in mathematics?

19. Who was the first British golfer to win the US Masters?
    a) Nick Faldo
    b) Sandy Lyle
    c) Ian Woosnam

20. In feet, how long is a tennis court?
    a) 74ft
    b) 76ft
    c) 78ft

Answers to Quiz 184: Pot Luck

1. Edinburgh
2. Jack Nicholson
3. Snoop Dogg
4. Seven years
5. Shallow Grave
6. The Winchester Club (in 'Minder')
7. Alan Carr
8. Tango
9. Eva Green
10. Sudoku
11. Germany
12. Microsoft
13. John Huston
14. Chess
15. Munich
16. Chicago
17. Uruguay
18. Francis Ford Coppola
19. Castle
20. Photography

DIFFICULT

Quiz 186: Pot Luck

1. 'Dr No' in 1962 was the first film in the James Bond franchise. What was the second?

2. What was the first name of Dr Beeching who implemented a raft of cuts to Britain's railways in the 1960s?

3. Which former UK Foreign Secretary resigned as an MP in March 2013?

4. Michaela Tabb and Zhu Ying are referees in which sport?

5. Mary O'Brien was the real name of which chart-topping singer who died in 1999?

6. Who was the president of Argentina during the Falklands War?

7. Which former pop star was nominated for an Olivier Award in 2013 for her performance in the play 'The Effect'?

8. Which comedian starred in and wrote the sitcom 'Grandma's House'?

9. Willy Loman is the central character in which play by Arthur Miller?

10. The 2014 World Cup will be held in Brazil. Who were the winners the last time Brazil hosted the tournament?

11. Which actress is older – Kristen Stewart or Jennifer Lawrence?

12. Who was the first left-handed player to win snooker's world championship?

13. Which writer and poet is the subject of David Hare's play 'The Judas Kiss'?

14. Reid Hoffman was the founder of which social media and networking website?

15. 'Old Times', 'The Caretaker', and 'Remembrance of Things Past' are works by which British playwright?

16. Which actress and 'Loose Woman' wrote the 2010 autobiography 'Pulling Myself Together'?

17. Which American singer founded the social network Littlemonster.com?

18. The mother of which notable British broadcaster and journalist in 1971 became the first person to produce and license an official Paddington Bear soft toy?

19. Which film icon was the subject of the 2013 opera by Philip Glass called 'The Perfect American'?
a) Walt Disney b) John Wayne c) Orson Welles

20. What was used by police in London for the first time in May 1983?
a) rubber bullets b) water cannon c) wheel clamps

Answers to Quiz 185: Sport part 3

1. Exeter Chiefs
2. Ronnie O'Sullivan, Peter Ebdon, and Shaun Murphy
3. John Francome, Peter Scudamore, Richard Dunwoody, and Tony McCoy
4. Stevenage
5. Jonathan Marray
6. Steaua Bucharest
7. Finnish
8. Newmarket
9. 128
10. Black and white halves
11. Budapest
12. Speedway
13. Pittsburgh Steelers
14. Maria Sharapova, Amelie Mauresmo, and Petra Kvitova
15. Japan
16. Ice hockey
17. Nigeria
18. Nathan Cleverly
19. Sandy Lyle
20. 78ft

DIFFICULT

Quiz 187: Movie Taglines

Identify the film from the following taglines:

1. 'In space no one can hear you scream' (1979)

2. 'You don't get to 500 million friends without making a few enemies' (2010)

3. 'Love is a force of nature' (2005)

4. 'Escape, or die frying' (2000)

5. 'The last man on earth is not alone' (2007)

6. 'Fifty million people watched but no one saw a thing' (1994)

7. 'The man with the hat is back. And this time, he's bringing his Dad.' (1987)

8. 'When he said "I do", he never said what he did' (1994)

9. 'If Nancy doesn't wake up screaming, she won't wake up at all' (1984)

10. 'Who will survive and what will be left of them?' (1974)

11. 'Twelve is the new eleven' (2004)

12. 'When you can live forever, what can you live for?' (2008)

13. 'You know the name. You know the number.' (1995)

14. '... look closer' (1999)

15. 'Nothing spreads like fear' (2011)

16. 'He's out to prove he's got nothing to prove' (2004)

17. 'What if this guy got you pregnant?' (2007)

18. 'The mission is a man' (1998)

19. 'Earth. It was fun while it lasted.' (1998)

20. 'Whoever wins ... we lose' (2004)

Answers to Quiz 186: Pot Luck

1. From Russia with Love
2. Richard
3. David Miliband
4. Snooker
5. Dusty Springfield
6. Leopoldo Galtieri
7. Billie Piper
8. Simon Amstell
9. Death of a Salesman
10. Uruguay
11. Kristen Stewart
12. Mark Williams
13. Oscar Wilde
14. LinkedIn.com
15. Harold Pinter
16. Denise Welch
17. Lady Gaga
18. Jeremy Clarkson
19. Walt Disney
20. Wheel clamps

DIFFICULT

Quiz 188: Pot Luck

1. The Latin motto 'Superbia in proelio' appears on the crest of which Premier League football club?

2. Which Greek island was also the title of the 2013 novel by Michael Frayn?

3. Spanish is the official language of which African country?

4. 'The Winslow Boy' and 'The Deep Blue Sea' are works by which British playwright who died in 1977?

5. 'The Elephant to Hollywood' is the title of an autobiography by which veteran British actor?

6. Daniel Ek is the founder of which music-streaming service?

7. Which religious order was founded in 1540 by Ignatius of Loyola?

8. Discovered by Tennant in 1804, what hard, white metallic element has the atomic number 77?

9. 'Naughty', 'School Song', and 'Revolting Children' are songs from which hit West End musical?

10. Which Italian footballer was named one of 'Time' magazine's 100 most influential people in 2013?

11. The Aces were the backing band for which reggae artist?

12. 'Fidelio' was the only opera written by which composer?

13. The Astros and the Rockets are professional sports teams based in which American city?

14. Which landlocked central Asian republic is surrounded only by other landlocked countries?

15. Jerry Yang and David Filo were the founders of which giant Internet company?

16. Humphrey Bogart won his only Oscar for his performance in which film?

17. Which English city is also the name used by Americans for a bowler hat?

18. Which pop star had Mally, his pet monkey, seized by customs officials in Munich in 2013?

19. 'Strine' is a word used to describe English spoken in which accent?
    a) American
    b) Australian
    c) Jamaican

20. 'Letter to Coroticus' and the spiritual autobiography 'Confessio' are works by which saint?
    a) St Andrew
    b) St David
    c) St Patrick

Answers to Quiz 187: Movie Taglines

1. Alien
2. The Social Network
3. Brokeback Mountain
4. Chicken Run
5. I Am Legend
6. Quiz Show
7. Indiana Jones and the Last Crusade
8. True Lies
9. A Nightmare on Elm Street
10. The Texas Chainsaw Massacre
11. Ocean's Twelve
12. Twilight
13. Goldeneye
14. American Beauty
15. Contagion
16. Napoleon Dynamite
17. Knocked Up
18. Saving Private Ryan
19. Armageddon
20. Alien Versus Predator

DIFFICULT

Quiz 189: Transport part 2

1. JAT Airways is the national carrier of which European country?

2. The Elvis Presley Bar is a feature of which British airport?

3. Grantley Adams Airport is the main airport on which Caribbean island?

4. SAIC Motor and FAW Group are car manufacturers from which country?

5. Which British airport offers direct flights to the most destinations around the world?

6. 'The Day We Caught the Train' was a top five hit in 1996 for which band?

7. Which international airline is wholly owned by the government of Dubai?

8. Which French word, which means feathers on an arrow, is also used to describe the tail section of an aeroplane?

9. True or false – in 2012, a Scottish distillery agreed a deal with a car company to supply by-products from its whisky production for fuel for cars?

10. In 2013, which fashion designer gave the uniforms of airline Virgin Atlantic a makeover?

11. The SNCB/NMBS is the national rail operator of which country?

12. In terms of passenger numbers, what is Britain's busiest railway station?

13. In which country is Angkor Air the national flag carrying airline?

14. The railway station serving which UK airport was used by just 14 passengers in the 12 months up to March 2012?

15. TXL is the international code for which European airport?

16. The truck manufacturer DAF is based in which country?

17. Which TV detective drove a red 1947 Triumph Roadster?

18. Which Arab capital is served by Houari Boumediene Airport?

19. The M55 links Preston with which town?
    a) Blackpool
    b) Southport
    c) Whitby

20. Which of the following cities is closest to London?
    a) Beijing
    b) Buenos Aires
    c) Tokyo

Answers to Quiz 188: Pot Luck

1. Manchester City
2. Skios
3. Equatorial Guinea
4. Terence Rattigan
5. Michael Caine
6. Spotify
7. The Society of Jesus (Jesuits)
8. Iridium
9. Matilda
10. Mario Balotelli
11. Desmond Dekker
12. Beethoven
13. Houston
14. Uzbekistan
15. Yahoo
16. The African Queen
17. Derby
18. Justin Bieber
19. Australian
20. St Patrick

DIFFICULT

Quiz 190: Pot Luck

1. Which cult American author wrote the novels 'Junkie', 'Naked Lunch', and 'The Soft Machine'?

2. Which French photographer, who died in 2004, was associated with the theory of 'the decisive moment'?

3. What were the first names of the author GK Chesterton?

4. Starring Viggo Mortensen, the 2009 film 'The Road' was based on a book by which American author?

5. What are Standard & Poor's, Moody's, and Fitch?

6. How many weapons are there in the board game Cluedo?

7. +61 is the international dialling code for which country?

8. Which is the smallest of London's eight royal parks?

9. In 1928, a greyhound called Primley Sceptre was the first winner of what competition?

10. What is England's oldest Football League club?

11. Ted Danson plays DB Russell in which American drama?

12. The son of which Rolling Stone is the founder of the London art gallery 'Scream'?

13. The Beatles are one of two acts to have two songs in the top 15 best-selling UK singles of all time. Who is the other?

14. 'I first met Dean not long after my wife and I split up' is the opening line of which 1957 'beat generation' novel?

15. The largest Hindu mandir outside of India is located in which London suburb?

16. The jazz musician Thelonius Monk was associated with which instrument?

17. Who directed the 2013 film adaptation of 'The Great Gatsby'?

18. How many feet are in a furlong?

19. In what field is Ferran Adria a world-renowned name?
    a) architecture
    b) fashion design
    c) gastronomy

20. What sort of animal was Mary of Exeter, who was awarded the Dickin Medal for her activities in World War II?
    a) dog
    b) dolphin
    c) pigeon

Answers to Quiz 189: Transport part 2

1. Serbia
2. Glasgow Prestwick Airport
3. Barbados
4. China
5. Manchester
6. Ocean Colour Scene
7. Emirates
8. Empennage
9. True
10. Vivienne Westwood
11. Belgium
12. London Waterloo
13. Cambodia
14. Teesside Airport
15. Berlin Tegel
16. Netherlands
17. Bergerac
18. Algiers
19. Blackpool
20. Beijing

DIFFICULT

Quiz 191: Sport part 4

1. Which country was runner-up in the 1979 and 1987 Cricket World Cup finals?

2. Sir Alex Ferguson won his first trophy as a manager with which club?

3. Who scored the winning goal in the 2013 FA Cup Final?

4. Australian Chris Holder was a world champion in 2012 in which sport?

5. A sports stadium called The Shay can be found in which English town?

6. Who was the last player whose surname starts with a vowel to win the ladies' singles at Wimbledon?

7. In which country is a famous horse race called the Velka Pardubicka held?

8. Cal Crutchlow is a notable British performer in which sport?

9. Which footballer, who joined Accrington Stanley in 2013, scored on his one and only appearance for England against Australia in 2003?

10. What was the name of the Olympic sailing gold medallist who died in a tragic training accident in California in 2013?

11. Which was the first team to win the FA Cup final after a penalty shoot-out?

12. In a Formula One grand prix, which colour flag warns a driver that he is about to be lapped and to let the faster car overtake?

13. Which tennis champion helped rescue guests after a hotel caught fire in Rome in 2004?

14. Which was the last team to win the FA Cup final after a replay?

15. Which left-handed player, who started the tournament as an 80/1 outsider, was the runner-up at the 2013 World Snooker Championship?

16. Who was the only German on the 2012 European Ryder Cup golf team?

17. Who in 2013 became the second player to be sent off in an FA Cup final at Wembley?

18. Which county won cricket's County Championship in 2012?

19. British cyclist Chris Froome was born in which country?
    a) Kenya b) Uganda c) Zimbabwe

20. Sir Alex Ferguson was in charge of Manchester United for how many games?
    a) 1400 b) 1500 c) 1600

Answers to Quiz 190: Pot Luck

1. William Burroughs
2. Henri Cartier-Bresson
3. Gilbert Keith
4. Cormac McCarthy
5. Credit-rating agencies
6. Six
7. Australia
8. Green Park
9. The Best in Show at Crufts
10. Notts County
11. CSI: Crime Scene Investigation
12. Ronnie Wood
13. Boney M
14. On the Road
15. Neasden
16. Piano
17. Baz Luhrmann
18. 660
19. Gastronomy
20. Pigeon

DIFFICULT

Quiz 192: Pot Luck

1. Anne of Denmark was the wife of which English monarch?

2. In 2007, lawyer Pratibha Patil became the first woman to serve as president of which country?

3. 'I still remember the day my father took me to the Cemetery of Forgotten Books for the first time' is the opening line of which 2001 novel by Carlos Ruiz Zafon?

4. Which action-movie star, born in 1957, has a master's degree in chemical engineering?

5. 'The Millers' is the nickname of which English football club?

6. What nationality is the Formula One driver Esteban Gutierrez?

7. Francis Henshall and Stanley Stubbers are the central characters in which hit West End play?

8. 'Hellblau' is the German word for what colour?

9. A Zamboni machine is used to prepare the playing surface in which sport?

10. After resigning as manager of the England football team, Fabio Capello went on to manage which country?

11. Onika Tanya Maraj is the real name of which Caribbean-born US singer and rapper?

12. Who played Captain Kirk in the 2009 film 'Star Trek'?

13. Terry de Havilland is a noted maker of what?

14. In which sport do teams compete for the Vince Lombardi Trophy?

15. Who was born first – Margaret Thatcher or Marilyn Monroe?

16. Which deal-of-the-day website was founded by Andrew Mason in November 2008?

17. Which comedian's 2013 world tour was called 'Force Majeure'?

18. What nationality is the champion golfer Nicolas Colsaerts?

19. The writer Thomas Hardy was also trained in which profession?
    a) architecture
    b) law
    c) medicine

20. In which field is the Helmerich Award given?
    a) biology
    b) music
    c) literature

Answers to Quiz 191: Sport part 4

1. England
2. St Mirren
3. Ben Watson
4. Speedway
5. Halifax
6. Chris Evert
7. Czech Republic
8. Motorcycle racing
9. Francis Jeffers
10. Andrew Simpson
11. Manchester United
12. Blue
13. Andy Roddick
14. Arsenal (in 1993)
15. Barry Hawkins
16. Martin Kaymer
17. Pablo Zabaleta
18. Warwickshire
19. Kenya
20. 1500

DIFFICULT

Quiz 193: Books

1. Brobdingnag is a fictional land in which novel?

2. Dan Kavanagh is a pseudonym of which Booker Prize winning novelist?

3. 'Last night I dreamt I went to Manderley again' is the opening line to which novel?

4. Which best-selling author served as a representative in the Mississippi state legislature from 1984 until 1989?

5. 'Joseph Anton: A Memoir' is an autobiographical book by which British author?

6. In the novel 'Pride and Prejudice', what is the first name of Mr Darcy?

7. Jack Torrance is the central character in which 1977 novel by Steven King that was later turned into a film?

8. 'If Morning Ever Comes', 'The Amateur Marriage', and 'Back When We Were Grown-ups' are novels by which contemporary American author?

9. By what name is the Belgian author Georges Prosper Remi more commonly known?

10. 'The Rotters Club' and 'What a Carve Up' are novels by which British author?

11. Which star of the 'Carry On' films was the subject of a biography called 'The Man Who Was Private Widdle'?

12. 'Between the Lines' was the title of the 2012 autobiography by which British Olympic gold medalist?

13. 'The Binman Chronicles' is the title of the autobiography of which scruffy goalkeeper?

14. Which Pulitzer and Nobel Prize winning author wrote the 1944 Alfred Hitchcock thriller 'Lifeboat'?

15. Since 2007, the ISBN book identifcation code has featured how many numbers?

16. 'An Act of Treachery', 'The Clematis Tree', and 'An Act of Peace' are novels by which former Member of Parliament?

17. Which broadcaster and comedian, who shares his name with a footballer who won a single England cap, wrote the books 'Charlotte Street', 'Join Me', and 'Yes Men'?

18. Dan Brown's 2013 novel 'Inferno' is primarily set in which city?

19. How did author Albert Camus die?
    a) in a car crash
    b) by drowning
    c) from tuberculosis

20. Harry Patterson is the real name of which thriller writer?
    a) Len Deighton
    b) Frederick Forsyth
    c) Jack Higgins

Answers to Quiz 192: Pot Luck

1. James I (James VI of Scotland)
2. India
3. The Shadow of the Wind
4. Dolph Lundgren
5. Rotherham United
6. Mexican
7. One Man, Two Guvnors
8. Light blue
9. Ice hockey
10. Russia
11. Nicki Minaj
12. Chris Pine
13. Shoes
14. American football
15. Margaret Thatcher
16. Groupon
17. Eddie Izzard
18. Belgian
19. Architecture
20. Literature

DIFFICULT

Quiz 194: Pot Luck

1. 'Enduring Love', 'Solar', and 'Sweet Tooth' are novels by which British author?

2. The Irish Literary Theatre was co-founded by which poet?

3. Adopted in 2001, the flag of Rwanda is made up of which three colours?

4. The Battle of Shiloh was fought during which conflict?

5. In 2012, Enrique Peña Nieto succeeded Felipe Calderon as the president of which country?

6. Which 1999 number 2 hit by Blur draws on a novel by F Scott Fitzgerald?

7. Walton, Wavertree, and West Derby are parliamentary constituencies in which city?

8. The massive Kariba Dam is on the border of which two African countries?

9. Which British actress was born Julia Elizabeth Wells on 1 October 1935?

10. Which four African countries are members of the oil organization OPEC?

11. What colour blood does an octopus have?

12. 'Let me at 'em!' was the catchphrase of which diminutive animated character?

13. What international body has the initials WIPO?

14. The word 'robot' derives from which language?

15. After how many years is an emerald anniversary celebrated?

16. Best known for designing the Sydney Opera House, what nationality was architect Jørn Utzon?

17. Of all the England football managers since the war, which one won the highest proportion of matches?

18. The scene of a major battle in the Crimean War, Balaklava is in which modern day country?

19. The World Snooker Championship final is played over the best of how many frames?
    a) 31
    b) 33
    c) 35

20. In what field is the David Cohen Prize awarded?
    a) architecture
    b) chemistry
    c) literature

Answers to Quiz 193: Books

1. Gulliver's Travels
2. Julian Barnes
3. 'Rebecca' by Daphne Du Maurier
4. John Grisham
5. Salman Rushdie
6. Fitzwilliam
7. The Shining
8. Anne Tyler
9. Hergé
10. Jonathan Coe
11. Charles Hawtrey
12. Victoria Pendleton
13. Neville Southall
14. John Steinbeck
15. 13
16. Ann Widdecombe
17. Danny Wallace
18. Florence
19. In a car crash
20. Jack Higgins

DIFFICULT

Quiz 195: Fill in the Blank

Fill in the missing word in the following sequences:

1. St Louis, London, Stockholm, _____

2. West Indies, West Indies, _____, Australia

3. 'The French Connection', 'The Godfather', _____, 'The Godfather Part II'

4. Selwyn Lloyd, George Thomas, Bernard Weatherill, _____

5. Kate Winslet, _____, Natalie Portman, Meryl Streep

6. _____, Sedgefield, Kirkcaldy and Cowdenbeath, Witney

7. 'Million Dollar Baby', _____, 'The Departed', 'No Country for Old Men'

8. Bern, Solna, Santiago, _____

9. _____, Boutros Boutros-Ghali, Kofi Annan, Ban Ki-moon

10. Danny Boyle, Kathryn Bigelow, Tom Hooper, _____

11. Milk, Littlewoods, _____, Coca-Cola

12. Michael Ramsey, Donald Coggan, _____, George Carey

13. Carl Lewis, Carl Lewis, Linford Christie, _____

14. Argentina, Czechoslovakia, Hungary, _____

15. Alex McLeish, George Burley, Craig Levein, _____

16. _____, Basil Hume, Cormac Murphy-O'Connor, Vincent Nichols

17. Durham, Nottinghamshire, _____, Warwickshire

18. _____, Colin Firth, Jean Dujardin, Daniel Day-Lewis

19. Helmut Schmidt, Helmut Kohl, _____, Angela Merkel

20. Norman Lamont, _____, Gordon Brown, Alistair Darling

Answers to Quiz 194: Pot Luck

1. Ian McEwan
2. WB Yeats
3. Blue, yellow, and green
4. The American Civil War
5. Mexico
6. Tender
7. Liverpool
8. Zambia and Zimbabwe
9. Julie Andrews
10. Algeria, Angola, Libya, and Nigeria
11. Blue
12. Scrappy-Doo
13. World Intellectual Property Organization
14. Czech
15. 55
16. Danish
17. Fabio Capello
18. Ukraine
19. 35
20. Literature

DIFFICULT

Quiz 196: Pot Luck

1. 'So we beat on, boats against the current, borne back ceaselessly into the past' is the closing line of which 1925 novel?

2. The award-winning London restaurant Le Gavroche takes its name from a character in which novel?

3. Writer, actor, and director Julian Fellowes was born in which African country?

4. For what did the J in J Edgar Hoover stand?

5. What 2012 sporting event was dubbed 'the Miracle of Medinah'?

6. Chance to Shine is an organization that encourages children to play which sport?

7. Which scientist said, 'Nationalism is an infantile sickness. It is the measles of the human race'?

8. Which former 'EastEnder' plays PC Sean McCartney in detective drama 'Scott & Bailey'?

9. In relation to finance, for what do the initials LIBOR stand?

10. Who was the most talked about British sportsman on Twitter during the 2012 Olympic Games?

11. Richard Esterhuysen is the real name of which British actor?

12. The title of which James Bond film was also the codename of an allied plan to defend Gibraltar from Axis forces during World War II?

13. In 1967, which team became the first to win English football's League Cup competition at Wembley?

14. Played by Kevin Spacey, John Doe was the main antagonist in which 1995 film?

15. What colourless inflammable gas, sometimes used as fuel, is made from carbon and hydrogen has the chemical formula C_3H_8?

16. Which London borough incorporates the former boroughs of Paddington and St Marylebone?

17. What girl's name is also the name of the outermost moon of Saturn?

18. Edward Teach was the real name of which pirate, who terrorized the Caribbean in the early 18th century?

19. A person in which occupation would wear a garment called an amice?
    a) lawyer b) priest c) soldier

20. What was the name of Rupert Murdoch's tablet-only newspaper app that ceased publication in 2012?
    a) The Daily b) The Globe c) The Tap

Answers to Quiz 195: Fill in the Blank

1. Antwerp (Olympic host cities 1904 to 1920)

2. India (Cricket World Cup winners 1975 to 1987)

3. The Sting (Best Picture Oscar winners 1971 to 1974)

4. Betty Boothroyd (Speakers of the House of Commons)

5. Sandra Bullock (Best Actress Oscar winners 2008 to 2011)

6. Huntingdon (constituencies of British prime ministers)

7. Crash (Best Picture Oscar winners 2004 to 2007)

8. London (World Cup final host cities 1954 to 1966)

9. Javier Perez de Cuellar (UN Secretaries General)

10. Michael Hazanavicius (Best Director Oscar winners 2008 to 2011)

11. Rumbelows (sponsors of the Football League Cup)

12. Robert Runcie (Archbishops of Canterbury)

13. Donovan Bailey (100m Olympic gold medalists)

14. Brazil (Runners-up in the World Cup 1930 to 1950)

15. Gordon Strachan (Managers of the Scotland football team)

16. John Carmel Heenan (Archbishops of Westminster)

17. Lancashire (Winners of cricket's County Championship 2009 to 2012)

18. Jeff Bridges (Best Actor Oscar winners 2010 to 2013)

19. Gerhard Schröder (Chancellors of Germany)

20. Kenneth Clarke (Chancellors of the Exchequer)

DIFFICULT

Quiz 197: Pop Music part 3

1. The double A-side 'The Model / Computer Love' was the only UK number one hit for which European band?

2. Tramar Lacel Dillard is the real name of which US rapper who topped the UK singles charts with 'Club Can't Handle Me' and 'Good Feeling'?

3. 'Forever Love' and 'Love Won't Wait' were the two solo UK number one singles for which boy band favourite?

4. Which one of Madonna's UK number one singles was taken from the soundtrack to the 2000 film 'The Next Best Thing'?

5. In which year did the Rolling Stones have their last UK number one hit single?

6. 2001's 'Asleep in the Back' was the debut album from which award-winning band?

7. Andy McCluskey is the lead vocalist with which influential synth pop band?

8. 'Opposites' was a 2013 number one album from which Scottish rockers?

9. GOOD Music is an American record label founded by which recording artist?

10. What was Blur's first UK number one album?

11. 'Collapse into Now' was the fifteenth and final studio album by which American rock band?

12. What was Robbie Williams' first solo UK number one?

13. Mike Joyce and Andy Rourke were the lesser known members of which band?

14. The 1994 number 2 hit 'Love Spreads' was the best performing chart single from which band?

15. Madonna has had four UK number one singles made up of just one word. Name them.

16. William Ashton is the real name of which veteran Liverpool rock and roller?

17. Which crooner had the UK's first ever official number one album?

18. The Drells were the backing band for which 1970s R&B singer?

19. What was the title of Muse's 2012 UK number one album?
    a) The 2nd Law
    b) The 3rd Law
    c) The 4th Law

20. What sort of warning did Take That's Mark Owen have a 2003 top 4 hit with?
    a) Two Minute Warning
    b) Three Minute Warning
    c) Four Minute Warning

Answers to Quiz 196: Pot Luck

1. The Great Gatsby
2. Les Miserables
3. Egypt
4. John
5. Europe's victory in the Ryder Cup
6. Cricket
7. Albert Einstein
8. Sean Maguire
9. London Inter-Bank Offered Rate
10. Tom Daley
11. Richard E Grant
12. Goldeneye
13. Queens Park Rangers
14. Seven
15. Propane
16. Westminster
17. Phoebe
18. Blackbeard
19. Priest
20. The Daily

DIFFICULT

Quiz 198: Pot Luck

1. What is the largest province of Canada by area?

2. Everton FC run out to the theme music to which 1960s drama?

3. Which British film director owned a Mayfair pub called The Punch Bowl from 2008 until 2013?

4. The Barada River flows through which Middle Eastern capital city?

5. 's Gravenhage is the local name for which European capital city?

6. Who was the first British cyclist to win the points competition in the Tour de France, Giro d'Italia, and Vuelta a España?

7. What is the only tile in Scrabble that is worth 5 points?

8. 'The Captain' is the nickname of which snooker player who was runner-up in the 2012 World Championship?

9. Which pop band took their name from a character in the 1968 film 'Barbarella'?

10. What is the first event on the second day of an Olympic decathlon?

11. Which actor from the TV comedy 'Cheers' played the lead role in the 2011 police drama 'Rampart'?

12. What was the first sequel to the novel 'Fifty Shades of Grey'?

13. What was the last single released by The Beatles before they announced their split?

14. In computing, for what do the initials PDF stand?

15. Oliver Cromwell was born in which Cambridgeshire town?

16. What are the first names of pop siblings The Jonas Brothers?

17. The Borg-Warner Trophy is awarded to the winner of which annual motor-sport event?

18. Which Scottish actress played Lady Jane Felsham in 'Lovejoy' and now plays Mrs Hughes in 'Downton Abbey'?

19. Which city is home to the oldest annual marathon in the world?
    a) Boston
    b) London
    c) New York

20. 'Levels of Life' is a 2013 book by which award-winning author?
    a) Julian Barnes
    b) Ian McEwan
    c) Salman Rushdie

Answers to Quiz 197: Pop Music part 3

1. Kraftwerk
2. Flo Rida
3. Gary Barlow
4. American Pie
5. 1969
6. Elbow
7. Orchestral Manoeuvres in the Dark
8. Biffy Clyro
9. Kanye West
10. Parklife
11. REM
12. Millennium
13. The Smiths
14. The Stone Roses
15. 'Vogue', 'Frozen', 'Music', 'Sorry'
16. Billy J Kramer
17. Frank Sinatra
18. Archie Bell
19. The 2nd Law
20. Four Minute Warning

DIFFICULT

Quiz 199: Colours

1. Anne Shirley is the central character in which novel by Lucy Maud Montgomery?

2. Which football team beat Marseille in the final of the 1991 European Cup?

3. Which former Secretary of State for Wales unsuccessfully challenged John Major for the leadership of the Conservative Party in 1995?

4. The 1968 number one 'Fire' was the only UK hit single for which British rock band?

5. Stan, Big Blue, Harvey, and Nipper are characters in which BBC children's animation?

6. Which Canadian-born scientist and author wrote the books 'The Blank Slate' (2002), 'The Stuff of Thought' (2007), and 'The Better Angels of Our Nature' (2011)?

7. Famous as a boxing venue, York Hall is in which part of London?

8. What is the name of the Australian thoroughbred racehorse that retired undefeated in 25 races in 2012?

9. 'Sequoia sempervirens' is the scientific name for which species of tree?

10. What was the first novel to feature serial killer Hannibal Lecter?

11. Michael Caine played an ex-serviceman turned vigilante in which 2009 film drama?

12. 'Anyone Who Had a Heart' was the first UK number one single by which female singer?

13. Tom Hanks played Paul Edgecomb in which 1999 drama that was based on a novel by Stephen King?

14. Seattle Grace Mercy West Hospital was the setting for which medical drama?

15. Norman Osborn is the alter ego of which comic-book super-villain?

16. Which member of Take That recorded the solo album 'Green Man'?

17. Hester Prynne is the central character in which novel by Nathaniel Hawthorne?

18. The 2002 song 'Just Like a Pill' was the first UK number one single for which singer?

19. What is the name of the music festival that is held each year in the Brecon Beacons, Wales?
    a) The Blue Man b) The Green Man c) The Red Man

20. Who was the lead singer with 2 Tone band The Selecter?
    a) Pauline Black b) Pauline Brown c) Pauline White

Answers to Quiz 198: Pot Luck

1. Quebec
2. Z Cars
3. Guy Ritchie
4. Damascus
5. The Hague
6. Mark Cavendish
7. K
8. Ali Carter
9. Duran Duran
10. 110m hurdles
11. Woody Harrelson
12. Fifty Shades Darker
13. Let It Be
14. Portable Document Format
15. Huntingdon
16. Nick, Joe, and Kevin
17. The Indianapolis 500
18. Phyllis Logan
19. Boston
20. Julian Barnes

DIFFICULT

Quiz 200: Pot Luck

1. In which part of the body will you find the tragus?

2. The original version of the board game 'Monopoly' was based on which American city?

3. The 1968 hit 'I Love My Dog' was the unlikely sounding first UK top 40 single for which artist?

4. Which actress, who later found fame in another sitcom, was originally cast as Roz in 'Frasier'?

5. Which name is shared by an actor from the TV sketch show 'The Fast Show' and a former world snooker champion?

6. For what does the E in the author's name EL James stand?

7. The 2012 Oscar-nominated documentary 'The Gatekeepers' is about the secret service of which country?

8. Which award-winning contemporary play is based on the 1783 Italian play 'The Servant of Two Masters' by Carlo Goldoni?

9. In the 1941 classic 'Citizen Kane' what were the first and second name of the title character?

10. The 2011 film 'Rise of the Planet of the Apes' is set in which American city?

11. What nationality is Warren Gatland, coach of the 2013 British and Irish Lions rugby team?

12. Which crime writer wrote novels featuring Inspector Ramsey, Vera Stanhope, and the Shetland Island quartet?

13. In which field of literature is the Frost Medal awarded?

14. Germany shares a border with how many different countries?

15. The 1945 Charter of the United Nations was signed in which American city?